MARX AND WEBER
ON ORIENTAL SOCIETIES

Classical and Contemporary Social Theory

Series Editor: Stjepan G. Mestrovic, Texas A&M University, USA

Classical and Contemporary Social Theory publishes rigorous scholarly work that re-discovers the relevance of social theory for contemporary times, demonstrating the enduring importance of theory for modern social issues. The series covers social theory in a broad sense, inviting contributions on both 'classical' and modern theory, thus encompassing sociology, without being confined to a single discipline. As such, work from across the social sciences is welcome, provided that volumes address the social context of particular issues, subjects, or figures and offer new understandings of social reality and the contribution of a theorist or school to our understanding of it. The series considers significant new appraisals of established thinkers or schools, comparative works or contributions that discuss a particular social issue or phenomenon in relation to the work of specific theorists or theoretical approaches. Contributions are welcome that assess broad strands of thought within certain schools or across the work of a number of thinkers, but always with an eye toward contributing to contemporary understandings of social issues and contexts.

Also in the series

The Puritan Culture of America's Military
U.S. Army War Crimes in Iraq and Afghanistan
Ronald Lorenzo
ISBN 978-1-4724-1982-8

A Genealogy of Social Violence
Founding Murder, Rawlsian Fairness, and the Future of the Family
Clint Jones
ISBN 978-1-4724-1722-0

Liquid Sociology
Metaphor in Zygmunt Bauman's Analysis of Modernity
Edited by Mark Davis
ISBN 978-1-4094-3887-8

Marx and Weber on Oriental Societies

In the Shadow of Western Modernity

LUTFI SUNAR
Istanbul University, Turkey

Routledge
Taylor & Francis Group

LONDON AND NEW YORK

First published 2014 by Ashgate Publishing

2 Park Square, Milton Park, Abingdon, Oxon OX14 4RN
711 Third Avenue, New York, NY 10017, USA

Routledge is an imprint of the Taylor & Francis Group, an informa business

First issued in paperback 2016

British Library Cataloguing in Publication Data
A catalogue record for this book is available from the British Library

The Library of Congress has cataloged the printed edition as follows:
Sunar, Lutfi
  Marx and Weber on oriental societies : in the shadow of western modernity / by Lutfi Sunar.
     pages cm
  Includes bibliographical references and index.
  ISBN 978-1-4724-1716-9 (hardback : alk. paper) -- ISBN 978-1-4724-1717-6 (ebook) -- ISBN 978-1-4724-1718-3 (epub) 1. Marx, Karl, 1818-1883. 2. Weber, Max, 1864-1920. 3. Civilization, Oriental. 4. Civilization, Modern. I. Title.
  B3305.M74S768 2014
  301.095--dc23

2013034189

ISBN: 978-1-4724-1716-9 (hbk)
ISBN: 978-1-138-27394-8 (pbk)

Cover image: Jean-Léon Gérôme, *Oedipus, or Napoleon Bonaparte before Sphinx* (1867–68)

To my beloved wife, Dilşad.

Contents

PART III: CONVERGING POLES OF SOCIOLOGY

List of Tables

In this book, Lutfi Sunar offers a new perspective on the modern attitude toward the Orient found in the works of Karl Marx and Max Weber. In painstaking detail, Sunar shows that both Marx and Weber were ethnocentric and arrogant in their attitudes toward societies, religions, and cultures that used to be called Oriental, including but not limited to Russia, Islam, India, Buddhism, and China. Sunar's thesis is far from obvious. In academia, Marx is hailed as the champion of the working classes and as the philosopher of the concept of alienation. But, to pick one of many counterexamples to this general perception, Sunar shows that in his writings on British Imperialism in India, Marx sympathized with the British—not the oppressed Hindus. Marx perceived the British as the harbingers of civilization that would deservedly wipe out alleged Hindu backwardness, superstition, and tradition. Similarly, Weber is best known today through the prism of George Ritzer's *McDonaldization of Society*, namely, as the discoverer of modern, Western, rationality, efficiency, predictability, and control. But the dark side of this interpretation of Weber is that he regarded all cultures that were based on non-Protestant roots as irrational, inefficient, unpredictable, and chaotic.

To the small extent that these ethnocentric attitudes in the works of Marx and Weber have been noticed, they have been dismissed in various ways. Thus, Sunar shows that Marx and Weber influenced the contemporary social theorist, Anthony Giddens, to depict modernity as a monster. More precisely, Giddens uses the metaphor of the juggernaut to depict Western modernity, but he does not challenge the Marxist assumption that his juggernaut must, inevitably, crush all non-Western cultures in its path. On the other extreme, in his book, *Orientalism*, Edward Said lumps all the founders of sociology (not just Marx and Weber) with Western artists, philosophers, and writers as depicting the Orient in deprecatory, negative ways. Said's brush is too broad. For example, the sociologist Émile Durkheim was a champion of cultural relativism and he argued against the attitude that is known today as ethnocentrism. Durkheim believed that all religions and cultural habits were "true in their own way" so long as they helped any given society function. Similarly, the philosopher Arthur Schopenhauer stands out as an exception in the pantheon of Eurocentric philosophers in that he explicitly appreciated the insights and values of Chinese and Hindu philosophy. Unlike Giddens and Said, Sunar is very precise and meticulous in his depiction of the ethnocentrism found in the works of Marx and Weber: he cites works by them that are not widely known; he compares and contrasts how their views have been received in a vast, secondary

literature; and he finds similarities as well as differences in their attitudes toward
the Orient.

The issue that emerges from Sunar's book is this: How have these two
particular strands of what is broadly known as Western ethnocentrism and
Eurocentrism—namely, Marxism and Weberianism—influenced the paths of
various civilizations? Sunar shows a historian's attention to detail in tracing the
various paths these two doctrines took geographically as well as intellectually.
It is ironic that Marxism migrated into the very, "backward," cultures that Marx
did not believe were ripe for a modern, Communist, revolution, especially Russia
and China. The other irony is that a form of Western modernity was imported into
tradition-directed Russian and Chinese cultures. It is important to keep in mind
that Communism was and still is a form of modernity. And various Communist
regimes used this Marxist version of modernity to fulfill Marx's vision of British
Imperialism in India, namely, to attempt to wipe out backwardness, superstition,
and tradition. On the other hand, it was Talcott Parsons who translated Max
Weber's *The Protestant Ethic and the Spirit of Capitalism* and in that way brought
Weber to America. The cultural affinities for this connection are numerous, from
the fact that Parsons was the son of a Congregationalist minister to the fact that
the Puritan traditions of America are still strong. As Ritzer correctly points out,
the twentieth century in America was fundamentally Weberian in its grand vision
of efficiency, McDonaldization, and the exponential growth of bureaucracy. But it
was also a century of demonizing the "other," from fighting "the Huns" in the First
World War through fighting the "Evil Empire" during the Cold War to the current
War on Terror.

As of this writing, the outcome of the clash of these civilizational trajectories
based upon Marx and Weber is still unclear. China is still Communist, although
it is simultaneously becoming McDonaldized. Russia is an ambiguous mixture of
pro-Western, Weberian tendencies while it maintains some of the social structure
of its old, Marxist regime. But the biggest contest is for the biggest prize in this
civilizational struggle: the nations of Islam. President George W. Bush proclaimed
war on Iraq as a way to bring Western democracy to Iraq and the surrounding region.
During the past 20 years, wars have been justified primarily on "humanitarian"
grounds, not hatred of the enemy. The outcome of this Weberian strategy is unclear.
Meanwhile, China has become Iraq's biggest trading partner. The direction and
fate of numerous, former Soviet republics that are primarily Muslim—the so-
called "stan countries," because their names all end in—stan—is undetermined.
The fate of Turkey vis-à-vis the European Union (which may or may not survive)
continues to be debated, and Turkey is a unique country in that it was established
on the intellectual base of the theories of Emile Durkheim. Beneath and behind
the power struggles for the Muslim countries of North Africa based upon Western,
military superiority there lies the cultural struggle of China trying to win cultural
inroads in those countries as it competes with McDonaldization. The cultural and
civilizational trajectories of Marxism and Weberianism that Sunar uncovers and
describes are still at work in the world today. The weakest civilizational force

today, as was the case since the nineteenth century, is the one promulgated by Durkheim: the anti-ethnocentric and pro-cultural relativism doctrine that each and every culture has its own history, its own right to existence, and an obligation to live with other cultures in a peaceful, division of labor.

Stjepan G. Mestrovic
Texas A&M University

Acknowledgements

This book grew out of a dissertation written for the Department of Sociology at Istanbul University, and I am indebted to the department for its intellectual support. I am particularly grateful to Ismail Coskun for his guidance and encouragement. I would also like to thank Besim Dellaloglu, Korkut Tuna, Hasan Karatas, Necmettin Kızılkaya and Ali Kaya for their insightful comments in the several stages of this study. Some parts of this study have been written at NYU where I have been as a visiting scholar. I am very thankful to Robert Young for his support and guidance during this term.

Stjepan G. Mestrovic encouraged me to publish this study. His advice and suggestions have been invaluable to me as I have revised and reformulated my argument. My friend, Yunus Kaya helped me in the process of writing and editing. Without his endless support this study could not have been completed. The editorial team of Ashgate Publishing, especially Neil Jordan, made the publishing process easier and quicker. Kayhan Ali and Rashid Nasibov have made proofreading and editing. Their contributions made this study more fluent and readable.

Above all I want to thank my wife, Dilşad and the rest of my family, who supported and encouraged me in spite of all the time it took me away from them.

Chapter 1
Introduction:
The Marx–Weber Relationship in Sociological Literature

One can argue that the history of sociology has been built on a comparison of Karl Marx and Max Weber. Weber's sociological theory was generally understood in comparison to those of Marx and presented as a response to Marxism. Although, since 1970, a variety of different readings and attempts to combine the theories of these two thinkers has been made, the dominant reading has kept its place in mainstream sociology until today.

Marx and Weber, who dealt with fundamental problems of the modern age in connection with the conditions in which they found themselves in, worked on subjects that were closely related to one another and searched for answers to similar questions. The basic aim of both was to analyze the structure and functioning of modern society in connection with the birth and development of modern capitalism. Thus, they sought the definition of modern society and its positioning historically. In the light of this aim, the analysis of Oriental societies held an important position for both of them, and, in the context of the theoretical opportunities provided to them by the studies of the Orientalists, they carried out discussions on Oriental societies as a means of defining modernity.

With this definition, Marx and Weber, who differ from one another in their approaches to political questions in the West, become closer when the subject matter is the Orient. Even though this convergence in their conceptual systems, sources and conclusions has attracted the attention of some researchers, it has not been addressed to the extent it deserves in sociology. In this study, I claim that the study of Oriental societies is the central element of their respective sociological theories, and this makes Marx and Weber incredibly close to one another.

According to the approach that has taken roots in sociological literature, Weber is an alternative to Marx and his interpretive explanations replace materialist ones in a switch to a non-positivist position. He explains the birth of capitalism in relation to intellectual and religious effects in opposition to Marx, who approaches the problem with reference to economic factors in a progressive understanding of history. According to this view, Weber exchanges Marx's materialist single-line history with a multi-dimensional understanding of historical development. This perspective has a function in contemporary sociological theory; in the atmosphere of the Cold War, Weberian sociology offered a defense of the liberal world against Marx's socialism.

The first work to conduct a comparison of Marx and Weber was by Karl Löwith (1897–1973) *Max Weber und Karl Marx*, written in 1932 (Löwith, 1993).[1] This work had an effect on later views in many ways. According to Löwith, both Marx and Weber carried out works concerned with Capitalism and were spurred into action by similar impulses. But, because their epistemological hypotheses and perception of humanity were very different, they came up with very different solutions. In addition, as no explicit idea of opposition had yet been developed, Löwith, while stressing the differences between Weber and Marx, expressed their similarities as well. More specifically, Löwith thought that their closeness to one another from a sociological perspective was caused by their closeness in the philosophical anthropological framework. According to him, even though they took contrary political positions, both were interested in the human problems inherent to bourgeois capitalism. Thus, the attitudes of both about the negative character of bourgeois capitalism are similar. But while one explains this via alienation, the other approaches it through the idea of disenchantment (Löwith, 1993, pp. 79–80). According to both Weber and Marx, capitalist society is unavoidably problematic, however, at the same time it is revolutionary in comparison to the traditional societies of both the West and the Orient. In all, Löwith believes that Weber's sociology is a rival to Marx's *Das Kapital*. He prepares the ground for claims that Weber was searching for an alternative to Marx. By 1964, under the influence of contemporary literature, Löwith speaks more clearly on the subject matter in a later article, *Die Entzauberung der Welt durchWissenschaft* and expresses the view that Weber's works as a whole represent a counterpart to Marx's *Das Kapital* (Bottomore and Outwaite, 1993, p. 34).

In the 1930s, economic historians took up the critique of Weber and approached him as being in opposition to Marx. One of these was Hector Menteith Robertson (1905–84). In his work *Aspects of the Rise of Economic Individuals: A Criticism of Max Weber and His School*, was written in 1933, he tries to establish a different causative chain from that developed by Marx and claims that Weber was looking for a psychological determinant of economic events. According to him, Weber, who saw the rise of capitalism in particular as being the result of the birth of the capitalist spirit, represents an alternative to Marx (Robertson, 1933, p. 54).

The person who placed Weber entirely in opposition to Marx was Talcott Parsons, who introduced Weber to the English-speaking world. He had an important influence on Weber's position in contemporary sociology and for many years his 1930 and 1958 forewords to the translation of *The Protestant Ethic and the Spirit of Capitalism*, significantly shaped views on the relationship between

---

1   This article, written in 1932 and published in *Archiv für Sozialwissenschaft und Sozialpolitik* (Vol. LXVI, 1932, pp. 53–99, pp.175–215), was republished after being edited in 1960. (*Gesammelte Abhandlungen. Zur Kritik der geschichtlichen Existenz*, Stuttgart: Kohlhammer, pp. 1–67.) I am citing the second edition of the revised English translation.

Marx and Weber.[2] According to Parsons, Weber designed *The Protestant Ethic* to refute the Marxist thesis and to directly settle accounts with Marx. With this understanding, Parsons established the basis of his functional sociology by synthesizing Weber with Durkheim in his magnum opus, *The Structure of Social Action* (1937). His earlier works (Parsons, 1968, pp. 502–503) argue that Weber used some Marxian themes in the matter of the jurisprudential development, but that from *The Protestant Ethic* onwards had switched to an opposing position.[3]

Albert Salomon[4] was the scholar who named this opposition that Parsons foreshadowed. He wrote articles (1935a, 1935b, 1935c) on Weber in the *Social Research* and played an important role in the spread of Weber's ideas to the American world. In addition, his remark that Weber developed his theory "in a long and intense debate with the ghost of Marx" (Salomon, 1945, p. 596) became a motto repeated in the literature. Salomon claimed that the main purpose of *Economy and Society* was to serve as a critique to the *Marxist sociological thesis*. This idea became a settled belief in the post-war environment and established Weber as an opponent and alternative of Marx.

The introduction of *From Max Weber*, written by Hans Heinrich Gerth and C. Wright Mills, contributed greatly to the developing perception of Marx and Weber's theoretical opposition. According to these authors, Weber's intellectual biography was formed in direct engagement with Marx. By stating that throughout his life Weber was waging a war against historical materialism (Gerth and Mills, 1946, pp. 46–50), they secured Weber's anti-Marx position with expressions in keeping with the period. In this environment, Robert King Merton's *Social Theory and Social Structure* (1949) canonized Weber as a sociological classic after Durkheim. In the 1950s, Norman Birnbaum expressed that Weber's theory had been

---

2   Parsons's effect on the perception of Weber is not limited to his own writings and circle. For a long period he made a deep impression on the translation map of Weber's works and the conceptual world of these translations, thus determining the perception of Weber's thought. Parsons's "destructive" effect on the perception of Weber was criticized by Cohen, Hazelrigg and Pope (1975). For a short answer in the same journal by Parsons to this critique, see Parsons, 1975.

3   Later on, however, Parsons realized that in the context of this contrast, Weber was perceived by scholars as a pure idealist as compared to Marx's materialism and he attempted to rectify this situation. In 1963, in his long introduction to Ephraim Fischoff's translation of Weber's *The Sociology of Religion*, Parsons suggests that *The Protestant Ethic* had initially been perceived as an attack against the Marxist materialist views. But according to Parsons, although Weber's orientation towards sociological solutions as a whole were completely different from Marx, this simple contrast was not absolutely accurate (Parsons, 1963, see also 1967, p. 37). Parsons cautiously suggests that Weber confronted not Marx himself, but rather the "historical Marx" of Marxists. That which is being rejected is Marxist historical materialism (Parsons, 1968, pp. 504, 715).

4   Salomon emigrated from Germany to the USA in the 1930s and worked with the other members of the Frankfurt School.

formed by a deep polemic with Marx. Thus, he made a serious contribution to the deepening of the widespread thesis of the period (Birnbaum, 1953, pp. 125–141).

American sociology entered a relationship with Weber "as the prophet of Western values against Marxism" (Munch, 1993, p. 52). Under contemporary political influences, many sociologists and political theoreticians perceived the existence of a pertinent confrontation between Weber and Marx and this oppositional image was presented as: "Weber is superior to Marx, The *Protestant Ethic* is superior to *Das Kapital*, ideas and values are superior to material factors, leadership is superior to sovereignty, and finally, rational capitalism is superior to illogical socialism"[5] (Antonio and Glassman, 1985, pp. xii–xiii). The perception of the period is even reflected in the names given to the translations of Weber's works. In particular, we can see this in works concerned with India and China. The translator and editor of these works, Hans H. Gerth, (1968, p. ix) states that in order to escape "isms" (probably as at that time in the bipolar world "isms" reminded him of something else) he added the title *The Religion of China* and *The Religion of India* above the original names. Even these preferences show the degree to which Weber's texts were influenced by the existing political environment. By not using the name of the work, the translators ensured that the "ism" was not brought to the fore and in fact attempted to ensure that Weber's ideology would not be negatively received by prejudiced view.

However, the positioning of Weber in opposition to Marx is not just something peculiar to Western or American sociology. On the socialist side, Weber is approached as a bourgeois sociologist.[6] The Hungarian sociologist Georg Lukács, who had a personal relationship with Weber, depicts him as presenting an extension of German imperialism and the defender of bourgeois values against socialism in his work *Die Zerstörung der Vernunft*, written in 1954 (Lukács, 1981, p. 609). According to him, Marxism is a science that explains society, and sociology is a science that was brought out to oppose historical materialism (Lukács, 1972). In this context, the German Marxist Karl Korsch wrote in his work *Karl Marx* (1938) that sociology is another name for opposition to modern socialism (Korsch, 1938, p. 19).

Soviet academics deepened the opposition between Weber and Marx. An important work about how Weber was perceived in the socialist world by Johannes Weiss states that in Socialist countries Weber was politically prohibited. *Bol'šaja Sovjetskaja Enciklopedija* (The Great Soviet Encyclopedia), in its second edition in 1951, "dismissed Weber as a 'reactionary German sociologist, historian and economist, Neo-Kantian, the most malicious enemy of Marxism' and as an 'apologist for capitalism'" (Weiss, 1986, p. 16).

---

5   For an evaluation of the literature concerned with the relationship between Weber and Marx, see Schroeter, 1985, pp. 2–19. For the use of Weber in the Cold War environment, see Whimster, 2005, p. 878.

6   For the relationship between sociology and socialism, see Bottomore, 1984.

Within *Structural Marxism*, led by Louis Althusser, new aspects were added to the thesis of the Marx-Weber opposition. In 1965 Althusser, in *Pour Marx*, denied the possibility of an individualistic and scientific sociology opposing Marxism, which is a scientific theory of social structure. By this means, in the context of methodological individualism and political liberalism, Weber is characterized as a "bourgeois sociologist" (Althusser, 1969).

This opposition, which thus took roots in sociological literature, was later reproduced by a variety of Weber's interpreters. At the end of the 1950s, Wolfgang J. Mommsen, who had produced an important work on Weber's view of German politics, proposed that Weber was perhaps the most important theoretical bourgeois opponent of Marx (Mommsen, 1977a, p. 374, 1977b, p. 43, 1989, p. 53). On the other hand, at the beginning of the 1960s, Arthur Mitzman, (1985, p. 182) had made a Freudian analysis of Weber's work. He claims that *The Protestant Ethic* was built on a critical study of Marx's historical materialism. After that, H. Stuart Hughes has declared Weber to be one of the founders of contemporary social thought along with Freud. He states that Weber formed a social theory that challenged Marx. According to him, the most important duty of Weber's generation, a generation that established twentieth century social theory, was to surpass the thought of the nineteenth century. In his view, Weber offers a view of society in which the economic impetuses in Marxism force the deepest spiritual values of humanity into a tense and contradictory relationship (Hughes, 2002, pp. 42, 67, 321). Hughes insists that there is a division at the fundamental level between the thought of Weber, who prepared the way for the twentieth century, and Marx's thought, being a product of the nineteenth century.

The work by Raymond Aron, frequently-referred to in the context of sociological history, has made an important contribution to the deepening of the thesis of opposition. Aron, who brings Weber to the fore as a liberal theorist in the history of sociological thought, writes an account of opposition. According to him, Weber believed that Marxist philosophy was incorrect (Aron, 1965, p. 202). However, he also writes, "Weberian thought is not an inversion of historical materialism. Nothing would be more untrue than to imagine what Weber maintained a thesis exactly opposite to Marx's and explained the economy in terms of religion instead of in terms of the economy" (Aron, 1965, pp. 264, 267). Aron states that this difference results from fundamental approaches, supporting the ideas that Parsons had earlier expressed.

Irving Zeitlin, another scholar who has written on the history of sociology, takes as his basis the role of the conflict between Marx and Weber in the creation of sociological theory in the twentieth century (Zeitlin, 1968, p. vii). He states that Weber established his own sociology in a long and serious conflict with the specter of Marx. In this context, he states that Weber forms his own approach, in particular, directed towards a criticism of Marx's methodology, emphasizing that he achieved different results in the same subjects (Zeitlin, 1968, pp. 111–112). However, Zeitlin (1968, pp. 321–322) is also of the opinion that this was not merely Weber's unique rendering, but rather, that the contrast with Marx's thought was effective in the formation of sociological theory as a whole. According to him, had this not happened, sociological theory would have been greatly deprived.

Tom Bottomore, when writing about the relationship of Marxism with sociology, also defends the idea that Weber's thought was formed in response to Marx. He states that "Weber, in greater part of his work, was engaged in a critical confrontation with Marxist thought, in formulation of an alternative account of the origins of modern capitalism." (Bottomore, 1975, notes 18–19). Another influential name, Julien Freund (1978) writes that Weber brings criticism of Marxism to the realm of academia, with the assistance of Georg Simmel (1858–1918) and Werner Sombart (1863–1941), and establishes its limits. According to Freund, throughout Weber's work Marxism was a veiled enemy. Thus, Weber refutes the scientific excesses of Marxism and defends a value-free science.

In this sense, we can include Carl Mayer and Robert J. Antonio among those who searched for the basis of the Weber-Marx opposition in the internal tension of German thought. They establish the tension between Marx and Weber on the opposition between Kant and Hegel (Antonio, 1985, p. 26; Mayer, 1975, p. 719). According to this position, Marx was a Hegelian, while Weber was a Kantian, and when the components are examined starting from the methodology, the differentiation in the formation establishes the basis of this type of evaluation.

From the middle of the 1960s, and more particularly after the 1970s, when the classics started to be approached in a new way,[7] the ideas about the opposition between Marx and Weber started to take different forms. With the effect of the *détente* that was experienced between the blocks in the political arena and the emphasis put on the similarities between Marx and Weber, some scholars even discovered Marxist tendencies and periods in Weber's thought. In this period, the former clear-cut oppositions receded, and the idea of *common heritage of the classics of social theory* became popular. As Dennis Wrong (1984, p. 72) stated, after 1970, particularly in studies in historical sociology, the traditional barriers between Marx and Weber had been torn down and there were attempts to unite them as common forefathers of interdisciplinary works.

In this context, Benjamin Nelson draws attention to the closeness between Weber and Marx which resulted from their common grounding in German thought (Nelson, 1965, p. 153). Similarly, scholars like Tom Bottomore and Randall Collins claimed that Weber's sociology had been established on the bases set up by Marx (Bottomore, 1978; Collins, 1981). Bottomore even stated that Weber could be seen as an interpreter of Marx. In this period, there is an important place for Giddens's *Capitalism and Modern Social Theory* in emphasizing their closeness, even their synthesis (Giddens, 1971). Giddens (1984, p. 1) tries to combine interpretative and structuralist sociologies, by going beyond the orthodoxies. He builds his *structuration theory* on the common heritage of Marx and Weber.

---

7   For the formation of Marx, Weber and Durkheim as the trinity of sociology, see Connell, 1997, p. 1542. Dirk Kaesler (2004) accurately summarizes Weber's sociology in the process of becoming a classic and the formation of the "holy trinity" of sociology.

Giddens states that Weber had respect for Marx and appreciated his contributions to contemporary social thought. By differentiating between Marx and the Marxism that was prevalent at his time, Giddens (1970) softens the rhetoric of opposition by expressing that the criticism of historical materialism is in fact directed towards contemporary Marxism, and that it is possible to examine Marx and Weber together in the concept of a "third way." Giddens reduces the opposition between Weber and Marx to a solely methodological distinction, ignoring the class values that had been attributed by Weber himself to his own writings. Giddens needs such a positioning in order to achieve a synthesis between Marx and Weber. Another name that has been important in the synthesis of the theories of Marx and Weber is Immanuel Wallerstein. In his *World System* approach, which combines *Annales School* and Marxist inclinations, Wallerstein has a special role in establishing the methodical approach between Marx and Weber (Ragin and Chirot, 1995).

The most variant views in the relationship between Marx and Weber are on Weber's early studies. Some assert that Weber holds a Marxist perspective in his early studies. According to this, setting out from his contemporaries, Weber was affected by Marx in the studies written before 1896 (Dibble, 1968, p. 99; Kozyr-Kowalski, 1968). In fact, Weber's works during this period, particularly his *habilitus* thesis concerning the collapse of Roman civilization, use the concepts of infrastructure and superstructure as a ground of his analysis. However, this does not mean that Weber held Marxist ideas, but rather that he was affected by the historical materialist approach that was widespread at that time (Roth, 1971a).

There is also a significant line of thought around *Grundrisse* that holds Marx and Weber complement one another in their analysis of Oriental societies. George Lichtheim was the first scholar who observed such a connection between them. He thinks that Weber's studies in the sociology of world religions accords with Marx's scheme of historical development, in particular that found in *Grundrisse*. According to Lichtheim (1961, p. 385), if Weber had had an opportunity to read *Grundrisse*, he could have related his own studies of the Orient with Marx's research. Ernest Mandel (1971, p. 123, fn. 26) states that the views of cities and craftsmanship in Oriental societies identified in Weber's work are in fact the same as those concerning Oriental societies as expressed by Marx in *Grundrisse*.[8] Mohammad R. Nafissi (2000, 2005, p. 104), who stresses the similarities in Weber and Marx's examination of antiquity, states that Weber's explanation of underdevelopment in Near Eastern societies due to the effects of primitive bureaucratic administration, which he conceptualized as Oriental despotism, coincides with the approach of Marx in *Grundrisse*. Jack Goody, (1996, p. 3) one of the scholars to most clearly express that Marx's construction of a "stationary Asian state" in the form of despotism based on irrigation, prepared the ground for

----

8   Paul Hirst tries to purify Marxism from being Eurocentric by accusing Weberian sociology of being Western oriented. According to him, Marx gave only a priority to the West and did not see the West and capitalism as unique. (Hirst, 1975, p. 460).

Weber's explanations. He states that the works of both were formed by an Asiatic exceptionalism (Goody, 1996, p. 82).

The German sinologist, Karl Witfogel (1981, pp. xxvii–xxviii), tries to delve further into the matter of Marx's approach to Oriental societies from a Weberian perspective in his controversial book written in 1957. In this work, which provoked a number of discussions, he synthesizes Marx and Weber, re-establishing their approaches to Oriental societies in the framework of "hydraulic bureaucracies" starting from Marx's Asiatic Mode of Production (AMP) thesis and working towards the analysis of Weberian patrimonialism. Even if his principal aim was to demonstrate that the Soviet system was an Oriental despotic power, he wants to open a debate about the form of Marxism prevalent in the Soviet World (Wittfogel, 1981, p. xxviii). Witfogel is important in that he is aware of the capacity of Weber's studies in providing a completion to Marxist theory.

In this context, Bryan S. Turner holds an important place in the literature. He denied the integrated opposition between Weber and Marx and emphasized the similarities in the context of their studies of Oriental societies. In his study examining Weber's sociological analysis of Islamic societies, Turner saw that the Marxist scheme is subject to similar problems. Subsequently, he wrote a separate treatise on this subject matter. He is of the opinion that the two thinkers worked around the same problems, and thus were not only led to similar perspectives, but also developed the same conceptual systems and were fed from the same Orientalist sources. Turner states (1974, pp. 75, 173, 1978, p. 1, 1981, pp. 234, 248, 1992, pp. 25–26) that Weber's patrimonial dominance theses and Marx's AMP model were very close to one another. What is more, because they offered the same explanations for the stagnation of Oriental societies before capitalism, the thesis that the two thinkers are in conflict is invalid in this context. Turner, who states that there is a difference between Weber and Marx in the way in which they examine these issues, absolutely denies the idea that Weber developed his own thought in a dialogue with Marx's ghost (Turner, 1974, pp. 16–17). Turner's study, which separately examines both the approach of Marx and Weber to Oriental societies and expresses the closeness of their perspective on the Orient, fills an important gap in the literature. As an expert on the sociology of Islam, Turner continued his work in the context of Islamic societies, but nevertheless was unable to evaluate Marx and Weber's approach to Oriental societies as a whole. Thus he could not implement a systematic method of comparison.

Whether positively or negatively, we can see from the account given above that Weber in some way has been evaluated according to his relationship with Marx and Marxism. In this sense, although it is correct that Weber criticized Marx with the desire to form an alternative to Marxism without mentioning his name or openly taking sides, the fact that he also has been positioned as an integral theoretical alternative to Marx has to do with the political atmosphere of the period. After 1970, the rapidly increasing discovery of theoretical similarities and the attempt for synthesis continued to be motivated by the political environment.[9] Ultimately, both approaches remain far from understanding the core logic of either Marx's or Weber's sociology. Opposition discourses achieved by working from purely polemical expressions or methodological arguments and convergence theses which are achieved by working from some of Weber's personal evaluations[10] towards Marx, are both undermined by an integral evaluation of their sociology. In this sense, although we can see that the array of studies mentioned above indicates the existence of some similarities concerning Oriental societies, it is also clear that the subject has not been studied in depth. And even though a number of references and evaluations in the literature touch upon the subject, incidentally forming a very contentious debate, it is remarkable that there has not been one individual work which examines the subject thoroughly.

My thesis in this work is that although a strict divergence exists in Marx and Weber's analyses on modern society, they have a converging perspective on Oriental societies, as the fundamental aim of their sociology, as with other early pioneers of sociological thought, is to define modern Western societies. Both Marx and Weber examined Oriental societies in the light of Occidental societies, and made analyses that were incredibly close to one another, even complementary. By following nineteenth century Western social thought, they used the information provided by the Orientalists to define the position of modern society in world history.

---

9   Moreover, the Marx-Weber opposition in mainstream sociology, for example in text books, maintained its dominant position.

10   Eduard Baumgarten, Weber's student, states that Weber said two weeks before his death, "Today an academician, in particular a philosopher, is defined by their attitude towards Nietzsche and Marx. Anyone who says that an important part of their study has been formed without any contribution from these two men is deceiving themselves and others. Our intellectual universe has been formed to a large extent by Marx and Nietzsche" (Roth, 1971b, p. 22) These words are often presented as evidence for the claim that Weber was not opposed to Marx, but rather that he was nurtured by him.

PART I
Karl Marx and Imagining the Orient

Chapter 2

The Development of Marx's Vision of the Orient: The Cultural and Social Background

Karl Marx's interpretation of modern society led him to become one of the three classics in sociology. It could be said that he had a greater tendency to make sociological explanations than either Saint-Simon or Comte although he was not concerned with pure sociology. For this reason, those who followed Marx were forced to shape the main works of sociology while keeping his theory in mind.

During the era in which sociology was born, classification of societies held an important place in the explanation of the modern social form. In this context, analyses of Eastern societies became a permanent part of the explanation of the modern society, and Marx, who used Oriental societies in this way, pursued this tradition. Proposing that social forms were basically formed by modes of production, he analyzed them according to the stages that humanity had experienced historically. It was in this framework that he formulated the AMP in order to analyze Oriental societies.

Even if Marx did not devote much room to the analysis of Oriental societies in his work, they do hold an important place in his sociology. Nevertheless, his explanations of Oriental societies are generally studied in a fragmented way, and have not been examined thoroughly. Marx's writing style, the fragmented nature of the development of his theory, the manner in which his works were published and the political environment in which the matters were debated all contributed to this.

In the following five chapters, the functions of Oriental societies in his theory will be discussed. In order to evaluate his theory of Oriental societies, the sources, conceptual system, manner in which he used Oriental societies in his theory and his analyses of Oriental societies will be analyzed.

The Political and Intellectual Environment of Young Marx

Marx (May 5, 1818, Trier–March 14, 1883, London) was born in the German city of Trier into a Jewish family that converted to Protestantism. It is necessary to understand the formation of Marx's thoughts and sociology in the context of the revolutionary intellectual and political environment of the day.

In order to understand Marx, one must first become well acquainted with the world in which his philosophical and intellectual development took place. There are clear traces of the nineteenth-century's intellectual climate in Marx's thought.[1] Marx's intellectual development can be dealt with in three layers. The first of these regards his family, the environment in which he spent his adulthood and the educational system in which he was raised. As for the second layer, it consists of the German political and social environment present at the beginning of the nineteenth century. Here, the French Revolution and the counter-revolution, Romanticism, issues concerned with formation of German national history and German unity are matters that particularly come to the fore. In the third layer, the Enlightenment, which affected the formation of the nineteenth century, German historical philosophy, the development of Orientalism and the attempts to define modern society took place. These three layers were integral to the *weltanschauung* in which Marx was situated.

Due to the characteristics of the era, Marx's parents—first his father and then his mother—converted from Judaism to Protestantism when he was a child. His father, Hirschel Marx, who was raised amidst Enlightenment ideals and whose personal connection with religion had weakened, made this choice so that his children would have better prospects in life. Marx's father, a lawyer, was a liberal seriously influenced by the Enlightenment thinkers and adopted the ideas of the French Revolution. Marx's childhood was spent in his father's library, which was full of works from the Enlightenment.

Trier, the oldest city in Germany, where Marx's family lived, is in the Rhineland region on the border with France. Here the political effects of the French Revolution displayed themselves widely and liberalism was the dominant political thought. It had spread after Napoleon's campaign, and was found, in general, among the *petite* bourgeoisie enlightened thinkers of which Marx's father was one. These thinkers, who criticized the aristocracy, demanded a democratic Germany. Thus, this was a region in which radical democratic petite bourgeoisie and labor movements were common.

In addition to the effect of the French Revolution, there is the fact that the Rhineland region was one of the first regions in Germany to be industrially developed. Unlike the rest of Germany, which took upon the industrial development relatively late, it was the first place to encounter the problems that made their stamp on the nineteenth century. In addition to this, the region played host to a number of major political developments in Germany. In this environment, Marx was raised as an enlightened humanist revolutionary and radical democrat.

The educational system in which Marx was schooled influenced the development of his ideas and intellectual character in many ways. In 1810, in the quest of realizing the ideal of German national unity, the Prussian minister of education, Wilhelm von Humboldt (1767–1835), who was significantly influenced by leading thinkers of the period, such as Goethe, Winckelmann, Herder and Schiller, played an important role in the classical education that was part of the education system. After these reforms in Gymnasiums Latin, Greek and Classics

---

1   As Foucault (2005, p. 285) writes, "Marxism exists in nineteenth-century thought like a fish in water: that is, it is unable to breathe any-where else."

were specifically thought. As a result, Marx not only started to learn these languages while still in high school, but also attained an in-depth knowledge of antiquity and European history. The effect of this education, apparent in all German thinkers of the nineteenth century, showed itself in the interest Marx took in the ancient period from the view of European historical uniqueness.

This familial and educational layer was augmented by the political and intellectual effects of the environment with which Marx was surrounded (Garaudy, 1967). At the beginning of the nineteenth century Germany opened its eyes on the century with Napoleon's campaign. With the influence of this campaign German thinkers tried to fight off the threats of the age with intense Enlightenment criticism and romanticism. In contrast to the scientific and rationalist ideals of the Enlightenment, the German intellectuals who had brought naïvely to the fore the love of nature and earlier periods of humanity, also aimed to explain the roots of the German nation and thus make a contribution to the realization of German unity. The attempts to redefine the nation opened the way to the development in the philosophy of history in Germany. While a unique perspective was introduced by human history in the framework of the return to nature offered by Romanticism, attempts to discover the roots of the nation opened the way to create the most influential area for the German philosophy of history. Herder, Kant, Schelling and Hegel played the most fundamental role in nineteenth-century European thought.

This second layer was one that pervaded the general situation of nineteenth-century European thought. Progressivism was not only a privileged concept of eighteenth-century Enlightenment thinkers, but also a popular idea in nineteenth century (Koselleck, 2007, p. 21), and in fact has become one of the cornerstones and distinguishing characteristics of modern Western thought. The scientific developments that prepared the ground for progressivism at the time formed the belief that with these a new world could be established. Humanity's progress appeared possible with the establishment of sovereignty over nature. According to nineteenth-century thought, a human being who had established sovereignty over nature had the power to redesign society.

In this sense, progressivism made sociology possible. It was used to demonstrate the uniqueness and superiority of modern society, and to prove that modernity is the peak of historical and social development (Plamenatz, 1992, p. 301) in comparison to others. Marx's theory of the development of modern society was formed in this progressive environment.

Yet although Marx's thought was shaped in such an intellectual and political environment, he had a dialectical relationship with the French revolution; he was affected by a variety of attitudes towards the revolution and later formed his own system of thought based on its criticism.

The Development of Marx's Thought and His Interest in Oriental Societies

The formation of Marx's philosophical perception was a long process based upon the criticism of different schools of thought. More specifically, the philosophical development of Marx can be studied in four phases. The first consists of his youth, when he was with the left-wing Hegelians. This period, lasted until 1844. In this period Marx was a radical democrat who made abstract religious and philosophical criticisms. In the second phase, he was influenced by the thought of Feuerbach, and by criticizing Hegelian idealism and utopian socialism, he formed his own view of dialectic materialism. This period lasted from 1844 to 1848. In the third period, he carried out political economy studies and tried to gain a theoretical framework for his thought. This phase, representing the mature phase in Marxist theory, continued until the Paris Commune in 1871. After this, Marx searched for new bases for his own model; this forms the final period in which he pursued fragmented interests.

Marx developed his approach to Oriental societies in three different stages which ran parallel to this process. In his youth, he dealt with Oriental societies, without a deep assessment, by using direct quotes about Oriental despotism which was found in European thought. After 1850, in the second stage, Marx attempted to create political and economic analyses of Oriental societies in his studies on political-economy. Finally, in the period after *Das Kapital*, he started to take an interest in ethnologic studies of ancient and contemporary non-Western societies, ensuring the material foundations of AMP.

Marx started to form his own thought while at university. In this sense, according to Lenin's (1990:99) generally accepted view, Marx's sources were German philosophy, British economic policies and French socialism (Krader, 1974, 1975, 1982). In addition to these three sources, the Enlightenment occasionally provided a source of philosophic inspiration. He had a unique relationship with his sources. First, he would digest the sources completely and would then criticize the ideas that he had attained from another, forming his own approach. Thus, Marx's thought was the product of a simultaneous engagement with multiple sources and was formed in the shape of a new interpretation (Lichtheim, 1969, pp. 185–214).

Starting with Hegel, German philosophy was an important philosophical source for Marx. Even though he did not live at the same time as Hegel, he was under the influence of Hegel's philosophy due to the intellectual milieu in which he was included and the context in which he found himself. As a university student, Marx spent time in Bonn and Berlin, two cities where the influence of Hegel was intensely felt. His teacher in Berlin, Otto Bauer, introduced Marx to Hegel's works. In this period, in a letter he wrote to his father, dated November 10, 1837, Marx (1975a, notes 18–20) states that he wanted to study Hegel from beginning to end. After Hegel's death in 1831, Hegelian thought was maintained by two branches; while the conservative branch proposed that Hegel's philosophy was the last stage of philosophy, the Left Hegelians or Young Hegelians, to which Marx belonged, tried to establish a radical political extension of Hegel's philosophy. In this group, which, rather than criticizing Hegel's metaphysical inferences, broke away from the theological dimension and used the dialectic method in religious and political analyses, Marx became acquainted with the possibilities offered by Hegel's thought. However, over time he fell under the influence of Feuerbach and French materialism, and began criticizing Hegelian thought from the perspective of materialism. His PhD thesis, presented to Jena University in 1841, is the beginning of this transitional phase. In this study Marx compares the philosophies of Democritus and Epicurus. He was a party to the materialist philosophy of Epicurus against that of Democritus.[2]

In this period, Marx broke away from Hegel and the left-wing Hegelians formulating his own dialectical materialist philosophy with a criticism of Feuerbach.[3] However, Marx had a complex relationship with Hegel from which he did not find it easy to extricate himself. Even if Marx states that he had severed the connection with Hegel with *German Ideology* in 1844, he returned later several times to this philosopher. Marx qualified himself as a disciple of Hegel at the time he formed his own theory in 1872 (Marx, 1996, p. 19). At last, Engels stated that German Socialists were proud to be "descended not only from Saint-Simon, Fourier and Owen, but also from Kant, Fichte and Hegel" (Engels, 1989, p. 459).

After completing his PhD thesis, understanding that he would not be able to find the position he hoped for at Berlin University, Marx left Berlin and started to work as an editor for a radical democratic newspaper in Bonn, *Rheinische Zeitung*. In this period, Marx, who encountered the current social problems and the question of laborers and peasants for the first time, started to collect articles, particularly those addressed to the problems of forest villagers. However, while the publication of these articles increased, so did the political pressure on the newspaper, forcing Marx to resign. This process had a significant effect on Marx's thought. When he had joined the paper he was a radical democrat who was only interested in the social and economic conditions of the villagers; when he left he was much closer to socialism. What is more, this is the period in which Marx started to shift from philosophy and law to economics and sociology (Riazanov, 1990, pp. 40–41).

After leaving the newspaper; towards the end of 1843, Marx went to Paris to publish a journal with Arnold Ruge. They were able to produce only one issue of the *Deutsch-Französische Jahrbücher* in February 1844. In this journal Marx published two articles that were the first critical products of his own thought. In the first, *Contribution to the Critique of Hegel's Philosophy of Right [Introduction]* (Marx, 1976a), he questioned Hegel's idealist philosophy; and in the other article, *On the Jewish Question*, written as a response to Bauer, the distance between Marx and the Young Hegelians became clear (Marx, 1976b). Due to a difference of opinion with Ruge, Marx was not involved any further

---

2 For a comparison between them see Krader, 1975, note 3
3 To follow traces of this transition from the earlier manuscripts see Marx and Engels, 1897

in the publication of the journal, but started to write articles for the most radical German newspaper in Paris, *Vorwärts*, stating that he openly supported the assassination attempt carried out against the Prussian king, Frederick William IV. Eventually, in response to a request from the Prussian government, Marx was exiled from Paris in February 1845 and went to Brussels, where he would stay until the 1848 revolution.

Even though the *Deutsch-Französische Jahrbücher* was unsuccessful, this journal had another influence on Marx. Friedrich Engels, the son of a German industrialist from England, contributed an article entitled *The Condition of the Working-Class in England* to this journal. After this article had attracted Marx's attention he met with Engels on August 28, 1844 in Paris at the *Café de la Régence*. They spent 10 days together until September 6, 1844. Thus, the foundations of the continuous friendship and cooperation that was to last a lifetime between them began. In these meetings, not only did they criticize the young Hegelians and Hegelian idealism, but they also decided to carry out a joint project. They completed *Holy Family*, in Brussels and get it published in Frankfurt in 1845.

In 1846, another joint project with Engels formed a turning point in Marx's thought. This work, *German Ideology*, represented the young Marx's liberation from the influence of Feuerbach. It was the first systematic study to realize Marx's materialist conceptualization of history, and includes the fundamentals of his later conceptual system. The basic concept of historical materialism, mode of production, was first developed in this study.[4] According to this study, the development of modes of production is affected by the internal laws of the powers of production and the dialectic influence of production relationships. *German Ideology*, which tried to demonstrate scientifically that the historical role of the working class, as a social force, was to fulfill the duty of destroying the capitalist system and constructing a Communist society, represents an important step in the development of Marxist theory (Marx and Engels, 1976).

Marx's settling of accounts with Hegelian thought and German idealists, in one sense, represents his settling accounts with utopian socialists.[5] During the years that Marx spent in Paris, particularly 1843 and 1844, he became acquainted with the philosophers mentioned to him by his father-in-law, Ludwig von Westphalen, and later Professor Gans in Berlin. He became closely acquainted with and read the works of utopian thinkers like Saint-Simon, Fourier, Cabet, Proudhon, Robert Owen and Weitling. The criticisms that Marx made of the utopian socialists, whose ideals he shared, were due to their methods. *The Poverty of Philosophy,*

---

4   The concept of social form was used for the first time in *Grundrisse*, while the concept of the socio-economic form was used for the first time in the forward to *Contribution to the Criticism of Political Economy*. In order to understand the developments of social order that followed one upon the other it is necessary to examine the general scheme of *German ideology*.

5   For socialist thought before Marx, see Marx and Engels, 1969. The other articles in this encyclopedia about early socialism are short but explanatory.

which Marx produced as a critique of *The Philosophy of Poverty* by Proudhon, is an important work that expresses these thoughts (Marx, 1976c). In this text, a forerunner to the *Communist Manifesto*, Marx exhibits his own thoughts that had now been well-developed on communism (Riazanov, 1990, p. 80). According to Marx, when utopian socialists criticized capitalism, they emphasized the immorality of the latter, but they did not offer a real solution or alternative system. In contrast, Marx was searching for an organized body of socialist thought that he could scientifically prove. For this reason, he preferred to separate his own theory from the utopians and called his theory communism.[6]

Thus, Marx had realized an important transformation. He formed his scientific socialism by criticizing radical democrats, left Hegelians, vulgar materialism and utopian socialism. He gave an important place to the historical role of the working class, and carried out studies in Cologne in a pre-revolutionary environment with Engels. In January 1847, they joined the *League of Justice*, which they subsequently re-organized. After this they changed its name to the *Communist League*. *Communist Manifesto,* which is written as a manifesto of the *League*, appeared at the beginning of 1848. It was the first example of the crystallization of Marx's thoughts. So, it represents Marx's transition to the mature period. In this period he carried out fundamental analysis concerning the nature of modern society.

In the works of the early period mentioned above, in the texts which gave shape to historical materialism, Marx was also aware of the discussions concerning Oriental societies thanks to the Enlightenment thinkers and other sources which he had studied. However, there is no direct analysis of Oriental societies in his works from this time. But in the work called *Contribution to the Critique of Hegel's Philosophy of Right,* Marx compares the character of political authority in Asiatic, ancient, feudal and capitalist societies. While explaining a text by Hegel and criticizing the Hegel's defense of monarchism, Marx makes two references to despotism (Marx, 1976d). Similar references are made in the article *Debates on Freedom of Press* (Marx, 1975b). In this period, Marx accepted the existence of a separate society and political form, that is, Oriental despotism, and used it polemically.

In *German Ideology*, Marx and Engels (1976, pp. 32–35 and 89–90) classified the development of the division of labor before Capitalism as communal, classic and feudal. However, there are no comparisons to non-European societies. The focus of the *Communist Manifesto* is on the historical development in the West and there is no social analysis concerning the Orient. However, there are references to Oriental societies in the context of the spread of capitalism and its progress.

With the failure of the 1848 revolutions and his expulsion from Germany and France, Marx went to London in 1849, where he would spend the rest of his life. In this period, which forms a new stage in his life, Marx (Marx, 1978a, 1978b) first questioned the development and results of the 1848 revolutions, and then

---

6 Engels says that in order to separate himself from the utopians and bourgeoisie radicals, in 1847 they did not name it as socialist manifesto (Marx, 1968).

turned to political economic studies, trying to re-establish his thought once again. This period represents the start of an intensification of his efforts to understand and define modern society. By analyzing the development and nature of modern society, Marx was aiming to create an opportunity to bring about a revolution.

In this period, he re-read the English political economists that he had first studied from French and annotated between 1843 and 1844. In this reading, Marx established the basic views of his own theory and based it upon a criticism of the modern political-economy that had been developed by Adam Smith (1723–90) and David Ricardo (1772–1823). Reinterpreting their value theory and labor theory of value, Marx created a surplus-value analysis based on his own studies on political-economy.

Marx started to write his own "economics." One of his letters to Engels he says that he will complete is in a short time. But he was forced to constantly put it off due to hardness of his daily life and theoretical problems. During the 1850s, he was writing for the *New York Daily Tribune* (NYDT).[7] The articles he produced ranged from colonial issues to the administration of the French budget, the Crimean War and the American foreign policy, as well as many current events. More than forty of these articles were concerned with Oriental societies. The general subject in these articles was the political, social and military effects of British rule in colonized India and China. Additionally, Marx and Engels (Marx and Engels, 1897) created an important corpus in the framework of the Eastern question in the context of the Crimean War.

In these years, which were spent in intense journalistic activities, Marx was making notes for his most important work. In these notes, known as *Grundrisse,* Marx criticized political-economy and established his own thought. In the *Einlaitung* (Introduction) of this "difficult text"[8] the methodological bases for critique of political economy are explained (Oakley, 1983, p. 55). For this reason, it occupies an important place from the aspect of understanding Marx's basic analyses. It demonstrates the stages of development of Marx's concepts and studies and includes basic forms of many unique analyses. *Grundrisse* is also particularly important as it helps us to understand the structure of Marx's thought.

Grundrisse occupies an important place from the aspect of containing the first systematic analysis concerning Oriental societies. Here in the section entitled *Pre-Capitalist Economic Formations,* Marx analyzes ancient, classic Germanic, feudal and Oriental modes of production, and emphasizes the stagnant and immutable nature of Asian societies. Marx also recasts the approach that he presented

---

7 These articles demonstrate Marx's attitudes to many current problems. Marx and Engels corresponded and developed their thoughts on these subject matters before writing the articles. As a result, the correspondence of this period is important for following the development of Marx's thought.

8 Marx (Avineri, 1971) states that *Grundrisse,* "were written not for publication but for self-clarification at widely separated periods."

in his earlier newspaper articles concerning Oriental societies into a general theoretical framework.

In *Contribution to the Critique of Political Economy,* Marx mentions modes of production as stages of economic development, presenting the final style for his historical periodization. Even if these stages sometimes continue simultaneously, they demonstrate the progressive development of humanity. This is the first place that Marx covertly formulated the Asiatic style as an alternative to the Western path.

One of Marx's most important works in this period was the *Theories of Surplus Value,* consisting of notes and manuscripts that he created between January 1862 and June 1863. In these notes, which can be considered to be a continuation of *Grundrisse,* a preparation for *Das Kapital,* or perhaps its fourth volume, Marx analyzes Asiatic societies from the perspective of political economists who had adopted three different stances: (1) Adam Smith's productive and unproductive labor (Marx, 1989, pp. 12–13, 74 and 192), (2) Simon-Nicolas-Henri Linguest's criticism of Montesquieu (Marx, 1989, pp. 241, 245), (3) and the theories of the British political economist Richard Jones (Marx, 1991, pp. 48–49, 321, 335, 338, 340 and 356). In this work, it is possible to see that after *Contribution to the Critique of Political Economy,* Marx had not changed the framework in which he handled these subjects.

He published the first volume *Das Kapital,* in 1867. It reflects Marx's own system in the most fundamental way. But it was greeted in Marx's words with a *resounding silence* and remained for many years a work that was neither read nor critiqued. Probably due to disappointment, Marx did not complete the second or third volumes of *Das Kapital,* which were only published posthumously by Engels after being compiled from Marx's notes.

It is possible to find analyses of Oriental societies in the context of studies on political economy in the first and third volumes of *Das Kapital.* Marx mentions Asiatic societies in five different places in the first volume.[9] He deals with them in (1) the first section, which is entitled "Commodities," in a reproduction of the footnote from *Contribution to the Critique of Political Economy* concerning primitive communal property, (2) in the third section, entitled *Money, or the Circulation of Commodities,* when discussing the protection of the excess value in gold or silver against user-value in money circulation, (3) in the thirteenth section entitled *Co-operation,* when arguing that no advanced level of division of labor existed in ancient times or in Asian, Egyptian or Etruscans societies, but rather that they had established a simple co-operation, (4) in the fourteenth section, entitled *Division of Labor and Manufacture,* when dealing with the data provided in the 1853 Indian article, which reiterates the comparison of primitive communism and Asiatic societies, and (5) in the sixteenth section, entitled *Absolute and Relative Surplus Value,* when discussing the place of the Orient in the development of Capitalism and stating that it was as if this development had been imposed by

---

9   Here, it is surprising that there is no mention of AMP, and that the reader is pushed towards a vague understanding of the difference between primitive communism and AMP.

the Orient on Western society, thus examining the differences that resulted from irrigation in Western societies and Oriental societies.

In the third volume of *Das Kapital*, Marx mentions Oriental societies in five places. (1) In the tenth section, entitled *Equalisation of the General Rate of Profit through Competition*, he states that the value of goods is not historical, only theoretical. At the same time as discussing the prioritizing of prices, Marx emphasizes the value of goods in primitive Communist societies. However, he does not state whether or not these societies are Asiatic. (2) In the twentieth section, entitled *Historical Facts about Merchant's Capital*, Marx states that the terms primitive communism and Asiatic have the same meaning. (3) In the twenty-third section, entitled *Interest and Profit of Enterprise*, and while making a functionalist explanation of the state in AMP, Marx examines the relationship between modes of production and the general structure of political administration, claiming that in despotic states the state interferes in all matters. (4) In the sixth part, entitled *Transformation of Surplus Profit into Ground Rent*, Marx discusses the modern form of property rights and states that land only became private property in the West; it has been brought into the Orient by the West in the modern era. Here Marx makes some explanations concerning the land rent in Asia. These explanations become more frequent in the forty-seventh section, *Genesis of Capitalist Ground Rent*. (5) Finally, in the fifty-first section, *Distribution Relations and Production Relations,* Marx criticizes the normalization of production and distribution relationships found in capitalism. He positions oriental societies at the opposite pole by defining them as primitive, or, in some places, as developed communism.

Marx underwent a rapid political evolution, due, in part, to the fact that the publication of *Das Kapital* did not attract attention, and in part due to the changing political environment. However, with the repression of the 1871 Paris Commune, his hopes for a revolutionary movement in Europe were crushed. After this, Marx took a close interest in Russia a country which he believed was a potential candidate for the revolution that would spark revolutions throughout Europe. He studied a number of sources concerned with Russian history and social structure,[10] and, in a similar way, delved into the newly developing ethnographic studies to secure new foundations for his own theory. Marx read ethnologists like Kovalevsky, Morgan, Maine and Sumner and took notes. However, he died in 1883 without converting these notes into a theoretical formulation. After his death, Engels compiled his works and had them republished; he also compiled his notes from many works and gave life to them.

---

10   Marx gathered quite a lot of studies and statistics concerned with the contemporary situation of the Russian society. According to Engels, he had a pile of books on Russian statistics that was more than two meters squared. (Avineri, 1990)

Chapter 3
Discussions on the Asiatic Mode of Production

There is a great deal of literature about Marx's approach to Oriental societies. Indeed, his arguments were realized in the framework of historical phases of transition to socialism. These arguments, which were generally shaped by the political atmosphere of the period, have been greatly affected by the internal divisions of Marxism and the general intellectual environment. In this regard, the arguments about AMP took a journey of several stages. The arguments began in the 1920s after the Russian Revolution, in order to identify the societies that were dominant in the Soviets. This stage came to an end with the removal of AMP from the literature in 1931. In the second stage, the view that Marx had never had any such concept or approach was taken up by many. With the re-publication of *Grundrisse*, Stalin's death and the changes experienced in international politics, the discussions started again in the middle of the 1950s. From the 1960s to the 1980s, the AMP discussions experienced their most lively period, and played an important role in the debates about modernization, the transition to Socialism and the Third World. From the 1980s on, the debates on Marx's theory of Oriental societies and the AMP arguments have gradually been extinguished.

Early Soviet Discussions

The discussions that started in the 1920s and came to a conclusion at the beginning of the 1930s in the Soviet Union were more concerned with the Russian social structure, and therefore, the character of the revolution. In 1928, after the Sinologue Liudvig Mad'iar published a book that analyzed the Chinese economy in the context of AMP, corresponding discussions began among Soviet intellectuals. As a result of this, two meetings were organized by the *Marxist Orientalist Society* in 1930 in Tbilisi and in 1931 in Leningrad. Here, the AMP in Marxist thought was discussed, but as a result of these meetings, it was concluded that Marx never discussed such a thing and that AMP were the equivalent of an Asian type of feudalism (Bailey and Llobera, 1981). Riazanov and Mad'iar, who defended opposing views, were purged in the 1930s.

The fact that the arguments ended in such a way was a determining factor in Stalin's theoretical outlook. In the work entitled *Dialectics and Historical Materialism,* Stalin (1940, 1947) put forward a five-stage view of history and society, consisting of primitive Communism, slavery, feudalism, Capitalism and

Socialism. This historical development thesis, subsequently improved in order to circumvent revolutions that could be realized outside the Soviet doctrine, became the official historical understanding, first in the Soviet Union, and then later in China. In this period, non-Soviet Marxists tried to prove the existence of AMP and those with a critical stance tried to reformulate Marx's concept in the axis of Kovalevsky's post-1870 work or to show that Marx had abandoned this idea.

Discovery of *Grundrisse*: The Rise and Fall of Discussions on AMP

In this environment, even though it was discovered that Marx directly mentioned AMP in *Grundrisse*, the publishing of this work took time. The section of *Grundrisse*, known as *Pre-Capitalist Economic Formations (Formen)*, which was to become the focus of later arguments, was published in 1939 in Moscow, and gained popularity. This is not only because of the wartime environment; it can also be thought that this was an attempt to put the work into circulation as a precaution against the Stalinist position. Until the publication of *Formen* in 1952 and *Grundrisse* in its complete form in 1953 in Berlin, this text had gone almost completely unnoticed. After this, it was translated into a number of languages and AMP became widely discussed.[1]

The reissue of the book and the fanning of the flames of debate ensured a number of political effects. First, Stalin's death and then the official cleansing of Stalinism from the Soviet Union removed the largest obstacle blocking the way to discussion. Also, when many non-Western countries gained independence and saw the development of their own socialist movements, AMPs came onto the agenda (Sezer, 2003, p. 27). From this date on, there was a great increase both in the number and scope of arguments on this subject.[2]

Evgeni Varga (1928) was one of the participants in the discussions in 1930 and 1931. Taking Marx's articles in NYDT as his point of departure, after 1950 in an article he wrote about China, Varga severely criticized these debates. With this he formed a new start for discussions on AMP. Varga (1970) stated that the concept was concerned not only with Oriental but with all non-Western societies. Another person to start the discussions in France was the French Marxist anthropologist Maurice Godelier. Godelier (1964), who had translated *Pre-Capitalist Economic Formations* into French, explained the framework that had been laid out for AMP and claimed that Oriental societies had to follow the typical and tested development present in Western societies. Jean Chesnaux (1964), who wrote about AMP in a

---

1   After *Formen* was published in 1939 in Moscow, it was translated into Japanese in 1948. In 1953 it was published again in Germany, and then translated in 1956 into Italian and Romanian, into English in 1964, and in 1966 into French, and in 1967 into Turkish (Hilav, 1970, pp. 10–11).

2   Samuel Baron (1975) lists over 100 works done in 20 countries between 1963–68. For the literature on this subject also see Bailey and Llobera, 1974; Dunn, 1982.

special issue of the journal *La Pensee* with Godelier and Ferenc Tokei in 1964, brought forward an idea that was in opposition to the entire argument, that the Western type was accidental/causal, while the Asiatic type was universal.

The Sinologue Karl A. Wittfogel has a special place in the discussions of AMP.[3] Wittfogel, a former Marxist, uses Marx's analyses in view of AMP concerning the socio-economic structure of Russian and Oriental societies in his work *Oriental Despotism,* written in 1957 as a means to attack Marxism. Wittfogel's work draws attention to the establishment of despotic power in non-European societies and the dimensions of the Communist interpretation of totalitarianism. Using Weberian terminology, Wittfogel (1981, p. xxiii, 1990) wrote in support of the Marxist analysis of Oriental societies. According to him, the structure of Oriental societies, in the scope of bureaucrats organizing irrigation tasks in the name of the state, formed a despotism that was based on water.

A short time after this work was published criticism directed against Wittfogel started, and in later works that were written on this subject matter, such criticism of this author became almost "traditional" (Bailey and Llobera, 1979, pp. 550–552, fn. 1–8). One of these critics, Arnold Toynbee (1958, pp. 196–197) states that the concept of Oriental despotism used in the work is unfounded and a part of American political propaganda. Wittfogel in turn claims that the reason for this criticism was that he had not given reference to Toynbee's historical perspective. However, he was unable to respond to the criticisms directed at him by Toynbee (Wittfogel, 1958). Joseph Needham (1959), a historian of science, states that in spite of his appreciation for Wittfogel's early works, his concept of Oriental despotism is sophistry. Needham, also argues that his evaluation of despotism based on water is not consistent with empirical data from Chinese history.

Wittfogel's study was subjected to an intense counter attack by Soviet academics (Gellner, 1985), and also caused Marxists in the West to feel incredibly uncomfortable. The truly disturbing point of Wittfogel's thesis is that he expresses Marx's explanations of Oriental societies in a similar way to liberal theorists. Despite Wittfogel's disturbingly self-satisfied Eurocentric analysis, it is incredibly important that some of its foundations can be found in Marx. Defenders of Marxism reject Wittfogel's theory however, either with accusations of misrepresentation or with outright denial. At most, they directed responsibility to Engels or official Soviet Marxism for the claims of Wittfogel. This is because having a scapegoat

---

3   Wittfogel, who paid particular attention to adding himself to the chain of knowledge about Oriental despotism states in one work that there are five stages to the development of "hydraulic" explanations of Oriental societies in the West: (1) The government policies based on irrigation in Oriental societies of Adam Smith and other classic statisticians; (2) Herder and Hegel's statement that the large valley bases of the Orient became residential areas; (3) Marx and Engels' hydraulic states; (4) Weber's statement that the administrative hydraulic bureaucracy was not a class but an "estate;" and finally (5) Wittfogel, own statement that the administrative class was combined with the agricultural administrators as a superior autocracy (Wittfogel 1969, p. 361).

like Stalin gives a certain comfort and there was an attempt to save Marxism from the charges of Eurocentrism. The reason that Wittfogel makes them uneasy is that he identifies the Eurocentrism in Marx's thought and brings it to the fore.

In the English-speaking world, the most influential name in the AMP discussion is that of Eric Hobsbawm, the Marxist historian who wrote a long introduction to the translation of *Pre-Capitalist Economic Formations* (1965). In his introduction, Hobsbawm states that Marx studied Oriental societies with an approach shaped by progressivism. More specifically, that Marx's basic problematic was the development of capitalism. He used the AMP as a non-Western Pre-Capitalist Modes of Production (PCMP) for a means of comparison. Hobsbawm draws attention to the insufficiency of sources concerning Marx's approach to the Orient in both periods; moreover, he claims that after 1870, in the period in which he became acquainted with ethnological studies, Marx changed his concept of a linear progression to a multi-lined historical analysis. Thus, Hobsbawm claims that even if Marx did not find the opportunity to revise his theory concerning Oriental societies, he was able to change his perspective. Unfortunately, this view, based on a few letters that Marx wrote after mid-1870, is not supported by a close examination of his ethnological studies. Therefore, while the first part of Hobsbawm's periodization is accurate, the second section, which removes Marx from progressivism, has no sound foundation.

In this sense, the works that completed this approach and which included this information were published by Lawrence Krader (1974, 1975, 1982). Krader, criticizing Marx's sources, emphasizes that it is necessary to evaluate his AMP theory within the context of nineteenth-century Western social thought. According to Krader, Marx shares many of the misconceptions that his contemporaries fell into, and was unable to harmonize his views concerning Oriental societies with his general theory. It was for this reason that, with the disappointment that he experienced in politics after the 1871 Paris Commune, he returned once again to his ethnological studies. Krader questions Marx's relationship with ethnology and criticizes the way that Engels later used these notes. He emphasizes that Engels explained and simplified Marx's works and also made them more progressive. However, by expressing that in ethnological readings Marx focused more on the points that supported his own social evolutionary perspective, Krader (1975, p. 3) contradicts himself.

The compilation of what Marx wrote in various works about Oriental societies plus their publication as individual works have seriously affected the arguments in the literature. The first of these works was the one known as *The Eastern Question,* which was compiled from the writings of Marx and Engels in 1897 by Marx's daughter, Eleanor, and her husband, Edward Aveling (Marx and Engels, 1897). This book, which was also printed at a number of different later dates, includes in particular the NYDT articles that Marx wrote concerning the Crimean War. Another influential work for the subject in question was the book published by the Soviet Foreign Languages Publishing House called *On Colonialism,* which included selections concerned on the subject from different works by Marx and

Engels (1969). Marx's notes on the history of Muslim administration in India are important in this context.[4] These edited works, which have made the job of the researcher much easier, have also in one sense determined the framework of evaluating Marx's approach to Oriental societies, but more importantly have been the reason why his writings have been removed from a general context.

The most commonly used of these collected works is the work *Karl Marx on Colonialism and Modernization* by Shlomo Avineri (1968a). In the introduction written to this book (Avineri, 1968b, pp. 27–28) and in another work (Avineri, 1971) which makes many references to Marx's social and political views, Avineri proposes that Marx's ideas about modernization sometimes conflict with his theory's supposed universal validity. However, emphasizing the Hegelian roots of Marx's theory (Avineri, 1990), and stating that Marx's criteria for modernization have, in a surprising manner, over time come to correspond with the views (universal superiority, special and goal-oriented norms, advanced change and development based on class structure) of the people whom he had criticized, Avineri fails to see that these views of Marx result from his own theory on historical development. On the other hand, Avineri, who (like other authors) states that Marx's perspective of the progress of humanity presents very questionable views about colonization, claims that after 1870 Marx returned to this issue, and that if there had been more time he would have revised his own theory. Here, he shows as evidence the letter that Marx wrote to the Russian socialist journal *Otechestvenniye Zapiski* in 1877. In addition to this, he mentions a speech Marx made in 1872 in Amsterdam, as reported by Hans H. Gerth (1958, p. 236), in which Marx states that one should not take into account the traditions and situations of various countries in the transition to socialism, and that there was not only one path for modernization (Avineri, 1969, p. 174, note 4). However, as Avineri does not quote the entire sentence, he covers up the fact that when speaking of various countries, Marx was only talking about Western countries and not all. Thus, the reader is misled.[5] In conclusion, these views which are presented to demonstrate the validity of the universality of Marx's theory are not based on a careful or integral interpretation of Marx's work and speeches.

In this context, a work that attracts attention in the literature was created by Bryan S. Turner. Turner (1978, note 50) constructs his book on the criticism that Avineri used Marx's theses in a selective manner to legitimize the Israeli invasion of Palestine. Turner, (1978, note 50) who states that Marxist Orientalism carries deep traces of a relationship with Hegelian Orientalism and the idea of historical phases, proposes that Marx's fundamental problem started with the hypothesis that the Occident is active and changeable while the Orient is passive and stagnant. As

---

4   These notes were published in the Soviet Union, first in Russian in 1947, and then in a 1970 revised and corrected version published in English (Marx, 1970).

5   Marx uses this sentence in a speech (La Liberté Speech) at September 8, 1872 in The International Working Men's Association's meeting at Amsterdam. For the full and original version of this sentence see Marx and Engels, 1962.

he did in his earlier work, Turner finds that the framework on the Islamic world used by Weber has more explanatory power than that found in Marx. The fundamental weakness in Marx's model is meanwhile explained by the geographic limitations at its foundations (Turner, 1978, p. 50). Although, Turner's work occupies an important place in the literature, it does not offer a comprehensive examination of Marx's work as a whole. The polemic with Avineri and the fact that this matter is examined solely from the aspect of Muslim societies both limit its significance. Given the absence of the kind of detailed explanations Turner used when dealing with Weber, this work appears to indicate a foray beyond his area of expertise.

In the work they wrote together, Barry Hindess and Paul Q. Hirst, (1975) who enter the discussion from a similar perspective as Turner, deal with Marx's AMP analysis from the view of economics and conceptualizing modes of production. They state that referring to the journal articles, notes and correspondence on the matter is problematic and also that the debate has been carried out on frail ground. According to them, the issue should be studied from theoretical texts and Marx should be evaluated as a theoretician (Hindess and Hirst, 1975, p. 178). In addition to this, the authors emphasize the dangers of selectivism in evaluating Marx. Thus, they try to develop a methodological defense against accusations of colonialist interests in reference to Marx's writings on India in NYDT and in his correspondence with Engels. Hindess and Hirst, following Althusser (1969, p. 35), consider the works subsequent to the shift in Marx's epistemology in 1857 (after *Grundrisse*) to be works of his mature period and, therefore, state that when evaluating Marx it is necessary to take this period as the basis. It is of course necessary to keep theoretical texts central when dealing with any issue in Marx. However, sources like the newspaper articles, notes and correspondence make it easier to understand his position, as they hold a light to the formation and background of these works. If one was to examine the subject matter from their perspective, many central theories that appear in the *1844 Manuscripts, Grundrisse* and the second and third volumes of *Das Kapital* would be left out of the evaluation, and this would greatly reduce the theoretical power of Marx.

Another name who contributed to the analysis of AMP from an economical viewpoint was Ernest Mandel. Mandel claims that he was able to be critical of Marx's analyses of Oriental societies by focusing on demonstrating that Marx wanted to show the unique nature of capitalism. According to him, Marx examined the developmental line in the West and the underdevelopmental line in the Orient (Mandel, 1971, p. 127, note 26). For Mandel, the fundamental problem of Marx's analyses on Oriental societies is not merely economic within a narrow context.

Perry Anderson devoted a section of his book *Lineages of the Absolutist State* (1974) to AMP. Anderson (1979, p. 495) deals with Marx's theories in the framework of the lengthy analyses which he makes about the historical development of the theses of Oriental despotism in the West. Anderson (1979, p. 495) states that no idea about Oriental societies exists in Marx's sources. According to Anderson, in this framework, the theoretical function of Marx's conceptualization of AMP was intended to demonstrate the unique nature of Europe by explaining the collapse of non-European empires which, unlike European ones, had been unable to achieve capitalist development. Thus, Anderson states that the AMP lacked consistency and was formed with insufficient knowledge. For example, in holding that there was both a very strong and centralized state and autonomous village communities, two forms that do not support one another, the two fall into contradiction. Anderson, (1979, p. 495) thinking that Marx's generalization of some specific forms to the all Orient cannot be scientifically approved, emphasizes that Marx's theories are proved unsound by empirical-historical research (Anderson, 1979, p. 490). However, it is surprising that Anderson concludes his analysis in a typical Orientalist-Weberian manner by offering "civilization" instead of "means of production" (Anderson, 1979, p. 495) as a better means of defining the Orient. After criticizing Marx and his conceptualization of Oriental despotism, Anderson states that from a cultural-essentialist perspective, the reason for the lack of development in the Orient depended on the failure to form a civic culture, the lack of development of trade, the central position of military success, and that failure of cities, particularly in the Islamic world, thus obstructing the development of capitalism. In this way Anderson is more fragile and Eurocentric than Marx, whom he is criticizing.

The Italian academic Umberto Melotti (1977) examined the different approaches to Marx's analysis of PCMP. Melotti notes that Marx studied the differences between three pre-capitalist modes of production within the context of slavery, village and city relationships; the state, land types, ownership of means of production; and the existence of public works. Melotti states that this three-fold differentiation formed around these factors and the birth of capitalism in the West created a historical chain. He draws attention to Marx's PCMP analysis and observes that the AMP was in fact simultaneous. On this basis, he demonstrates how the feudal modes of production (FMP) were differentiated in an artificial manner, and thus, that Marx's fundamental aim was not so much to explain Oriental social forms, but to differentiate and distinguish them from capitalism. Melotti states that Marx made a conscious decision not to apply the same analyses that he had used for the birth of AMP to that of FMP. So, he was able to depict the Orient as stagnant and the West as active. Furthermore, he considers the historical roots of a hydraulic despotic state are to be rather weak. By accepting the transcendent state, notes Melotti, Marx refutes his own basic argument in which the substructure determines the superstructure, and instead accepts a view in which the state determines the production relationship. Nevertheless, while evaluating how Marx dealt with Oriental societies over a wide scope, it cannot be said that Melotti dealt with his approach with conceptual depth. The fact that he does not discuss the place of Oriental societies in Marx's work in particular, theory renders his analysis deficient.

In addition to the works dealt with above, it is worth mentioning the works of Marian Sawer, (1977) Daniel Thorner (1980), who studied this subject at the end of the 1970s, and Brendan O'Leary (1989); the latter, one of the rare names to deal with the subject matter after 1980, studied the AMP argument in a comprehensive and detailed manner. The work of Sudipta Kaviraj (1983) deals with the matter from a methodological angle. This is not a view from which the subject is often examined and thus has a distinct importance. Kaviraj not only states that Marx applied Hegelian logic in order to express his own views, but also that studies of Oriental societies held a central place in the dialectic method. When viewed in this way, Marx's Oriental studies take on greater importance, as they become key to his own doctrine concerning modern society. With his examination of Oriental societies, Marx presents a contrasting model to modern society, thus trying to ensure methodological unity for his own theoretical model. Working from here, Kaviraj (1983) states that empirical accuracy took second place in Marx's analyses, and that the primary matter, the study of the Orient, methodologically held a primary position in the theoretical model. Kaviraj has made important contributions by putting forward the idea that understanding Marx's works is easier if we keep in mind the background to his logical system used in *Grundrisse* and subsequent works.

Turkish Debate on AMP

The discussion presents an especially interesting situation for Turkey. Although the discussion has arisen as an extension of these Western arguments, there are some original formulations related to the modernization of the third world. In Turkey, Marx's approach to Oriental society was, for the most part, concerned with the character of the Ottoman State and society, and therefore continued in the context of AMP as a question concerning the transition to Marxism. The fundamental problem is whether Turkey can be considered to be an AMP, and whether the social character of any possible socialist revolution seemed problematic. During this period, in 1967, Marx's *Pre-Capitalist Economic Formations* was translated by Mihri Belli into Turkish (Marx and Engels, 1977) and fanned the flames of discussion in the West. The novelist/thinker Kemal Tahir brought the AMP onto the agenda by stressing the difference between the Orient and the West. According to Kayalı (2008), he played an important role in expanding the discussion with a new theoretical context.

In 1966, under the guidance of Kemal Tahir, Sencer Divitçioğlu (1966) published the pamphlet *ATÜT ve Az Gelişmiş Ülkeler* (AMP and Underdeveloped Countries), the first independent study in Turkish, and a year later, the book, *Asya Üretim Tarzı ve Osmanlı Toplumu* (Asiatic Mode of Production and Ottoman Society), his main work on this matter (Divitçioğlu, 1967). In these works, Divitçioğlu states that Ottoman society was not feudal but something closer to the AMP. According to him, there was no private property in the Ottoman lands, rather, the state owned all property and took on the responsibility for public works in the Empire. Divitçioğlu, who transmitted the arguments taking place in the West (particularly in France) to the Turkish intellectual world, tries to analyze Ottoman history in a Marxist framework. However, when the discussion in the

West changed direction, his direction also changed, and Divitçioğlu never returned to the matter of AMP.

Another name who was directed to the discussion under the influence of Kemal Tahir was Baykan Sezer. In his *Su Boyu Ovaları ve Bozkır Uygarlıkları* (Valley Basin Plains and Steppe Civilizations), Sezer (1979) criticizes Marx's AMP conceptualization and deals with its deficiencies in the context of Oriental societies. Sezer says that AMPs are "considered to be acceptable, as they allow the characteristics of the Orient to be placed within the development line of the West." He states that if different historical data were to be used for the AMP, which present a deficient but valuable conceptual frame, they will then be able to act as a guide for understanding Oriental societies. Sezer defines his own thesis not in order to disprove the AMP thesis, but rather to complete it by benefitting from the works that had been carried out by Turkish historians on the Ottoman social and political system. He created models focusing only on the Orient and tried to discover general developmental laws of this model. In order to understand the historical conditions that prepared the way for the appearance of AMP Sezer states that it is necessary to go back to the dawn of history (Sezer, 1979, pp. 1–3). In this context, Sezer tried to discuss AMP outside the contemporary framework and to rebuild the model.

Main Features of the Debates on AMP

I may summarize the points that come to the fore in the debate about AMP as follows:

1. The AMP debate generally developed in a close relationship with the political atmosphere of the contemporary period. The debate underwent its most intense phase between 1960 and 1980, with a serious decline after 1980.
2. It can be said that the method of publication of Marx's works and the internal debates within Marxism determined the progress of the debate.
3. There is a consensus in the matter of whether AMP was the most important precursor of the concept of Oriental despotism.
4. It is commonly accepted that Marx's approach to Oriental society took a progressive outlook and adhered to the idea of historical stages.
5. From the end of the 1970s the Orientalist connections to Marx's thought were added to the agenda. Marx's selective use of insufficient sources was often criticized in this period.
6. It has been often expressed that Marx's basic thesis was empirically invalid due to the unreliability of the sources and the information that was available about the Orient at the time.
7. It is debatable whether Marx's thesis on history, and as a consequence, his approach to Oriental societies changed after 1870.

After 1960 a great change was brought about by the political atmosphere that formed with the development of the debate around AMP globally and in Turkey. Subsequent to the Second World War many colonies became independent, while socialist regimes spread throughout Eastern Europe and the Chinese Revolution occurred in the east. In this atmosphere, in which revolutionary movements also spread to South America, debates about the transition to Socialism began. Most of these semi-capitalist countries did not evince an historical structure similar to those of Europe, and this led Marxist intellectuals to bring the matter of AMP back onto the agenda. While debates initially progressed around whether AMP represented a distinct social form or not, over time the debate turned directly to Marx's conceptualization of the AMP. In the *détente* atmosphere of the 1970s, more moderate, rapprochement policies reigned, while in the 1980s, in an atmosphere in which different political problems appeared, the discussion about the AMP slowly fell off.

The most remarkable subject of debate in the AMP literature from this period was Marx's sources concerning Oriental societies and the nature of their relationship to his revolutionary concepts. Within these debates, it was generally argued that Marx's sources were problematic. Some experts state that this was because Marx had a discriminatory approach to sources, using those that supported with his own theory and views. This intensified the Orientalist discussions, and after 1980 opened the way to Marx being examined in the context of Orientalism.

In the literature, there is greater agreement in the matter of whether Oriental despotism was the most important component in the concept of the AMP. Marx used this concept as a base for dealing with Oriental societies, demonstrating his relationship with his age. As many experts have stated, he followed in the footsteps of Enlightenment philosophy, British Utilitarians and economic politicians, and developed economic political analyses that would shape the AMP.

Marx defines historical progress according to humanity's struggle with nature, that is to say, the fundamental indication of progress is the human being's freedom from nature. In this context, the literature that formed around the AMP, in particular, in the framework of historical materialism, hosts an important matter of debate about the staged development line of modes of production, in which one stage follows upon another. It is stated that Marx's depiction of the AMP in its initial stage as a stagnant social structure brought him to the point of denying the historical accumulation of the Orient. In this sense, Marx ascribes a progressive mission to capitalism that is similar to the mission of colonialists. This approval of colonialism in the name of progress is one of the most important criticisms directed against him. In order to defend Marx on this point, experts have proposed two basic theses. The first holds that after 1870 there was a change in Marx's views concerning historical progress such that he attempted to construct another type of view based on his notes from ethnological studies. These experts defend that in his last period Marx renounced a *single-line* historical development thesis and adopted a *multiple-line* perspective. This argument is rejected by those who claim that Marx's views remained static on the subject, or that even if the contents changed, theoretically Marx did not change. The second line of defense holds that Marx's historical materialism did not include a strict progression, but rather, Engels and other Marxists later imposed this on his theory. According to this view, Engels brought the progress and evolutionism to the fore and over time transformed this into a single interpretation.

Another point on which the literature concentrates is the question of the validity of Marx's theses regarding Oriental societies. The arguments on the subject concern whether the AMP historically reflects the economic character of Oriental societies or not. These arguments, which in general were debated by historians, examine matters concerning many societies, ranging from South America to China, Ancient Egypt, Russia, India and the Ottomans. Three basic attitudes appear in these arguments:

1. Marx's theses on AMP were totally incorrect. At no historical period did an Oriental society demonstrate the fundamental characteristics of AMP.
2. Marx's ideas are fundamentally correct, although empirically incorrect. The group that defends this argument has tried to re-establish the model.
3. Finally, that Marx's theory is incorrect, though some of the empirical data he used are accurate. From here they worked to develop new explanations.

In all these debates, it is rare to find the place and function of Oriental societies being dealt with in Marx's theory. Because of the conflicts between Marxist groups and the general political atmosphere of the day, the reason why Marx made space for Oriental societies in his model has generally not been dealt with. Indeed, Marx's approach to Oriental societies was shaped by the application of his general theoretical approach to the particular social and historical cases. For this reason, a consistent and realistic explanation can only be attained by evaluating the position and function of the approach to Oriental societies within a theoretical model. When the matter is examined in this way, the agreement found in the debate in regard to historical cases renders the accuracy of Marx's theses on Oriental societies of secondary importance to their position within general theoretical explanations. However, this does not mean that the argument about the consistency and accuracy of Marx's model is of no importance. On the contrary, these discussions are crucial to understanding the formation of an explanatory theory and integrated perspective since the process of forming a general model indicates theoretical preferences. Nevertheless, the discussions on empirical accuracy and validity are of little explanatory value without attention to the general theoretical perspective.

Chapter 4
Marx's Sources for Oriental Societies

The philosopher Michel Foucault said Marx's relationship to his intellectual environment was that of a fish to water. As a thinker who was trying to explain modernity in the climate of nineteenth-century thinking, Marx's sources for Oriental societies are significant for understanding his ideas. However, it is very difficult to trace them, especially those of the unpublished works. The sources of Marx's thought can be followed over the chronological biographies[1] formed by intense review of the records of the period, letters and the notebooks that have gradually been discovered,[2] the book list[3] that was prepared by Engels after his death, and the limited number of references in his works. With the opportunities presented by Orientalist studies, Marx benefitted from the works of Enlightenment thinkers, British political economists, German historical philosophers (especially Hegel), official reports and works by colonial officials, travelogues and ethnological studies post-1870.

---

1   See studies of Draper (1985), Institute of Marxism-Leninism (1934) and Rubel and Manale (1975) that show Marx's life day by day.

2   The contents of the notebooks are recorded in the *Karl Marx/Friedrich Engels Papers*, published by the International Social Historical Institute in Amsterdam, who are in possession of the notebook writings of Marx and Engels. The list enumerates Marx's notebooks and their contents, making it possible to see what he used, his relationship with the sources, and the sources of his concepts and analyses. (International Institute of Social History, 2008)

3   After Marx's death in 1883, half of his books were inherited by Engels and a large proportion of the other half went to his daughters Elanor and Laura and other friends and relatives. Engels combined the books that he had inherited with those of his own and made a list which consists of 3,200 volumes, with over 2,100 titles. Along with the books that came from other channels at a later date, these were transmitted to the German Social Democrat Party. The books were stored in the party's library but were later removed and kept in a separate library. This list of books first gives the contents of *Karl Marx: Chronik Seines Lebens* under the title "Namen und Bühertitel" (Institute of Marxism-Leninism, 1934: 409–439) . In 1967 Bruno Kaiser, the director of the Marx-Engels-Lenin Institute Library, and his assistant Inge Werchan published the list of this library in an expanded form, adding an introduction telling the story of the listed books in the Marx's library (Kaiser and Werchan, 1967). Finally, in 1999 as part of the *Marx-Engels-Gesamtausgabe (MEGA)*, book list, the list of notebooks and marginal notes were published. Even though these do not include any new works or notebooks discovered after this date, it is the most complete work (Harstick, Sperl, and Strauß, 1999).

Hegel's Dialectic: Marx's Methodical Source

Marx's general social theory and the place of Oriental societies within it can be understood with an examination of his method. Marx established his own method by adding the idea of modes of production to Hegel's idealist dialectic, which he perceived as the peak of idealist philosophy (MacIntyre, 1968, pp. 29–30; McCarthy, 1988, pp. 6–8). This methodological connection between Marx and Hegel is so deep that Lenin (1972) announced that one who had not read Hegel's *Logic* would not be able to understand Marx. In this light, Hegel occupies an important place in Marx's theory of modern society, and thus on Oriental societies and the relevant terminology (Avineri, 1990, p. 165; Carver, 1990, p. 188; Cooper, 1925; Hook, 1950, p. 15; McCarney, 2000, p. 66). Yet, the relationship between Marx and Hegel's dialectic is not stable. In 1844, after making his criticisms, Marx announced that he had surpassed Hegel, though he had to return a number of times to the latter's writings. With every return he was more bound to the limitations that Hegel's methodology drew. Because of this, after 1853 Marx concentrated on writing a work that was to concern the nature of capitalism, his own "Economics" and was forced to return to Hegel's logic.[4] But during this time, although he had very plentiful notes, he was unable to mould his ideas or write them down (Marx, 1983a, p. 226). In 1857 Marx wrote to Engels (Marx, 1983b, p. 248) that he had coincidently re-read Hegel's Logic and stated that *Logic* was very useful in solving his own methodological problems and indeed, that he had benefitted greatly from this method of approaching the material. Hegel provided a framework with which Marx could formulize his basic conceptual categories.

Much as he used Hegel's dialectic, Marx also used Oriental societies as a mirror to the Occidental in order to place the latter into an historical context. Here, he used the explanations about Oriental societies to find a solution to the problem of explaining the birth and nature of capitalism. Thus, Marx was not trying to develop an explanation or a theory concerning Oriental societies. The fundamental aim of Marx's interest in Oriental societies concerned finding evidence to develop a negation of capitalism.

The Enlightenment: A General Framework

The nineteenth century was shaped by the fundamental concepts and ideas of the Enlightenment where rationality was framed as the essence of progress and

---

4   The notes that Marx made in this period form his *Grundrisse*. A large proportion of these notes, which are included in his most important study of Oriental societies, *Pre-Capitalist Modes of Production,* form the basis for *A Contribution to the Critique of Political Economy* and *Capital*. In particular, after the 1970s, it began to be understood that *Grundrisse* took central position in the work of what was known as Marx's most productive period. For a detailed discussion, see Musto, 2008

Western civilization.[5] In his childhood, Marx was intensely influenced by the rich contents of his father's library, full of books by Enlightenment thinkers. Marx took rational progressivism and Oriental despotism as a basic tool for explaining world history and the position held by Oriental societies.

In this framework, the general implication is that Marx took the idea of progress from thinkers of the Enlightenment. The progressivism of the Enlightenment can be noticed in its most concrete form, particularly in the division of world history into stages. On the other hand, Hegel, who had transformed the speculative ideas of the Enlightenment into a systematic philosophy, was the main source for Marx's notion of progressive history. The thinkers of the Enlightenment had formulized the stages of historical progress as Ancient, Mediaeval and Modern; this scheme was continued by Hegel. Marx took this historical development scheme from Hegel's *Philosophy of History,* and reproduced it around the concept of modes of production with a political economic approach (Marx, 1980a, p. 16). He added a fourth stage to the chain of the classical three stages, which was represented by the Asiatic society. In this context, the stagnant and passive Oriental societies were placed in opposition to Western civilization, which was perceived as dynamic, active, and the vehicle of historical progress. Thus, two completely opposing models were formed.

Marx also took the concept of despotism, which was used as a fundamental component to explain Oriental social modes. From the time of Aristotle, despotism had become a fundamental concept in the evaluation of the Orient in Western thought. This concept was integrally used as the main idea to qualify the Orient as a political system. The theses on despotism were explained in light of geographic determinism. Marx quoted directly this concept from Bernier's travelogue. He used this concept to develop the ideas he took from Hegel and British political economists. He advanced this theory in the framework of his own materialist conception of history.

The French doctor and traveler François Bernier (1620–88), who had popularized the idea of Oriental despotism in the West, had a profound effect on Marx.[6] Despite the limited number of direct quotes from *Voyage dans les Etats du Grand Mogol* (1699), which describes the years that Bernier had spent in the Mongol Khan's court as a doctor, it can be understood that this work allowed Marx to form some basic ideas on many matters concerned with Oriental societies. The most basic component that Marx took directly from Bernier is the idea that there was no private property in land (Marx, 1983c, pp. 333–334). At the same time, in many areas on the Orient Marx adopted the ideas of Bernier, including the

---

5   In this framework, Marx's opinion on civilization is based on the work by the Scottish Enlightenment thinker Adam Ferguson's *An Essay on the History of Civil Society* (Marx, 1996b, pp. 133, 359).

6   Marx read Bernier in 1853 upon the recommendation of Engels. The notes that Marx made about Bernier are recorded in notebook no. 64, pp. 62–65 (International Institute of Social History, 2008).

character of the despotic state, the relationship between court and subjects and the formation of cities. (Marx, 1979a, p. 127, 1979b, p. 182).[7]

Beside this, Montesquieu (1689–1755) had an important influence on Marx, regarding the systematization of explanations about Oriental societies and despotism. Through his works, *Persian Letters* (1721) and *The Spirit of the Laws* (1748), Montesquieu's ideas were central in the formation of an approach to the Orient. Montesquieu's intention was not to make an analysis of Oriental societies, but rather to use the East as a mirror to criticize the monarchy in France. Others like Marx, who carefully read Montesquieu's ideas a number of times,[8] used them to compare despotism with democracy, and to explain the stagnant Oriental societies (Marx, 1975c, p. 161).

For Marx, another important source concerning Oriental societies in relation to Enlightenment thought were the British political economists, most particularly Smith, who explained the theory of Oriental despotism with economic terminology (1723–90).[9] In *The Wealth of Nations*, Smith (1976, p. 729) states that the principle reason for despotism in Asia was the state's absolute control over the economy. From Smith, Marx discovered that the most important manifestations of despotism were artificial irrigation (Smith, 1976, pp. 35–36) and tax-in-kind (Smith, 1976, pp. 683, 729–731 and 837–840). According to this approach, the ruler would prescribe public works such as the construction of irrigation systems, roads, and transportation channels in order to increase the products which provide income for the ruler in the form of taxes-in-kind (Marx 1998, p. 777). However, the most important point that Marx (1986, p. 24) takes from Smith is the idea that the general conditions of production indicate the degree of development in different societies. Thus, Marx established the concept of historical stages, an idea taken from Smith which he later developed in the context of modes of production. Moreover, it was Smith who divided human history into eras according to means of subsistence.

---

7   Another traveler who fed these ideas to Marx was Robert Patton (1809–85). Marx read Patton's *The Principles of Asiatic Monarchies* in June of 1853 and took notes in Notebook no. 66, pp. 37–39 (International Institute of Social History, 2008).

8   Marx read the work by Montesquieu *The Spirit of Law* first in July–August 1843 and the notes he took are in Notebook no. 16 (pp. 51–66). Later, in 1858, while preparing *A Contribution to the Critique of Political Economy*, he read this work again and took short notes. (Notebook 86 A, p.180). Lastly, he read this work again in 1867–68 and took brief notes again (Notebook C, p. 30) (International Institute of Social History, 2008).

9   Marx first read Adam Smith's work in between March to August of 1844 in French and recorded his notes in Notebook no. 20 (pp. 1–23). After this, in London in March, 1851 he read the work again, this time in English, taking notes in Notebooks 44 (pp. 72–81) and 45 (p. 1). In 1856 he took notes in Notebook no. 77, pp. 1–2 again from the French, p. 12 from the English. Moreover, in Notebook 86A, which he recorded between 1858–62 (pp. 171–172 and pp. 184–190) from the French and in the same notebook (pp. 195–203) there are notes from the English. This shows us that Marx always had Smith's work at hand and kept rereading it (International Institute of Social History, 2008).

Early Orientalist Studies: The Source of Marx's Fundamental Ideas

As mentioned above, Marx evaluated the information produced by Orientalists with regard to formulating his own philosophical methods and basic ideas, and he used these within his explanations. In this way, he provided details established around a series of theories about Oriental societies, for example, the stagnation of the Orient, the inwardly closed and stagnant structure of village communities, the lack of cities and independent classes, and the development of industry.

According to Marx, village communities exist at the center of Oriental social life. As they simultaneously carry out agriculture and crafts, these communities are self-sufficient and closed to the outside. For this reason, the social division of labor is underdeveloped. Marx identifies this as an essential cause of stagnation. In addition, it is deemed as an important component behind the perpetuation of Oriental despotism which became an obstacle to the development of cities.

Marx (1996, pp. 363–364, fn. 2) attained his basic ideas concerning the nature of village communities from Bernier, Hegel and Mill, and was further nurtured by Jones. He transferred the details of this subject from Wilks, the 1812 *The Fifth Report from the Select Committee on the Affairs of the East India Company*, Metcalfe, Elphinstone, Campbell and Raffels. According to Marx (1979a, p. 131, 1996, pp. 362–363), the foundation of the inwardly looking structure of village communities was found in the village craftsmen, who were separated into 12 guilds that fulfilled all needs other than agriculture. The actual source in the West of the idea of village economy and the guilds in the village, which Marx uses a few times in different works, was written by Sir Thomas Munro (1761–1827) in 1806 (Dumont, 1966). Marx records the list found in *The Fifth Report from the Select Committee*, though he never actually read this report. He took the ideas that he attributed to this report from Wilks and Campbell (Marx, 1996, pp. 362–363).

After a pause of 15 years, Marx returned to the village debate in 1870s. In this period some new sources and debates appeared in connection with the early village life in Europe, in particular, on the German village community known as *Mark*. These debates directed Marx towards developing his ideas concerned with village communities (Marx, 1987a). On the other hand, the development of ethnological studies from 1870 inspired him to explain the village communities as the beginning of civilization. In this framework, between 1879 and 1882, Marx studied the ethnological works of Lewis Henry Morgan (1818–81), Sir John Budd Phear (1825–90), Sir Henry Summer Maine (1822–88) and Sir John Lubbock (1834–1913).[10] Despite the variety of ethnological material, these notes

---

10   These notes, which Marx kept between December 1880 and March 1881, are recorded in Notebook no. 146: Lewis Henry Morgan, (1818–81) *Ancient Society* (pp. 4–101); J.W.B. Money, *Java, or How to Manage a Colony* (pp. 102–130); Sir John Budd Phear, *The Aryan Village in India and Ceylon* (pp. 131–157); Sir Henry Summer Maine, *Lectures on the Early History of Institution* (pp. 162–199). The notes for Sir John Lubbock's *The Origin of Civilization and the Primitive Condition of Man* are in notebook No. 150, dated 1882

demonstrate that Marx was searching for arguments that would support his own theses. During this time, he gathered material that would benefit him in developing ideas concerned with ancient communism and bring forward the developing character of Western villages.

Among the ethnologists whom he read, Morgan had a special place for Marx. According to him, like Darwin's indirect support from the data he had obtained from natural sciences, Morgan also supported his theory directly with his perspective on the development of human history and civilizations. As a result, Morgan's study encouraged Marx to put primitive communism, and therefore the AMP, at the elementary stage of the development of civilization.[11]

According to Marx, due to the simple division of labor in the Oriental village, the artisan was dependent on agriculture. There was no expertise or competition in economic life, and for this reason, cities did not develop in the Orient. Marx (1986, pp. 401–402, 1989, p. 357, 1996, p. 338) claimed that Oriental cities were military camps developed around courts. According to him these cities were dependent on rural land. Marx took this idea from Bernier, whom he saw as the most useful source on the subject (Marx, 1983c, p. 332). Because of the dependency of cities on the rural economy a market could not be raised. From the British political economists on, it was thought that the Oriental economy had not been monetarized due to taxes being collected in-kind or as corvée (forced public labor). Marx's basic perspective in this area was taken from Bernier and Smith, and developed in keeping with the views of Jones, a thinker to whom Marx also gave great importance (Marx, 1998, p. 782).

Accordingly, Marx attempted to prove that capital was not formed in the Orient, basing this claim on the Utilitarians' thesis concerning the failure of independent artisans and merchants there. Mill, Ricardo and Jones, made a variety of comparisons between modern society and economy in the context of the development of trade. In this subject, Marx's most important source was John Stuart Mill.[12] Working from his ideas, Marx claimed that the minority of small administrators who seized the surplus wealth of artisans and merchants in the Orient had continued their existence as bureaucrats. Due to the parasitic administrative class, there was no material security and the merchants kept their wealth in the form of liquid assets (such as gold) and did not transform it into permanent investments (Marx, 1996, pp. 153–157). Further supporting these ideas, Marx (1986, p. 224, 1987b, p. 363, 1987c, p. 446) turned to Bernier and expressed

---

(pp. 3–10). (International Institute of Social History, 2008) Krader published these notes in the work *The Ethnological Notebooks of Karl Marx* in 1974 (Krader, 1974).

11 Benefiting from Marx's notes on Morgan, Engels (1990) published the work *The Origin of the Family, Private Property and the State* 1884, which earned him more widespread fame than his main works.

12 Marx read J.S. Mill's *Essays on Some Unsettled Questions of Political Economy* before 1845–46 (Notebook no. 35 pp. 35–46) and then again in 1856 (Notebook no. 79 pp. 9–10 and Notebook no. 77 p. 15) (International Institute of Social History, 2008).

Table 4.1   Marx's sources on Oriental societies

Subject	Source
Oriental despotism, geographic determinism	Bernier, Montesquieu, Hegel, Smith, J.S. Mill, Patton, Custine, Machiavelli
Lack of private property, common property, state property in land	Machiavelli, Harrington, Bernier, Montesquieu, Jones, Smith, Patton, J.S. Mill, Raffles
Sovereign's property over land as a right of conquest	Jones
Public works being carried out by the state	Bernier, Smith, Mill
Inertia, stagnation	Montesquieu, Hegel, Smith, Jones, Mill, J.S. Mill, Raffles
Isolated village communities	Hegel, Jones, Wilks, Metcalfe, Elphinstone, Campbell, Raffles, The Fifth Report, Phear
Integration of agriculture and crafts/ production, agriculture predominant to industry	Smith, Bernier, Jones, Wilks, Campbell, Raffles, The Fifth Report
Lack of independent artisans and merchants, lack of development in division of labor	Bernier, Jones, Mill, J.S. Mill
Uniformity in taxes and rent, income in kind; low productivity and performance	Smith, Jones; J.S. Mill
Lack of cities, lack of distinction between city and village, cities dependent on the village	Bernier, Jones
General slavery; social equality similar to slavery	Hegel, Custine, Montesquieu
Slavery	Jones
Lack of judicial limitations	Bodin, Bacon, Montesquieu
Religion holding a central position	Hegel, Lubbock
Jurisprudence being replaced with religion and morals	Montesquieu, Hegel
Primitive communism, village communities	Maurer, Morgan

that in the Orient wealth was not transformed into capital, thus explaining how unlike Europe the Orient did not develop a trade or city economy in a way that was independent from the state.

Marx (1996, pp. 363–364) derived the idea that Oriental social development had frozen thousands of years in the past from his study of Jones and James Mill[13] (1773–1836), the latter of whom Marx read a number of times, and that there had been only limited political and administrative changes as a result of conquests. Marx (1986, p. 417) established his own explanation of colonialism on the basis of these theories, which were being voiced in order to legitimize British dominion and the installation of the land system they defended. J.S. Mill supported the necessity of developing private property in Asia, seeing it as a special duty of colonialism. He, like Marx, thought that the stagnation of Asia could only be overcome with development of private property by an external influence, and to him, colonialism was necessary for Indian development, even at the cost of famine and feloniousness (Marx, 1979b, pp. 217–218).

As can be seen, Marx's range of sources on Oriental societies was fairly restricted. In the period in which he wrote his fundamental works, he could only find limited sources on the Orient. But he also restricted himself through a selective use of this meager array of sources and generalized the information he found there to an extreme.[14] In some sources, a number of observational notes concerning one village or one region were transformed by Marx into an idea that explained the entire Orient, that is, the non-West. Nothing of this sort is to be found in his works on capitalism. For example, anyone who examines *Das Kapital* can easily see that Marx used dozens of sources to demonstrate just one point. In a similar way, his critical relationship with the sources in a number of other subjects did not exist for that of Oriental societies. For example, he uses the general thesis of political economists on the Orient without any criticism. The relationship Marx had with the sources as examined at the beginning of this section gains significance when evaluated together with his methodical sources and the place he gives Oriental societies in his theoretical model.

---

13   Marx read Mill's *Elements Political Economy* for the first time in 1844–45 in French and took notes in Notebook no 22 (pp. 20–36) and no. 23 (pp. 15–20). In 1856 he read it again in French and took notes in Notebook no. 77 (p .8 and pp. 13–14). In 1858 he read it again in English and took notes again. (Notebook 77 A, p. 154) (International Institute of Social History, 2008)

14   This relationship that Marx had with the sources has been criticized in a number of ways. In particular, modern Indian and Chinese historians have destroyed many of his ideas empirically. See Dirlik, 1982; Habib, 1985, 1999; Hambly, 1982; Lowe, 1966; Mukhia, 1985; Naqvi, 1973.

Chapter 5
Marx's Study of Oriental Societies

Marx's approach to Oriental societies was shaped by his formulation of historical stages into modes of production and a framework of social forms that corresponded to each of these stages. Marx sets out to demonstrate his idea that different production forces opened the way to different modes of production and thus different social forms. This is expressed in the famous sentence which is found in Marx's *Poverty of Philosophy* that "The *windmill gives you society* with the *feudal lord*; the steam-mill, *society* with the industrial capitalist"[1] (Marx, 1976a, p. 166).

From his earliest works on, Marx divided history into a number of periods and classifications of social forms. In this sense, the first periodization can be found in *German Ideology*. Here the basic principle of periodization is explained as (1976a, p. 32) "The various stages of development in the division of labor are just so many different forms of ownership, i.e. the existing stage in the division of labor determines also the relations of individuals to one another with reference to the material, instrument, and product of labor." Working from this fundamental principle, he explains the rise of three forms of property (tribal property and its transformation into shared property, feudal class property and private property) in three respective historical stages (antique, feudal and modern).

In the periodization in the *Communist Manifesto,* the development of capitalism gains a central prominence. Marx deals with the transition and change mechanisms between periods in a way that is directly related to the class struggle. Here, the principle of historical dynamics are explained as: "The history of all hitherto existing societies is the history of class struggles" (Marx and Engels, 1976b, p. 482). The idea of a three-tiered historical period (slavery, feudal and modern bourgeois society) is continued in the *Communist Manifesto.*

Grundrisse, the first fruit of Marx's political economy studies, forms a different model by dealing with ancient primitive societies under two separate headings. It's most important innovation is placing Asiatic society as a separate type of social

---

1   Another statement of this sentence in the same book is "The hand-mill presupposes a different division of labor from the steam-mill" (Marx, 1976a, p. 183). A more extensive evaluation about this can be found in *Wage and Labor Capital*: "The relations of production in their totality constitute what is called the social relations, society, and, moreover, a society at a definite stage of historical development, a society with peculiar, distinctive characteristics. Ancient society, feudal society, bourgeois (or capitalist) society, are such totalities of relations of production, each of which denotes a particular stage of development in the history of mankind." (Marx, 1976b, pp. 211–212)

form outside the classic trilogy.[2] In this scheme, the stagnant Oriental mode of production is placed in opposition to the dynamic Western modes of production. Thus, he approaches capitalism in the West and explains its appearance in view of the opposition between dynamic and passive societies developing since the beginning of world history. Upon this explanation in the *Preface* of *A Contribution to the Critique of Political Economy*, Marx (1987a, pp. 262–264) suggests four modes of production (Ancient, Asiatic, Feudal and Capitalist) and social types. This scheme, which is continued in *Das Kapital*, represents the mature form of Marx's analysis of social forms.

This description of historical development is built upon the classic three-staged thesis that is frequently encountered after the Enlightenment in Europe. Marx adds an earlier stage to this, the Asiatic form, and thus separates the Antique Occident and the Antique Orient from one another. By forming a universal developmental history, not only does he preserve the three Western stages, but in parallel, formulates a continuing Asiatic form.[3] He bases his explanation about this division between Orient and Occident on the Oriental despotism theses which were widespread in the West from the eighteenth century on. Marx speaks of two fundamental factors that distinguished the Oriental modes of production, and thus social types, from that of the Occident: (1) that means of production (land) are not private property, (2) relations of production are not free. Given these differences, the class struggle, the driving force of history, did not appear in the East.

Although using the term of Asiatic for labeling the Oriental mode of production, Marx examined a great variety of non-Western societies in the same category.[4] In different works, when Marx is analyzing Oriental societies, he includes, at the beginning and most frequently India and China; later Egypt, Iran and Turkey; *Tartary* (the regions stretching from Central Asia to Central Europe); from the Far East, Java and Indonesia; the Aztecs and Incas before Colombo; the Celts; and Russia, a half-Asiatic country. Moreover, he uses Asiatic terms for the Etruscans and Andalusia.

The framework of these basic distinctions and analyses, which concerned irrigation and the character of land ownership, can be found at the base of Marx's approach to Oriental societies. In a complementary way, there are analyses concerning insular village communities which are self-sufficient as far as the integration of agriculture and artisans is concerned. In this context, Marx questions the emergence and nature of the city in Oriental societies. There are some central analyzes concerning the stagnancy of Oriental societies. In the end, in the context

---

    2   Marx was influenced by the Arian ideas of the period. In *Grundrisse*'s last paragraph he states that "a more thorough research into history uncovers it [India] as the point of departure of all cultured peoples." (Marx, 1987b, p. 253)

    3   As Lekas (1988, p. 67) notes, Marx does not make any emphasis in any other place of the effects of the physical environment but only in Oriental societies. While the other modes of production are given named with terms, the AMP is labeled with a geographical location.

    4   In several places he uses Orient and Asiatic interchangeably (Marx, 1986, p. 401).

of all these analyzes, Marx's views concerning the position of colonization take shape.

The Despotic State, Irrigation and Land Ownership

The history of the formation and circulation of the concepts tells us much. The concept of "despot," which has not been in use since antiquity, came into wide circulation in the early sixteenth century. Tracing the history of this concept offers us a significant meaning to decode the conceptual map of modernity. While it was connoted the power and magnificence in the Orient at the beginning, toward nineteenth century it has gained a more general and comprehensive meaning, signifying the antonym/opposite of the modern social order.

Despotism, having its roots in Ancient Greece, had different uses in different periods, but in the age of Enlightenment it was constantly resorted to as a means of defining the West through the Oriental other. In the sense that it gained with Aristotle (1996, pp. 84, 99, 106, 169, 188), despotic government meant the Oriental society living under the rule of a master, without access to any rights. On the other hand, it dictates that in Greece, society had autonomy and rights against the political authority. This idea was frequently adopted in medieval times, re-emerged in the sixteenth century and gained a strong place in the Enlightenment. In the sixteenth and seventeenth centuries, there were attempts to portray the Ottoman Sultan as a despot that owns all property and his people as slaves, and to use this portrayal for self-positioning (Valensi, 1993). Early modern thinkers such as Niccolo Machiavelli (2005, p. 15), Jean Bodin (1967, pp. 48–52) and Francis Bacon (Bacon, 1632, p. 72) reentered despotism into use by saying that in the "Turkish Empire", all land was property of the Sultan and people had no choice but to obey to an absolute sovereignty. Upon this foundation, such voyagers as François Bernier (1914) and Jean-Baptiste Tavernier (2012) expanded the discussions of despotism and generalized the definition to whole Orient. The word "despotic" was trespassing the governing style and became a noun as "despotism" at the beginning of sixteenth-century by Pierre Bayle to connote a political and social system. (Rubiés, 2005, p. 110). In the Enlightenment period, the political system of the Orient as a whole began to be classified as despotic.

However no one has been as influential as Montesquieu on the political system of the East. Inspired by Bodin, Montesquieu was an important contributor for spreading the idea of Oriental despotism, by his climatic and geographic explanation for how, as he stated, despotism was the main character of the Orient. *Persian Letters* (2008) and *The Spirit of Laws* (2011) claimed that geographical conditions served to the formation of liberty in Europe and despotism in Asia. Montesquieu considered Asian despotism as the opposite of European monarchy and republic. After him British political economists, especially Smith added an economic analysis into concept. And lastly Hegel (1988) in a philosophical manner gave the last shape and ossified the concept for imaging the Orient as a whole.[5]

Deeply influenced by Montesquieu and Hegel, Marx developed his views concerning Oriental societies with an economic analysis of Oriental despotism through the studies of British political economists.[6] According to Marx, the geographical position of rivers in the Orient, the mountains that rise from alongside the river basins and the deserts all led to the formation of a land with a different level of fertility. As the rivers flowed through deep valley sand, irrigation was necessary in order to carry out agriculture. Domesticated lifestyles can only be created in such geographies if the problems associated with water supply are solved. This problem, which cannot be solved by a person on their own, can only be addressed with the organization of individuals. In this context, the need to make dams and canals created a strong centralized state. According to Marx, (1996, p. 515, fn. 2) in return for solving this problem, the state came forward as the sole land owner:

> The state is then the supreme lord. Sovereignty here consists in the ownership
> of land concentrated on a national scale. But, on the other hand, no private
> ownership of land exists, although there is both private and common possession
> and use of land. (Marx, 1998, p. 777)

Due to the special relationship that society formed with the state in this system, the individual had rights to use land as a part of society, but not the right to ownership of a certain piece of land. Therefore, the relationship between society and the individual was not like that in the Western world, where private property was commonplace. Marx's 'autonomous individual,' to whom he gives great importance, could not appear in such societies, rather the individual in the Orient is dependent on society for their very basic needs, resulting in a condition of social stagnation. When Marx (1986, p. 417) speaks of a generalized slavery in Oriental societies, it is to this type of dependency of the individual on society to which he is referring to.

In this sense, Marx is of the opinion that free labor, which he sees as a precondition for capitalism, cannot appear in Oriental societies since the necessary social production relationships for the liberalization of labor do not exist. Therefore, it cannot be expected that capitalism will appear within the processes of this society. For such a thing to happen, it would be necessary for labor to be liberalized first, followed by a, "release of the worker from the soil as his

---

5   See Koebner (1951), Venturi (1963), and Springborg (1992) for a detailed discussion on the history of despotism in Western thought.

6   Marx at first took the idea to define the Orient with despotism from Engels. However, in this correspondence, while Engels wrote (1983, pp. 339–340) that irrigation was the task of the villagers, the community or the state, Marx ignored the others and claimed that not only irrigation, but all the public works were carried out by the state.

natural workshop—hence dissolution of small, free landed property as well as of communal landownership resting on the oriental commune" (Marx, 1986, p. 399). The fundamental condition is that land becomes private property. In this sense, according to Marx, no matter to what degree this includes some social destruction, by starting from this point, the British in India did what was necessary—even if the British and Irish land systems were implemented as a caricature of this.[7]

In this context, for Marx (1986, pp. 410–411) the different forms of slavery are an important analytical subject. In Western PCMP, the relations of production are based on the individual, and slavery is used as a means in the production process. For example, the appearance of slavery and a monetarized economic system in ancient Rome ensured the individual's independence from society, and as a result, opened the way for progress in this form. From here, Marx repeats the general slavery thesis that was a fundamental claim regarding Oriental despotism. According to Marx, (1986, p. 417) in AMP the production relationship is communal and since in this form the individual never becomes a proprietor but only a possessor, they are below property the slave in whom the unity of the commune exists. Thus, in the Orient labor has been limited collectively (Marx, 1996, pp. 339–340) and the class struggle does not exist.

As there was no land property in the Orient, Marx thought that there was a natural economy. Working from Smith, Marx states that in the Orient land income and taxes constitute the same thing; the state, which is the owner of the land, does not take taxes, but rather income in return for the use of its own land. While Smith states that this is the reason for a lack of productivity, Marx, following him, states that this will lead to the stagnation of the economic system. This is because a monetarized economy will not form in such an economic structure and production geared towards foreign markets would not be generated.[8] Thus, as there is no change, a stagnant life begins; at the same time, this condition ensures the continuation of Oriental despotism.

Oriental Division of Labor, Village Communities and the City

Another note upon which Marx bases his analyses of Oriental societies is the distinction of village community and city. Marx thought that in the Orient the

---

7 "If any nation's history, then the history of the English in India is a string of futile and really absurd (in practice infamous) economic experiments. In Bengal they created a caricature of large-scale English landed estates; in south-eastern India a caricature of small parceled property; in the north-west they did all they could to transform the Indian economic community with common ownership of the soil into a caricature of itself." (Marx, 1998, p. 332 note 50)

8 According to Marx, the economic problem with the PCMPs (non-economic means, religious, legal, political and familial relations) was based on the use of force. For this reason, he qualified the accumulation in these societies as "primitive accumulation."

center of social life was the village community. This is because a weak division of labor combined with the political character of Oriental despotism prevented the formation of the city. Village communities have a life introverted by economic self-sufficiency, and agriculture and artisanship are combined economically. As a result, this form of society, which has continued for thousands of years, takes hold of the resources to perpetuate itself in the same stagnation.

The idea of self-administered village communities first appeared with Jean Chardin (1699–1779) in the eighteenth century. According to him, the distance between the central government and the villages in the Orient was too great for true state management, leading to autonomous village communities that administered themselves with a low-level relationship to the ruling power. This idea later took hold in European scholarship, and as noted above, after taking the general idea of an immutable, autonomous and introverted village community from Bernier, Marx filled in the details with data from Wilks, Metcalfe, Elphinstone, Campbell, *The Fifth Report* and Raffels. For one, Wilks (1869, p. 73ff.) worked from his observations of Southern India and notes on ancient texts, to write that within every Indian village there was a republic. However, he speaks not of the non-existence of private property of land in the Indian village, but rather of the fact that the village community has authority over all the land. In discussions of the village community there are frequent references to the Select Committee's *Fifth Report*, based completely on Wilks's articles (even being written in his style). The definition of the village in there belongs to Wilks, and this was followed in another report presented to the House of Commons by the Select Committee in 1830, where Sir Metcalfe writes that the villages had their own autonomy. Metcalfe's views were in turn affirmed and used by Elphinstone (1889, p. 68) and developed by Campbell (1852, p. 84).

In general, the contents of the discussions about village communities were concerned with either the economic situation or the colonial administration. The Conservatives defended the *mahalwari* (village style) system, while the Utilitarians defended the *ryotwari* (farmer style) system. As a result, two opposing depictions of the village appeared. For example, Metcalfe, who was on the Conservative side, wrote to the Select Committee preparing the main contract of the East Indian Company in 1832 that the village communities had their own internal, introverted republics. According to him, generations would pass, kingdoms change, wars occur, but the village community would remain the same. The village community protected society against chaos, but in the eyes of the Utilitarians was a sign of stagnation. For the Utilitarians the goal was not order, but progress which was only possible if the individual became independent from society.

After 1850, with the development of anthropology as an academic field, the debate on the village community took off in Europe.[9] Starting with J.M. Kemble, Georg Ludwig van Maurer and August von Haxthausen, discussion about the basic

---

9 For an evaluation of the debate on the village in the West in the nineteenth century, see Ertürk, 1997, pp. 10–15.

ideas concerning the phases of the village in world history and how the Teutonic (and Slavic) village effected the modern situation began. After 1870, both the radicals and the conservatives made attempts to find evidence to support their views concerning the reorganization of land in connection with the discussions on history. In this context, the Indian village community and shared property, or the periodical re-distribution of property, was once again used in support of the arguments. In the 1870s, in a meeting organized by the Cobden Society, Campbell stated that the Indian village community could not be a basis for communism. According to him, what was periodically redistributed in Indian village communities was not land, but oxen. Thus, there was no component that would equate with property as such (Dewey, 1972, pp. 319–320). The contribution of Maine to these arguments in this period is important. Using the resources provided by the newly-developing study of comparative languages in German academia, he presented the theory that the bases of the Indian village and Indo-European communities was identical once again by using new methods and added fresh evidence in a form that would be acceptable to the age. Maine, supporting the thought of Indo-European relationship, searched for traces of the Indian village community in the European past.

In this context, by using these new sources Marx began studying once again the German *Mark*, Slavic *Zadruga* and Anglo-Saxon village communities as the basis for civilization. In a footnote added to the English edition of the Communist Manifesto in 1888, Engels expresses the effect of these developments on his own thought:

> That is, all *written* history. In 1847, the pre-history of society, the social organization existing previous to recorded history, all but unknown. Since then, August von Haxthausen (1792–1866) discovered common ownership of land in Russia, Georg Ludwig von Maurer proved it to be the social foundation from which all Teutonic races started in history, and, by and by, village communities were found to be, or to have been, the primitive form of society everywhere from India to Ireland. The inner organization of this primitive communistic society was laid bare, in its typical form, by Lewis Henry Morgan's (1818–1861) crowning discovery of the true nature of the gens and its relation to the tribe. With the dissolution of the primeval communities, society begins to be differentiated into separate and finally antagonistic classes. (Marx and Engels, 1976b, p. 482)

In general, Marx (1996, pp. 362–363) defines village communities in the context of communal landownership. According to him, only the use of the land, not its ownership, was transferred to the villager.[10] For this reason, even if there are village communities that differ from one another and different implementations in

---

10 The debate on property and possession is presented in context of the modern reflections of Roman law by Friedrich Carl von Savigny (1779–1861) who is one of the most respected and influential nineteenth-century jurists and historians in his famous treatise, *Das Recht des Besitzes* (*The Law of Possession*) published in 1803 (Von Savigny, 2003).

different places, in the most basic form, there is a *communal* sowing and reaping and distribution of crops.

Marx says that the existence of insular village communities has been sustained in a form that is dependent on the state's monopoly of water and land. Due to their physical isolation, these village communities, which need a strong central administration to carry out major public works, are not very interested in political matters. Whether the ruler is living or dead or altered does not distress them much; every village is trapped within its own borders.

At the same time, village communities are traditionally the fundamental actors limiting the individual. The community members are kept in the village, their movements are restricted and a dependency is formed. In the AMP, the variety in this dependency of village communities does not appear in an overt form as feudality (as in Mediaeval Europe) or slavery (as in Ancient Rome-Greece), rather the members are bound with traditional invisible bonds (Marx, 1986, p. 417). Thus, the area of movement for the individual is limited and there are no opportunities for social change.

According to Marx, these isolated and self-sufficient communities are like small states. Their self-sufficiency is "based on possession in common of the land, on the blending of agriculture and handicrafts, and on an unalterable division of labour." According to Marx, in addition to the spinning and weaving carried on in each family as subsidiary industries to meet their own needs, there are also a dozen of other crafts in the village, to fulfill communal needs:

> Side by side with the masses thus occupied with one and the same work, we find the "chief inhabitant," who is judge, police, and tax-gatherer in one; the book-keeper, who keeps the accounts of the tillage and registers everything relating thereto; another official, who prosecutes criminals, protects strangers travelling through and escorts them to the next village; the boundary man, who guards the boundaries against neighbouring communities; the water-overseer, who distributes the water from the common tanks for irrigation; the Brahmin, who conducts the religious services; the schoolmaster, who on the sand teaches the children reading and writing; the calendar-Brahmin, or astrologer, who makes known the lucky or unlucky days for seed-time and harvest, and for every other kind of agricultural work; a smith and a carpenter, who make and repair all the agricultural implements; the potter, who makes all the pottery of the village; the barber, the washerman, who washes clothes, the silversmith, here and there the poet, who in some communities replaces the silversmith, in others the schoolmaster. (Marx, 1996, pp. 362–363)

Marx is of the opinion that this simplicity in the village is the main cause of the perpetual stagnation in the Orient.

As his student, Marx thought that the legal expression of the Oriental village lay not only in modes of production but in the mutual relationship between property and possession.

The simplicity of the organisation for production in these self-sufficing communities that constantly reproduce themselves in the same form, and when accidentally destroyed, spring up again on the spot and with the same name this simplicity supplies the key to the secret of the unchangeableness of Asiatic societies, an unchangeableness in such striking contrast with the constant dissolution and refounding of Asiatic States, and the never-ceasing changes of dynasty. The structure of the economic elements of society remains untouched by the storm-clouds of the political sky. (Marx, 1996, pp. 363–364)

According to Marx, even with an increase in the population, no changes or variety in village crafts occur. This is because even if the population increases, another similar community (a village) will be formed on the land that is not being used. Thus, the production system continues without any changes in the material base or relations of production (Marx, 1996, p. 363).

Marx was of the opinion that there was no commodity production in village communities, that there was no exchange value, rather production value was used. In the village, excess produce was transferred to the state as rent-in-kind. The state used some of this excess produce that it collected, while exchanging the rest for imported luxury goods. That is, there was limited excess production in society, and what surplus there was used in exchange for luxury consumption by the ruling classes. For this reason, no independent merchant class that could transform the wealth into capital appeared in Oriental societies. Trade was carried out only as foreign trade for luxury goods.

For Marx, due to the nature of the AMP, the division of labor in the village did not lead to specialization.[11] This was because products were made for a limited market and there was no idea of economic exchange or inclination to outside markets. Thus, specialization could only appear if there was an increase in the number of artisans. The necessary surplus goods were not produced for exchange in the market, since production would only be carried out in keeping with the instant demands of the village. According to Marx, this lack of exchange and specialization was, in turn, the reason why cities did not appear in Oriental societies, for without a market, the artisans remained dependent on agriculture. Thus, "Cities proper here form alongside these villages only at exceptionally good points for external trade; or where the head of the state and his satraps exchange their revenue (surplus product) for labour, spend it as labour-fund" (Marx, 1986, pp. 401–402).

This relationship between cities and villages, and the absence of an independent artisan class meant that social relationships were under the control of the despot. In Marx's view, this type of rule could only be transformed by external effects

---

11   Indeed, Marx (1996, pp. 371–372) makes references to Plato, Xenophon, and Socrates to state that there was a developed division of labor even in ancient times in Oriental societies.

like invasion and raids. Other than this, there was no means of eliminating the dependency of individual to society, and the society to despot (Marx, 1986, p. 418).

Marx was constantly in search of explanations underlining the development of CMP. His interest in the city was directly related to the possibilities of economic and social development that led the way to capitalism.[12] Capitalism, Marx says, appeared in modern bourgeois societies due to the changes in classic and feudal societies. The most important support of this transformation is the division between country and city, the appearance of independent artisans and the development of divisions of labor. At the end of this process, the appearance of the free individual is vital to explaining the historical chain of the development of capitalism.

Marx connects the origin of the process leading to capitalism with the appearance of the city in the West. Urbanization reached its peak with capitalism and "Capitalist production completely tears asunder the old bond of union which held together agriculture and manufacture in their infancy" (Marx, 1996, pp. 506–507). Marx sees the occidental city as the bases of progress. As an extension of the ancient relations of production, with the appearance of the city in the Occident the relationship between agriculture and production became clear. Even though the incomes of the cities in the ancient world were still coming from the country from agriculture, the Occidental city differs from the Oriental city, which is a collection of villages. The fact that the city is placed as the point of differentiation is no coincidence. According to Marx, agricultural production in antiquity could only be generated by cities, as it was the citizens of the Polis who had the means of production (land). Thus, from antiquity on, cities in the Occident appeared as economic areas:

> The history of classical antiquity is the history of cities, but of cities founded on landed property and on agriculture; Asiatic history is a kind of indifferent unity of town and countryside (the really large cities must be regarded here merely as royal camps, as works of artifice [*Superfötation*] erected over the economic construction proper); the Middle Ages (Germanic period) begins with the land as the seat of history, whose further development then moves forward in the contradiction between town and countryside; the modern [age] is the urbanization of the countryside, not ruralization of the city as in antiquity. (Marx, 1986, p. 406)

Marx views the feudal society of the city as the womb of capitalism. For him, the fact that the merchants and artisans owned their own means of production, that these means were detached from social bases and that they thus separated labor from the objective conditions of production, all acted as precursors to the development of capitalism.

---

12   Marx sees the city as a place where the means and relations of production are intensified as the place where capital is formed and distributed (Isin, 2006, pp. 326–327).

In summary, Marx was nurtured by the literature of the era and, working from his own scheme of historical development, claimed that the Oriental societies were based in form on the self-administering village communities which saw no economic transformation. Rather, since social life in village communities composed a unification of agriculture and craft, no sufficiently advanced division of labor ever emerged, thus resulting in a failure to form the conditions necessary for the city to appear. This type of interpretation, which is empirically incorrect, is used by Marx to help explain the development of capitalism in the West.[13]

Change and Stagnation in Oriental Societies

Marx was of the opinion that the historical process was a kinesthetic occurrence and that at the basis of the development of production was a need for a constant development of new stages in society. His stages of historical development were based on Hegel's progressive scheme of world history, which he transposed onto a political economic basis. This idea of modern society based on economic developments was taken from earlier political economists before attempting to define how social forms evolved as such. In this context, it was possible for there to be no change of social form, but for there to be change in the infrastructure of society.[14]

According to Marx, in the developmental process of the forces of production, the individual enters a relationship with other individuals and establishes cooperation within the arrangement of the division of labor. In the historical development, like Hegel's "cunning of reason" and Adam Smith's "the invisible hand," Marx attributes a role to class conflict.[15] According to Marx, the class conflict is the driving force of history and brings about historical progress. In this sense, classes appear as a fundamental dynamic in history, a natural result of the development of forces of production. Every advance in the struggle of mankind against nature and their struggle to take nature under control developed a new means of production; as a result of this, social production was diversified into the

---

13   See the studies criticizing the empirical validity of Marx's perspective on village communities and the city in Oriental societies (Habib, 1985, pp. 44–53, 1999; Hambly, 1982, pp. 434–452).

14   In the context of dialectic materialism, Marx thinks that the later form matures in the womb of the earlier form and that a new and more advanced form is possible only with the completion of the life of the older one.

15   In the work *Ludwig Feuerbach and the End of Classical German Philosophy*, Engels states that they adopted the idea of Hegel's "historical role of evil" (Engels, 1990, p. 378). In the context of this idea, Marx declared in *The Poverty of Philosophy* that the utopians were not aware of the revolutionary potential in poverty (Marx, 1976a, pp. 177–178).

class struggle. According to Marx, "The history of all hitherto existing society is the history of class struggles" (Marx and Engels, 1976b, p. 482).

Marx sees private property and the free relations of production as preconditions for the appearance of classes. When examined from this framework, it is clear why classes only appeared in the Occident. The absence of classes and the presence of a despotic state with complete sovereignty over society are the corollary of private property's non-appearance. Given that there are no classes in such a social form, there is also no social change. For this reason, Oriental societies are stagnant according to Marx (1996, pp. 363–364), and are capable of change only in the political arena and not in the modes of production which will lead to real social change.[16]

According to Marx, the fundamental reason for this unchanging society was the basic social form of the self-sufficient insular village community which traditionally connected the individual to the community. The combination of agriculture and crafts in these villages created the internal conditions for reproducing themselves within the same form without cessation. "When accidentally destroyed" as a result of a natural disaster or conquest, these villages "spring up again on the spot and with the same name" and "[i]f the population increases, a new community is founded, on the pattern of the old one, on unoccupied land" (Marx, 1996, pp. 363–364) since the basic mode of production continued without change.

According to Marx, the conquerors of Asia had a role in the unchanging nature of these structures. They took the place of the earlier despots but continued the same policies, and so the society continued its existence under the same conditions. In this sense, for the first time the British, representing a higher level of mode of production, interfered in the mode of production, creating real social change. Western colonialism served the flow of history by destroying the Oriental social form that had been continuing for centuries.

According to Marx, another reason for the stagnation in the Orient was that the economic system did not produce an exchange value. In his view, trade did not develop in Oriental societies and as there was no production of merchandise, small, self-sufficient village communities did not create a production directed towards use value. Marx perceived societies that produced exchange values as being dynamic. This is because a short time after exchange values appear, capital emerges and the mode of production changes accordingly. Societies that only produce use value are stagnant, change is slow and the mode of production is created according to this. In this system, the surplus value is not intense enough to form capital accumulation. Marx is of the opinion that this is one of the reasons for the slow development and change in Oriental societies.

In contrast, the Western system, which is based on the individual, is viewed as being essentially competitive, thus producing social dynamism; and it is only after

---

16   In another place, Marx states that as there was no conflict between the religious and political elite in the Islamic world, advancement in these societies was out of the question. (Marx, 1979c)

studying the formation of energy, power and change in the capitalist cooperation system at length that Marx turns to the reasons why such an event did not occur in Oriental societies. Given that there is no individual in Oriental societies, there is thus no competition. And the most important reason for this is the strong presence of the restricting social ties and a traditionally closed insular community. According to Marx, while the capitalist cooperation was based on free individual competition, Oriental cooperation was based, "on the one hand, on ownership in common of the means of production, and on the other hand, on the fact, that in those cases, each individual has no more torn himself off from the navel-string of his tribe or community, than each bee has freed itself from connexion with the hive" (Marx, 1996, pp. 339–340). As a result of a lack of individualism and competition, while one society was productive, the other was not; while one was open to development and dynamism, the other was closed and remained stagnant.

The non-appearance of a competitive structure is accorded responsibility for the appearance of a non-monetarized natural economy. The most important reflection of this natural economy is that production directed towards change, and as a result, specialization, did not occur. According to Marx (1996, p. 344), craftsman in the Orient did not specialize. This was because there was no economic or social environment that demanded such a thing from them, whereas, due to the competitive social structure in the West, it was vitally important for there to be specialization in craftsmanship. The establishment of a system to create greater and better quality production, which was more competitive to the outside, made the Western social system dynamic, and as a result, the CMP appeared. The CMP represents the severing of all the social ties of an individual and the peak of competitiveness.

In this context, Marx compares merchant wealth and modern capital and defends the idea that merchant wealth is only a means of exploitation, and lacks the dynamism to change the production conditions of society. According to him, as there is no economic change, merchant wealth in the Oriental economy does not turn into capitalist wealth as it does in the West since the political structure in the Orient brings the economic arena under the sway of the political structure and the merchants are prevented from using their wealth in a transformative manner. Moreover, as there is no private property, the merchant wealth is kept or instantly spent on ingots, and the capital is not placed into liquid circulation. Again, wealth that is not transformed into investment is only spent on luxury consumption and thus does not bring about an economic transformation for society. Capitalist wealth, as opposed to merchant wealth which does not enter liquid circulation, "thus forces the development of the productive powers of society, and creates those material conditions, which alone can form the real basis of a higher form of society, a society in which the full and free development of every individual forms the ruling principle" (Marx, 1996, pp. 587–588). As a result, while capitalist wealth is the creator of a dynamic social structure, merchant wealth is not, no matter how great the amount is.

Accordingly to Marx, Oriental societies have no history (Marx, 1979a, p. 217). This is because he (1986, p. 24) sees historical progress as being equal to a change in production relations that transform the modes of production, and since the Orient only experiences change in the political arena, no such thing is reflected in the social conditions of production. Rather, the kind of change which does occur does so with conquests or change of despots, so there is no real progress.

From the observations made above, in the comparison that Marx makes between pre-capitalist modes of production, AMP appears socially static and economically stagnant. The PCMP transforms into a higher production method as a result of internal development, whereas the AMP, of all the other modes alone, does not have the necessary internal dynamism to effect a transformation of the mode of production. According to Marx,

> The Asiatic form necessarily hangs on most tenaciously and for the longest time. This is due to its presupposition that the individual does not become independent *vis-à-vis* the commune; that there is a self-sustaining circle of production, unity of agriculture and manufactures, etc. (Marx, 1986, p. 410)

Moreover, Marx's classic relation of infrastructure and the superstructure, where the latter is determined by the former, is in the case of Oriental societies reversed. Here, the structure which Marx takes to be formed by institutions like religion, politics and law is the decisive one in the framework of despotism. In this way, Marx again demonstrates the distinct and exceptional position of Oriental societies in his model.

Given Marx's regard for the independent execution of economic processes as the basis of analysis, Oriental societies are found to lack the characteristics of Western societies listed above, and, with their stagnation, to remain outside the general process of history. In the Orient, the existence of a large, centralized bureaucratic state, the lack of private property and therefore of classes, the non-distinction of the city from the country and the lack of a city brings about economic and social stagnation and these societies do not attain social or political power against the state or an ideological or cultural independence. Civil society is not developed and the determinative nature of the state continues. Thus, the system enters and maintains a state of stagnation that will never end.

Colonialism and the Problems of the Transition to Capitalism

Marx's general social development theory is at the same time an explanation for colonialism. In Marx's writings, colonialism is often presented as a stage of the widening and spreading of capitalism, dictated by the latter's very nature. Thus, colonialism and imperialism are also perceived as a possibility for change in Oriental societies.

In Marx's work, capitalism is evaluated as a progressive step that has no equal in the history of mankind:

> The bourgeoisie has subjected the country to the rule of the towns. It has created enormous cities, has greatly increased the urban population as compared with the rural, and has thus rescued a considerable part of the population from the idiocy of rural life. Just as it has made the country dependent on the towns, so it has made barbarian and semi-barbarian countries dependent on the civilised ones, nations of peasants on nations of bourgeois, the East on the West. (Marx and Engels, 1976b, p. 488).

According to Marx, capitalism will rescue the Orient from the eternal stagnation via colonialism, thus joining the Orient into the main current of history. In this context, in an highly controversial article entitled *British Rule in India*, Marx states that the British shook the economic foundations of society in India and realized the first and unique social revolution,[17] extricating the country from a semi-barbarous state, advancing her towards civilization (Marx, 1979b, p. 131).

In general, Marx (1979a, pp. 221–222, 1996, p. 515 note 2, 740) is aware of the damage caused to Oriental societies by colonialism. However, as the Western social form in the end is at more advanced level, an exterior accelerator in the Orient like colonialism is seen to be a positive factor, as it grants a transition to the next stage in historical development. This is because, as in the analyses in earlier sections, according to the political, social and economic characteristics that Marx attributes to Oriental societies, it is not possible for these societies to progress to advanced stages by themselves. Marx places colonialism alongside the misery and suffering of the historical process through which Europe went on the way to capitalism, perceiving these as part of a natural law.

Yet for Marx, history's progress is realized in a rational manner, and he developed historical materialism to identify the general principles of the progress of humanity. With the study of the objective and subjective dimensions of events, which he took from Hegel, Marx separates how an event looks in and of itself from its place in the historical process. Thus, colonialism, even though painful

---

17 Marx states that from a military point of view the Arabs, Turks and Mongols who conquered India earlier were superior, but from the aspect of civilization these societies were backwards and with time these conquerors were Hinduized. Thus, the first real conqueror of India, superior in every way, was Britain, since under British rule India was able to transform its production system and social relations. Even though India had been invaded many times before, it had always been able to protect its own character, but with British administration this ability was undermined. In reality, the earlier groups of conquerors only wanted to administer the country and did not colonize it. Here the difference between Western imperialism and the earlier Oriental conquests is once more made clear. Because of his intellectual background, and his perspective based on the civilized-uncivilized dilemma, Marx could not understand this point.

and destructive from the point of view of the colonized people, is evaluated as a positive thing in the general flow of history.[18] Accordingly, history has a normal progress and every type of event has an effect in the process of this progress, no matter what their results are. As it is the sole system of creating the economic and technological infrastructure necessary for free social and individual development, capitalism, according to Marx, is a necessary step to be taken towards the final salvation. Due to this perspective, Marx was of the opinion that, "England has to fulfill a double mission in India: one destructive, the other regenerating the annihilation of old Asiatic society, and the laying the material foundations of Western society in Asia (Marx, 1979a, pp. 217–218).

For this reason, even if acting according to the most repulsive interests, and even if they acted stupidly, "whatever may have been the crimes of England she was the unconscious tool of history in bringing about that revolution" (Marx, 1979b, p. 132). This is because "without a fundamental revolution in the social state of Asia" Marx believes that there mankind could not "fulfill its destiny" (Marx, 1979b, p. 132).

Here Marx's thoughts on the historical process can be seen easily seen. Marx thought that over time the capitalist mode of production (industrial, scientific innovative, etc.) will generate a universal human who will use the same mode of production throughout the world. "Hence the great civilizing influence of capital; its production of a stage of society in comparison to which all earlier ones appear as mere *local developments* of humanity and as *nature-idolatry*." This is because when capital puts science and technology into the service of production, "For the first time, nature becomes purely an object for humankind, purely a matter of utility." For this reason, in order to enter the necessary path to progress "[i]t is destructive towards all of this, and constantly revolutionises it, tearing down all the barriers which hem in the development of the forces of production, the expansion of needs." And Marx's perception of the sovereignty of revolutionary capital is that although causing pain in the short term, in the long run it is beneficial for Oriental societies (Marx, 1986, pp. 337–338).

Marx's views on colonialism are in accord with the views of his contemporaries. What he has to say on Oriental societies can be seen as a legitimization of colonialism. For example, he claims that if dominance is not direct, but light and superficial, there might not be enough power to eliminate the socio-economic foundations of "Oriental despotism" (Marx, 1979a, p. 218). In this context, Marx (Marx, 1980, p. 539, 1998, p. 332) compares India and China in *Das Kapital* and as the economic sovereignty of Europe is not directly supported by political sovereignty, he states that the Chinese traditional society is not being broken up

---

18   This situation reminds us of Hegel's term "the cunning of history." Dellaloğlu (2008, pp. 136–139) states that the paragraph in which Hegel explains the cunning of history is his most striking paragraph. In the same place Dellaloğlu deals with how this thought is reflected in Marx.

quickly enough.[19] Due to this belief in the propelling force of Western colonialism, Marx (1982, pp. 297–300) did not approve of an independent insurrection against a Western capitalist colonialist power. Such a rebellion would mean that the traditional Oriental hegemony would take over the administration again and would lead to a continuation of the AMP and an end to the effects of Western modernization. This historical role that Marx imposed on the West stipulates that the Orient is given to the hegemony of the West.

Marx's belief that the technology and production systems that are brought to the Orient by the imperialists will transform the Oriental societies coincides with his belief that technology has a transformational power.[20] For him, one of the fundamental characteristics that separate capitalism from other modes of production is the unique role played by technology. When discussing the fundamental details of modernization in Europe he is of the opinion that the changes and renewal

---

19   When compared with Marx, Engels is even more enthusiastic about the benefits of colonialism for expansion of civilization. In the article entitled *Persia-China*, written on Marx's proposal, Engels gives an example of what colonialism can bring to India with the case of a small Anglo-Indian army defeating that of a large Persian one with modern equipment and trained by European experts. Here Engels tries to demonstrate that even though educated by European experts, as the social and political structure had not changed, the Persian army was unable to act according to modern forms, thus demonstrating the benefits that colonialism had brought to India (Engels, 1986, pp. 279–280). Again in 1847, in a report written for the *London Workingmen's Educational Society*, Engels states that China, refusing to develop, had remained in a stagnant state for thousands of years, but had finally been opened to civilization by the British (Engels, 1976a, p. 629). In a similar way, in an article written on January 22, 1848, in *The Northern Star*, he greets the conquest of Algeria by France as "an important and fortunate fact for the progress of civilization" (Engels, 1976b, p. 471). In an article he wrote for *Neue Rheinische Zeitung* on February 16, 1849, Engels *evaluates the taking of Mexican territory by America* (1846-48) with America taking half of Mexico, Texas, Northern California and New Mexico, from "the lazy Mexicans" in war, as this country's contribution to the advancement of a country that refused to participate in the compulsory historical progress (Engels, 1977, p. 365). On March 25, 1861, in an article in *Die Presse* Marx supports Engels (Marx, 1984, pp. 32–42). In a letter to Marx, Engels, says "Russian rule, for all its infamy, all its Slavic dirtiness, is civilizing for the Black and Caspian Seas and Central Asia, for the Bashkirs and Tatars." (Engels, 1982, p. 362)

20   Quite a lot has been written on the importance that Marx gave to the role of technology. Chakrabarty (1996, p. 838) claims that these analyses make Marx a technological determinist, while Rosenberg (1999, pp. 397–400) states that although he gave a central importance to technology, he was not a determinist. Llobera (1979) is of the opinion that it is not Marx himself, but rather Marxism that is the techno-economic determinist and thus indicates that this thought occurred after Marx. However, Ellul (1964, p. 54) makes clear Marx's perspective on technique by declaring that as Marx has showed the misuse of technology by the bourgeoisie, and that it should be re-established as a means to save the proletariat. For other evaluations of Marx's perception of technology, see Avineri, 1969, p. 177; Bimber, 1990, pp. 344–345; Shaw, 1979, p. 161.

of technology precede the changes in social institutions, traditions and behavior. According to Marx, technology brings automation in the production systems and thus an important increase in production takes place; historically, the social relations and the position of labor in the production process change. Marx thinks the same thing will occur in Oriental societies with the imperialist transfer of technology. According to him, when Oriental societies start to industrialize, these societies begin to modernize and change, breaking off from the traditional stagnant system.[21] The importance given to technology can be easily understood from the significance that was given to the railroad in India (Marx, 1979a, pp. 220–221). Ultimately, Marx thought that the industrial capitalism would carry out the historical mission of modernity.

In fact, in the era of capital development that Marx deals with, there were no components in which the Occident, economically or technologically, was superior to the Orient. At these dates, the exports from India, which was in the position of being the breadbasket of Asia and the workshop of the world, were greater than its imports, and British goods could not compete with Indian goods. However, after the British established political dominance, obstacles to reduce commerce and production settled down. As a result, there were no more business opportunities for the production sector in the cities, and the Indian looms were forcibly emptied by the British. What brought India to its knees was not the British steam engine, but British weapons. In the developmental era of capitalism, the Oriental economy had the power and dynamism to compete with the capitalists in many areas. However, the fact that the Europeans seized superiority in the Orient is related to many of the political conditions of the day, and Marx, although not voicing it, is very aware of this.[22]

---

21   For this reason, Marx, in opposition to Carey from *NYDT* defends free trade and industrialization in the name of progress (Marx, 1983, p. 346).

22   For a comparison of the details in this matter, see Hobson, 2004; Madan, 1979, p. 11.

Chapter 6
Marx's Oriental Mirror

Marx attempts no independent study of Oriental societies; rather he made his analyses of Oriental societies more in the context of the development of modern society. The fact that Oriental societies are not dealt with directly, but rather occupy a place in the context of the development of modern society demonstrates their great importance in Marx's work. The nature of Marx's study of Oriental societies is determined by his theoretical approach. According to the dialectic approach which Marx adopts, everything must be explained by its counterpart/ opposite. For this reason, fundamentally, while explaining the development of Western societies, Marx uses Oriental societies as an opposing model. This can be seen not only from his expressions concerning Oriental societies, but can also be identified in examples and studies of Oriental societies from the textual context. In general, these examples and studies are included in the text in connection with the exemplification and discussion of Western social formation or capitalist production means.

The "otherization" of Oriental societies in opposition to modern society is one of the basic characteristics of nineteenth-century Orientalism. The Orientalists defined Oriental societies as being non-developed and backwards, attributing this to different causes, such as the environmental and geographical factors, and the racial constitution or the people's lowly position on the evolutionary scale in contrast to the developed and civilized Europeans. In this context, the Orient is marginalized and identified as opposition to Western society. Thus, modernity was described as a negation of the Orient for the sake of intellectually guaranteeing the progress of the West.

Marx, who bases his approach on Orientalist sources, agrees with this unfortunate reading. In this context, his sources were too weak; they do not present enough information for a study of Oriental societies. Although an interest was developed in this period, no in-depth study had yet been carried out. Nevertheless, Marx included those ideas into his analysis without questioning. Indeed, when the same sources (for example British political economists) were used in studies of modern society, Marx used them within a critical perspective. Thus, when Marx dealt with matters like despotism, land ownership and village communities, he worked from sources whose weaknesses he was aware of. Despite this, he used them, even expanding their scope.

A second important point regarding Marx's sources is the problem of selectiveness. Marx did not undertake an independent study of Oriental societies, but rather selectively took ideas from certain sources in order to establish a point of affirmation within his own theory. In this context, to be honest, in that period it was not possible to find an objective study on Oriental societies. However Marx had the opportunity to benefit from a great variety of works which have opposing arguments. However, he preferred to select a restricted number of works that supported his own thesis from among the existing literature and make an evaluation of these alone. One who examines the bibliography of *Das Kapital* will easily see that the same fastidiousness shown in the studies concerned with modern societies is not present in the arguments concerning Oriental societies. Marx made sweeping generalizations based upon a limited number of works concerned with the subject.[1]

This weakness of the sources is not only connected with the intellectual atmosphere of the age, but also with the role that Marx gave to Oriental societies in his own model. When considering the function of Oriental societies in his theory, it becomes clear that this weakness was not very important to Marx. According to the methodology that Marx later referred to as dialectic materialism, in order to explain a social form there is a need for an opposing social form. In this framework, one who studies the connections in Marx's texts with Oriental societies can easily see that he uses them to better explain Western society. Marx constantly includes Oriental societies as a negation, as an opposing example to explain his point. Thus, Marx was not interested in the internal dynamics of Oriental societies beyond defining and positioning them against modern societies.

On the other hand, Marx does have a perspective and conceptualization that goes beyond his own sources. Marx transforms the partial thoughts about Oriental societies in the sources into a total explanation with his theory of modes of production. Thus, he creates a separate social form which runs in parallel to the progressive Western form.

According to Marx, the actual factor that gives character to a society is the mode of production that forms the infrastructure.[2] Thus, different societies formed some general categories in the context of the dominant mode of production. This allows for the appearance of the differentiation between the Occident and Orient, both theoretically and empirically. In this context, Marx, by following the perception of a three-staged historical progression of the Enlightenment, arrives at the conclusion that there is a variety of social forms that follow one another in successive historical stages. However, he widened this classification and, in parallel to these three stages implemented in European history, defined a

---

1   For a detailed discussion on Marx's use of the sources, see Naqvi, 1973, pp. 36–70.

2   While using the concept of modes of production in this context as a general category to explain a type of society among different societies, he also uses the concept of society for different structures within a mode of production. In this sense, it is a mode of production that gives the essential character to a society and differentiates it from others. For example, while modern society is defined in the context of CMP, Marx speaks of separate societies, for example France, Britain and Germany. In the same way, while using AMPs in general to speak of the Orient, he also deals with India, China and Iran separately (Marx, 1989a, p. 192).

fourth social form that had not changed throughout history, the AMP. Marx thus universalized the Western social forms in developing his own social analysis by posing the Orient against the Occident.

Historical bifurcation of Orient and Occident was based on the fractionation of their own modes of production founded on the following fundamental factors: ownership of means of production, the nature of production relationships and the social conditions of labor. The means of production had developed as private property in the West, and labor over time had been freed from a variety of social ties, becoming liberalized. As a result, societies progressed from the Ancient Mode to the FMP, to be followed by the CMP, finally resulting in the appearance of modern society. However, in the Orient, the means of production (land) never became private property[3] due to Oriental despotism, which appeared as a result of the special situation formed by the geographic conditions and the insular social structure. Thus, free labor never appeared. Indeed, according to Marx, a similar need for an irrigation organization appeared in Europe; however, here despotism did not emerge. In Marx's opinion, the irrigation channels that were formed in Italy and Flanders were not administered by a centralized state, but were worked voluntarily by the society. Here, Marx (1979a, p. 127) clearly differentiates between civilized Europe, formed upon volunteerism,[4] and the lesser civilized Orient, which used land in a futile manner in which there was no volunteerism. This explanation and comparison shows us why Marx did not perceive despotism as being only caused by geographic and climatic reasons, and gives us some of the cultural factors that he felt were also the causal factors.

The staging of history and classification of societies have a close relationship to the meaning that Marx gave to human nature and the development of humanity. According to Marx, history is formed by the progressive stages in the struggle of humanity with nature. The fundamental condition for the progression of history is mankind's establishment of dominance over nature. Marx assumes that in the West developing modes of production established dominance over nature and thus contributed to historical progress. However, he does not apply the same perspective for Oriental societies which had built dams, predicted rain, and increased production with canals thousands of years earlier. Marx does not see these developments as humanity's dominance over nature and thus does not

---

3   In fact, Marx is not sure whether or not land is private property in the East. In a letter that he sent to Engels, dated June 14, 1853, Marx says that private property of land in Asia was first introduced by the Muslims. Marx states that the matter of land ownership in India was still a subject matter of debate among British authors and that to the south of Kistna there was private land ownership. Indeed, he quotes from Sir Stamford Raffles that in Java absolute ownership of the land was prevalent. However, in order to support his own view and in keeping with his theses, Marx adopts the idea that there was no private land ownership in the Orient (Marx, 1983d, p. 348).

4   Marx returns to this point in the third section of *Das Kapital* and deals with the concept of voluntary unity in Europe.

perceive them as progress; he is able to claim that these societies are stagnant in the face of all these victories over nature.

Similarly, as these developments did not open the way to a change in production relations, Marx does not consider them to have formed an advance; historical progress can only appear and be realized with a class struggle. Social dynamism is procured by class divisions in society. In this context, the appearance of private property, which led to the appearance of classes in society, is of the utmost importance. As private property, classes and social dynamism did not appear in the Orient, there was no social change. In contrast to this, Western societies, which have a perpetual dynamism, saved humanity completely from the dominance of nature, and brought the modern social stages in which nature was dominated. In fact, it can be seen that even Marx was not sure of his thesis that there was no change in the Orient. In his work, in a number of places, expressions concerning some fundamental changes in the Orient can be found. For example, the fact that there was no private property in India is connected to Islamic law (Marx, 1983d, p. 348). This claim destroys Marx's claim that there had been no change over thousands of years since Islamic law entered India after 900 AC.

Due to the weakness and inconsistencies of Marx's sources and his own style of using these sources, none of these conclusions was attained with reliable empirical information. His analyses of Oriental societies, rather than being based on historical and social data, are explained with some empirical examples to support an idea that was formed from an abstract and logical perspective. Engels (1980, pp. 475–477) states that Marx's method requires surpassing the pure abstraction to create a constant contact with historical examples and empirical facts. However, due to the lack of sources, the only possible explanative model was the logical one. Marx makes a similar evaluation of his own method and says that a critical examination of the history of capitalism may give us explanation of the earlier stages. As a result of this method, Marx (1986, pp. 42–43) deals with pre-capitalist and non-capitalist forms from the perspective of capitalism.

As the logic of the dialectic required that every stage had to mature in the womb of the earlier stage and that it appeared as a result of the internal conflicts of the previous stage, Marx defines the last stage as the most mature form. Thus, capitalism contains within itself the explanation of the earlier stages. As a reflection of this thought, he proposed that the examination of capitalist political economy in a critical way would act as a beacon for societies in earlier stages. According to Marx, (1986, pp. 42–43) just as the human anatomy is a key to the anatomy of an ape, bourgeois economy held the key to antiquity and other ages.

In this context, while Marx showed care in establishing his own model of development of modern society working from empirical data, he studied Oriental societies with a logical analysis. This does not mean that there is no historical or empirical data in his analyses of Oriental societies; it shows that the empirical data that exists in the study has been selected to support the logical system that Marx had established. It is easier to see this in the dual attitude he displays to AMP and FMP. While the Western pre-capitalist modes of production were formed in a way that would lead to the birth of capitalism, the modes of production belonging to the Orient were formed in a way that could not possibly lead to capitalism. In order to reach a convincing argument concerning the modern form of Western society and its transformation in the future, Marx developed anachronistic teleological explanations.

In this approach, capitalism is seen as the *telos* of the historical development. Thus, this approach, which is the essence of the thought of every evolutionary thinker, evaluates historical events as evolutionary steps on the way to realizing the telos. Within this scope while imputing the idealist concept of history in *German Ideology*, by explaining history backwards and transforming the later stages into the purpose of the earlier stage (Marx and Engels, 1976a, pp. 53–54), he did the same thing.

On the other hand, one aim of Marx's analysis of Oriental societies was to find evidence for his claim that capitalism was historical. By basing his thought on the analysis of the primitive communism and common property attributed to Oriental societies, he claims that capitalism is not natural but historical, and that it will culminate in the future to the rule of the proletariat. Marx expected that research on Oriental societies would demonstrate the possibility of a social order in societies with no private property. Thus, he wanted to demonstrate that communism was not contrary to human nature; just the reverse, it was in harmony with it. If such a thing was possible once, then according to Marx, it would be possible for this higher social structure to be realized once again. In this sense, for example, in the rough drafts of the letter Marx wrote to Vera Zassulich, he explains modern communism, which he took from Morgan as "'the new system' towards which modern society tends 'will be a revival in a superior form of an archaic social type'" (Marx, 1989b, p. 351). In his correspondence with Engels, the traces of this thought can be seen, as Marx qualifies lack of private property in land as "the real *clef*, even to the eastern heaven" (Marx, 1983c, pp. 333–334).

In order to arrive at the essential meaning of what Marx wrote on Oriental societies, it is necessary to understand the central question he was answering. This question concerned the development of modern society and its nature. For this reason, he does not attempt to develop a theory or an explanation of Oriental societies. Rather, Marx used analysis of PCMP empirically and theoretically to demonstrate the unique aspects of capitalism. The basic aim of Marx's interest in Oriental societies was the concern to explain modernity with its negation.

PART II
Oriental Societies in the Theory of Max Weber

Chapter 7

The Formation of Weber's Sociology of the Orient and its Reception

Weber's position in twentieth-century sociology is closely related to his dealing with the basic issues of Western civilization. He defended modernity at a time when hopes for modern society were starting to be lost. In addition, he represents a turning point in the history of the science of sociology. The end of the nineteenth century was an era in which the questioning of evolutionist interpretations and positivist approaches along with the concept of modern society was taking place. It was in the context of finding solutions to these questions that Weber established his sociological approach. According to Julien Freund, (1968, p. 9) sociology became in practice an empirical and exact science with Weber. H. Stuart Hughes declared Weber to be the founder of twentieth-century social theory along with Sigmund Freud. Hughes states that by destroying the foundation of positivism, which had transformed into empty formulations and formalized idealism, Weber was able to revitalize the great traditions of the Enlightenment. According to him, Weber created new ways of perceiving historical realism, without prejudice or illusions, by breaking away from the dominant belief of shallow progressivism that had been prevalent in nineteenth-century social thought (Hughes, 2002).

However, Weber's central place in modern sociology is not just limited to this. His placement in opposition to Marx within American sociology has highlighted his analysis of social status, as opposed to Marx's theory of class, his interpretive method, as opposed to historical materialism, and his opposing opinions for analyses based on material components. In this regard, Weber's early critics emphasized his contributions to the various fields of sociology, proclaiming him as the founder of modern sociology. Talcott Parsons (1928, 1929, 1968[1937]) worked on and highlighted his analyses of capitalism and his theory on social action, while Edward Goldhammer and Edward Shils (1939) examined his analyses on power and status. Reinhard Bendix (1945, 1947) examined Weber's sociology of politics and the functioning of bureaucracy, while Paul Honigsheim (1946) looked at his theories on the rural sociology.[1] Ernst Moritz Manasse (1947) studied his thought on the sociology of race, while Oliver Cromwell Cox (1950) examined his theories on the sociology of stratification. Consequently, Weber

---

1 Honigsheim was a disciple of Weber. He attended the intellectual meetings at Weber's house and his studies on Weber were collected in 1968 in a book called *The Unknown Max Weber*.

is perceived as the founder of numerous basic fields of sociology, such as law, politics, economics and religion.[2]

Within this framework, the distinctive feature of Weber's sociology is his perspective on comparative history of civilizations, which has taken on more importance in recent times.[3] His comparative model prepared the ground for new sociological modeling and thoughts within a variety of syntheses. It cannot be said, however, that adequate research has been carried out on his analysis of Oriental societies, which presents theoretical and empirical significance in Weber's comparative sociology. Although various dimensions of the different theoretical effects of Weber's analyses of Oriental societies have been individually assessed, a complete and encompassing study has not yet been undertaken.

The Political and Intellectual Climate in Germany during Weber's Youth

Born into an industrial bourgeois family, as the child of a lawyer who was a liberal politician and a devout Protestant mother, Max Weber (April 21, 1864–June 14, 1920) was placed at an important transition period in the history of Western thought. Weber reflected the accumulation of thought which emerged during this time and offered conceptual and methodological innovations which would define the next period. In this regard, the intellectual and political climate that Weber grew up in defined the issues with which he dealt and his approach towards them.

Defined as the intellectual spirit in Germany during the period between 1897 and 1914 by Robert Michels (Antoni, 1962, p. 146), Weber's scientific understanding was formed by seeking solutions for the problems of the society and civilization in which he lived. Three principle issues held a crucial place in German intellectual and academic life during this period and in the climate in which Weber's thoughts were developing. These were: (1) growing academic and political debates centered on Marxism; (2) the questioning of positivism and progressivism as dominant trends, with a shift towards new philosophical methodologies; and (3) late nation forming with debates on the future of German society and state based on the problems caused by modernization and industrialization.

From the 1880s onwards, Marxism was on the rise both politically and, consequently, intellectually.[4] The reading and analysis of certain works by Marx and Engels were not widespread in the environment in which Weber grew up

---

2   For a short and impressive explanation of Weber's effect on German, European and American intellectual life in the first quarter of the twentieth century, see Mommsen, 1989, pp. 170, 179.

3   For Weber's place and importance in comparative historical sociology, see Kalberg, 1994.

4   A brief analysis of the debate on Marx's views in the academic world is presented in the preface of the third volume of *Das Kapital,* written by Engels (1998a) in 1894.

in, but deterministic and economic interpretations of history were fashionable among young German intellectuals and the educated bourgeoisie. However, due to the development of the German Social Democratic Party towards the end of the century, the necessity of a response to Marx and the claims of Marxism arose in bourgeois and liberal intellectual circles.[5] Therefore, as a person who defined himself as "a class conscious bourgeoisie,"[6] Weber's writings at such an intellectual period were interpreted as being directly focused on this purpose. His first contact with Marxism was through young members of *Verein für Sozialpolitik*,[7] such as Sombart, Gerhart von Schulze-Gävernitz (1864–1943) and Ferdinand Tönnies (1855–1936).[8] Members of the older generation of *Verein* were

---

As Roth quotes from Sombart, (*Das Lebenswerk von Karl Marx*, Jena: Fischer, 1909, p. 4ff) in the 1870s Marx was rarely read except by a "few extremely excited master tailors" as well as Marx Adolph Wagner, Albert Schäffle, and Adolph Held. "According to Sombart, before 1883 there were only 20 publications on Marx; between 1884 and 1894, when the third volume of Das Kapital was published, there were 58; between 1895 and 1904 this number jumped to 214" (Roth, 1971, p. 235 fn. 17). In this regard, Bottomore states that the effect of Marx's ideas after 1880 increased and "at the first international congress of sociology in 1894 scholars from several countries (including Tönnies) contributed papers which discussed Marx's theory" (Bottomore, 1984, p. 45).

5 Weber followed contemporary socialist politics. He attended Social Democratic Party (SDP) congresses and made observations on the structure, leadership and development of the movement. He also personally followed the developments in Russia, from the 1905 Revolutions onwards. In fact, he even learned Russian in order to be able to observe current events, and wrote lengthy articles analyzing developments (Weber, 1995). Weber had a strong dislike of SDP and its brand of Marxism. He viewed them as an obstacle to Germany's national interests and its becoming a power-state, seeing them as being politically inadequate for a national leadership.

6 In a letter dated November 6, 1907, written to Roberto Michels (1876–1936) during a debate about the German Social Democrats, Weber states that he saw himself as "a class conscious bourgeoisie" (Mommsen, 1989, p. 116). According to the information provided by Scaff, (1981) the letters he sent to Michels, numbering about 30, can be found in the archives of *Fondazione Luigi Einaudi* in Turin.

7 Established in 1873, the activities of the society were directed against liberal social politics (*laissez faire*) and the newly emerging revolutionary socialism. Within the context of these goals, the Society aimed to act as a consultant to the welfare practices of Bismarck, who had emerged with the same aims. The founders of the society advocated the improvement of education and the conditions of the lower classes for the continuation of the status quo. During the lengthy presidency of Gustav Schmoller (1890–1917), the society turned into an independent interdisciplinary association.

8 Among these names, however, Sombart had a greater effect in familiarizing Weber with Marx. At that period, Sombart was a name that was close to Marxism, and he played an important role in the presentation of Marx's ideas to academia with works such as *Sozialismus und soziale Bewengung* (1896) and *Der modern Kapitalismus* (1902). In the supplement of Volume 3 of *Capital*, Engels states that "Werner Sombart gives an outline of the Marxian system which, taken all in all, is excellent." According to him, "it is the first time that a German university professor succeeds on the whole in seeing in Marx's writings

known as *Kathedersozialisten* (Socialists of the Chair) by their opponents, such as Adolp Wagner, Gustav von Schmoller, Lujo Brenteno, Georg Freidrich Knapp and Rudolf von Gneist. Levin Goldsmith, a professor of law at Heidelberg and Berlin, the person to whom Weber dedicated his doctoral thesis, was one of these; writers such as Karl Kautsky and August Bebel, the joint founder of the Social Democratic Party, also had an influence in introducing Weber to Marxist literature.[9]

As Giddens (1995, p. 16) has stated, the younger generation in which Weber found himself were "concerned more broadly with the nature and origins of capitalism" than the former generation. The form of Germany's transition into capitalism formed the basic issues and intellectual identities for Weber's generation. Rapid industrialization enveloped German society under the governance of Bismarck. Under these conditions, in the last quarter of the century, the most important topic in German intellectual circles was the effort to position itself against the new model of German society and government and to explain these transformations. Leading figures of Weber's generation, such as Sombart, Simmel and Tönnies, followed up on questions about the roots of this process by depicting a critical and apprehensive perspective of Germany's process of modernization.[10]

Due to the social and political conditions specific to Germany, the most important problem among those which were encountered during the transition to industrial capitalism was that the Junkers, the land capitalists who were responsible for German unification, were incapable of adapting to the new capitalism. Because the bourgeoisie class was weak, political leadership problems became an issue in the period after Bismarck. At the same time, the views on the Junkers were also influenced by the opinions forming within academic and political circles in regards to Germany's place within global politics.

The reason Weber made some field studies on the current social problems alongside his historical-theoretical studies during his doctorate and *habilitus* was connected to the contemporary political agenda. In the research he carried out based on the request of *Verein für Sozialpolitik* entitled *The Conditions of Agricultural Workers in Eastern Germany (Die Lage der Landarbeiter im ostelbischen Deutschland)*, Weber developed analyses on the political conditions in Germany and its leadership. Here he stated that the migration of seasonal agricultural laborers from Poland to the east of the Elbe River had turned

---

what Marx really says, stating that the criticism of the Marxian system cannot consist of a refutation" (Engels, 1998b, p. 881). Moreover, he states his appreciation (together with his criticisms) in a letter he wrote to Sombart (Engels, 2004).

9 For Weber's circle in *Verein für Sozialpolitik,* and his work, see Marianne Weber, 2008, pp. 124–130.

10 This is in keeping with Marx's sympathetic approach to Russian primitive collectivism after complaining about the evils of capitalism, when he began research into primitive forms of society towards the end of his life.

East Germany into another Poland.[11] In this work, Weber touched upon the inseparability of Germany's political and economic problems from one another (Marianne Weber, 2008, p. 115). According to him, for Germany to become a *Machstaat (power-state)* it had to transform into an industrial country, while its national unity depended on demonstrating its power in the international arena.[12] In order for this to happen, the matter of German political leadership was important. Bismarck, however, had deliberately divided the liberals and pushed the working class outside the system by introducing anti-socialist laws. It was because of this, according to Weber, that the working class lacked the political maturity to take on leadership and the bourgeoisie was weak (Giddens, 1995, pp. 17–18). As a result, Germany's near future would depend on the development of incisiveness in the bourgeois political identity. In this regard, the Junkers' political positions, who acted only according to their class interests, lacked the foundations that would ensure the strengthening of the German state in the future. In this framework, starting with *Protestant Ethic*, Weber placed the development of the bourgeoisie at the center of the modern social structure.

The Conditions of Agricultural Workers in Eastern Germany introduced Weber to academic and political circles. He made his idea of the *power-state* clearer in 1896 during the Freiburg University inaugural conference, which received a huge response. As Marianne Weber relates, during this conference, entitled *The National State and Economic Policy*, both the audience and the speaker were excited about his power of articulation and the superb nature of his speech. Weber's ideas led to the debate taking place in academic and political circles (Weber, 1994).[13]

Describing Weber as a liberal nationalist, Aron (1965, p. 291) states that he placed the power of the state and the greatness of nation above all else. Claiming that it was necessary for Germany to take part in imperial politics as a power state, Weber was involved with instigative formations, such as the *Pan-German League (Alldeutscher Verband)* and *Naval League,* which provoked Germany into administering expansionist policies (Mommsen, 1977, pp. 31–32; Marianne Weber, 2008, p. 202). However, after seeing that these groups based their policies not on Germany's national interests but rather on the class interests of the Junkers and the industrialists, he parted ways with them in April 1899 (Turner and Factor, 1983, p. 13; Marianne Weber, 2008, p. 224). Weber maintained his

---

11   Only the part entitled "Entwickelungstendenzen in der Lage der ostelbischen Landarbeiter," published in *Preussische Jahrbucher* (1894, vol. 77, pp. 437–473) has been translated into English (Weber, 1979).

12   Aron (1965, p. 292) states that Weber has two basic missions. One is to protect the legacy of the founder of the German Empire, the other is to get Germany involved in world politics (Weltpolitik).

13   Subsequent to this speech, Weber says that it "gave a firm kick to 'ethical culture.'" Marianne Weber (2008, pp. 216–217) states that the speech had important political effects.

political stance throughout his life however, and worked for Germany's becoming a power state.[14]

The choice of the mediaeval period as the area of study for his doctorate corresponds with a new direction in European thought which Weber followed. The Enlightenment disdain of the Middle Ages, and its perception as the dismissible Dark Ages, slowly began to fall off after the 1880s. Instead of attempting to explain Western history by skipping over this era and ignoring its existence, an explanation through a more encompassing historical process emerged.[15] Starting initially with historians, this predisposition helped to establish schools of thought that studied mediaeval history, such as the Annales School. Weber's doctorate thesis, and in particular *Protestant Ethic*, holds a special place in these tendencies. As a result, continuity was being emphasized in the history of Western civilization, rather than discontinuity.

The Formation of Weber's Thought and Epistemology

In addition to the social and political conditions discussed above, the epistemological break in German intellectual circles which occurred at the end of the nineteenth century played an important part in the formation of Weber's thought. Comprehensive epistemological debates took place in Germany at the *fin de siècle*. It was also an era in which the power of evolutionism, progressivism and positivism, which had dominated throughout the nineteenth century, was beginning to be questioned. Through the debates being held on various central issues during this period, Weber formulated his own thoughts, with the most principal of these being about the separation of human sciences and natural sciences. Debates on historical materialism generated from Marxist analyses (which were on the rise at the time), and the disagreement in methodology between the Austrian School and the German historical school, of which Weber was a member, were both taking place as well. It should be added that there were also Weber's debates on objectivity, the relationships of science–politics and science–ideology too.

Towards the end of the nineteenth century, methodological debates *(Methodenstreit)*, which had the status of being the main context of humanities, were vibrant in German academia (Allen, 2004, p. 68; Freund, 1968, pp. 37–38). Zijderveld critically recommended that some thinkers who approached Hegel's metaphysics, Nietzsche's vitality, and Marx's materialism to turn towards Kant's

---

14 In this period Wolfgang Mommsen (1984) produced some significant work concerning Weber's political stance and relationship with German imperialism. Furthermore, the work written by Jacob Peter Mayer (1944) still holds value despite being affected by the atmosphere of the Second World War. In the second edition, published in 1956, Mayer tries to rectify this.

15 This transformation can be seen thanks to the emphasis on the Church as an institution in the development of Western civilization in Weber's work (Coşkun, 2000).

epistemology (Zijderveld, 2005, p. 29), which focused on the problematic relationship between knowledge and reality, concepts and experience. Neo-Kantianism[16] appeared in the framework of the methodological differences between spiritual sciences (*Geisteswissenschaft*) and natural sciences (*Naturwissenschaft*).[17] In order to escape positivism and scientism, a search for a logic and methodology equivalent to which is found in the natural sciences ensued in the newly emerging social sciences such as psychology and sociology. In the climate of this debate, Weber accepted that cultural sciences were based on principles that differed from those in the natural sciences (Freund, 1968, p. 41). He created his own cultural theory utilizing Neo-Kantian terminology. Weber went on to use this epistemological framework to formulate his criticism of both idealism and Marxist methodology (Giddens, 1972, pp. 30–31).[18]

Heinrich Rickert (1863–1936) and Emil Lask (1875–1915) were names among the Neo-Kantians who had a profound effect on Weber (Marshall, 1982, pp. 49–50; Schluchter, 1981, pp. 13–14, fn. 1). Rickert, who was a close friend of Weber's, changed the term *geisteswissenschaft* to *kulturwissenschaft* and established the methodological foundation of Neo-Kantianism. According to Rickert, *cultural* sciences also can seek general laws while investigating *value* and *meaning* at the same time. For him, while the unique, different and individual are at the forefront in cultural sciences, the focus of the natural sciences is the phenomenon that is more general, repetitive and law based. The solution Rickert proposes is that the classification of sciences and the demystification of the foundations of cultural sciences lie in the synthesis of the analytical and formal criteria. According to him, in contrast to the natural sciences, the unique values that create the principles which allow the establishment of individual scientific concepts in historical and social sciences which deal with explaining cultural phenomena exist in cultural entities. Over time, Weber's value-relationship conceptualization changed from Rickert's, even though in the beginning he was a Rickertian as far as fact-value, concept creation and the framework of explanation in cultural sciences were concerned. According to Weber, it is not possible for a universal system of values to emerge without paying heed to ethical, aesthetic or political views. As a consequence, a universally acceptable history is not possible.

---

16 According to this movement, while the purpose of cultural sciences is to understand human acts, or to make them understandable based on the meaning that the performer gives them, natural sciences seek causal explanations through the universal laws of nature (McNaron, 1999, p. 102).

17 Neo-Kantianism emerged in two different schools: *The Marburg School*, Ernst Cassirer (1874–1945), and the *South West German* or *Baden School*, Wilhelm Windelband (1848–1915) and Rickert. Weber was in close contact with the second one.

18 Weber's criticism of Neo-Kantian epistemology and the Hegelian methodologies of Roscher and Knies was viewed in terms of the Marx–Weber opposition, with Kant being opposed to Hegel. Nonetheless, there are those who argue that Weber's natural place is in German Idealism (Collins, 1986, pp. 33–37; Parsons, 1971, p. 29).

In this context, Weber was indicating to the tension in the thin line between objectivity and subjectivity, demonstrating that the conflict between value groups which are in competition with one another is irresolvable, thus transforming the cultural subjectivity into the basic component of cultural sciences.[19]

Another epistemological debate in which Weber took part is the one which took place between Carl Menger of the Austrian School and Gustav Schmoller of the Historical School. Brought up in the atmosphere of the Historical School in Heidelberg, Weber was not exactly a member, though members of the Historical School viewed him as part of the third generation along with Schumpeter, Sombart and Simmel.[20] Nevertheless, Weber was highly influenced by the Austrian School's "marginal revolution" in economy and this influence can easily be seen in his article on critical methodology which he wrote on Roscher and Knies.[21] This is why young members of the Austrian School such as Hayek, view Weber as belonging to their group. However, it can be said that Weber's methodological approach is not the same as that of Mengers. His work is more historical and comparative than being theoretical (Camic, Gorski, and Trubek, 2005, pp. 10–16; Ringer, 2004, p. 91).

Another area of debate in the context of the formation of Weber's methodology is historical materialism, a movement that became prevalent in German academia (in parallel to political developments) after the 1880s. Even though Weber had connections with Socialists of the Chair in his youth and had close connections with scientists who embraced the methods of historical materialism, he criticizes historical materialism, finding it to be a one-sided approach (Weber, 1949a, p. 68). Weber sees historical materialism as a "naive" idea and "that such 'ideas' arise as a 'reflection' or 'superstructure' of economic situations" (Weber, 2009a, p. 74). Yet, although he believes historical materialism is a type of economism, Weber clearly states that he has no intention of offering a one-sided explanation based on intellectual factors. Rather, he desires to show that "ideas" are generally effective in history (Weber, 2009a, pp. 159, 96). Such criticism of historical materialism by Weber and its polemical appearance in *Protestant Ethic* is an important factor in

---

19   For the effects of Rickert and Neo-Kantianism in Weber's epistemology, see Marshall, 1982, pp. 47, 50–51.

20   The Historical School was brought to its demise by those outside, such as Marx and Wenger, and those inside who ignored the rules, such as Weber. Older members such as Roscher, Hildebrand and Knies, were too scattered to establish a new sociological school. In methodological debates with the Austrian school led by Bücher, there was a tendency towards handling the heritage of classical political economics and a shying away from Schmoller's empirical historicism (Nafissi, 1998, p. 20).

21   While Weber was planning to edit a book entitled *Outline of Socio-Economics (Grundriss der Sozialökonomik)* which would form the basis of *Economy and Society*, he enhanced his relationship with Austrian Neo-Classicists by asking them to write the central parts of this book (Turner and Holton, 1989, pp. 34, 38–39). For an explanation of Weber's relationship with the German historical school based on the draft of *Economy and Society*, see Sumiya, 2001, pp. 120–138.

his being viewed in opposition to Marx. However, Weber's criticism of historical materialism is not part of an effort to establish himself as an alternative to Marx; it is an approach to determine his own stance.

Even though Weber actively joined in the debates discussed above, he did not choose to establish a methodology within marked boundaries or create a theoretical framework. He did not directly take on the task of establishing a methodology; his methodological works are more in the form of criticism to demonstrate what it is that he is opposed to.[22] In this regard, Weber's epistemological views can be examined within the framework of interpretation, ideal types, and historical developmentalism.

Weber rejected causal explanations, emphasizing cultural sciences which, in accord with the philosophy of the social sciences, favored interpretative explanations in opposition to those of naturalism. Developed initially around 1850 by the historian Droysen, Weber's interpretive (*verstehen*) method also contains elements from Dilthey, Rickert, Lask, Simmel, Gottlottlilienfeld, Lipps and Jaspers (Freund, 1968, pp. 63–93). While Dilthey saw the methods of explanation and interpretation as being different from one another, Weber combined these and developed an *interpretive understanding* (Freund, 1968, p. 100). Weber defines sociology as "a science concerning itself with the interpretive understanding of social action and a casual explanation of its course and consequences" (Weber, 1978, p. 4). According to Weber, this does not include free interpretation. The meaning of the action should be verified by *causal attribution, historical data, logical analyses* or *statistical data*. In this regard, Weber says that two types of understanding exist. The first one is based on direct observation, that is, on understanding the occurrence of actions through methods of observation such as reading or seeing. The other is explanatory understanding. This method serves the purpose of understanding the meaning the agent attaches to his/her action and the motives behind it. To understand the subjective meaning of the action, also known as the intended meaning, both methods of the complicated understanding processes should be utilized (Weber, 1978, pp. 8–9). According to Weber, for a

---

22   After falling ill in 1897, Weber returned to his work on methodological writings and continued to contribute to this topic until his death. First, he penned a critical piece on the two leading representatives of the historical school, Roscher ve Knies. After this, he wrote an article on objectivity in the social sciences, announcing the editorial policy of the *Archiv für Sozialwissenschaft und Sozialpolitik* magazine, which he took over with Sombart and Jaffe. Following his *Protestant Ethic* article, which was published in 1905, Weber returned to the discussion on methodology in 1906, and wrote on Meyer and the logic of cultural sciences. Following that, in 1907, he wrote an article on law in which he claims he applied Stammler's historical materialism, and put forward his most detailed criticism of historical materialism. Weber's articles on methodology continued after this and were collected in 1922 by Marianne Weber under the title *Gesammelte Aufsätze zur Wissenschaftslehre (GAzW)*. Although Weber complains about it, for Oakes, "[w]ith the exceptions of Hegel and Marx, no figure in the history of German social science contributed more prolifically to 'methodological pestilence' than Weber himself" (Oakes, 1977, pp. 13–14).

phenomenon to be understood, it is enough that it be understood, otherwise, one does not need to re-experience the entire event: "One need not have been Caesar in order to understand Caesar" (Weber, 1978, p. 5).

The most basic problem facing an interpretive explanation is the problem of objectivity. As there is no causality, it is difficult to capture objectivity when examining social events. However, Weber thinks that a scientist can achieve certain objectivity in cultural and social sciences by using this approach even though subjectivity is included, and that this objectivity can even be brought to the selection of the topic. Although unreality and single dimensionality may be characteristics of historical knowledge, the social scientists' approach will lead to a degree of objectivity. In the introduction of *Economy and Society,* Weber states that his work differs from Simmel's because he separates subjective intent from objectively valid "meanings" (Weber, 1978, p. 4). Weber thinks objectivity can be achieved by what has been intended subjectively and by possessing objective meanings. This, in turn, demonstrates that the analysis of social events should not begin with attributed meanings.

Another implication of objectivity as Weber understood it is that a scientist should abandon his political or ideological attachments when carrying out scientific work. As he frequently argued at the meetings of the German Sociological Society, this is an ethical responsibility of the scientist. In a similar way, in his speech *Science as a Vocation,* Weber states that he does not approve of scientists who have political attachments (Weber, 2008, pp. 25–53).

The second axis of Weber's methodology, which he used to actualize his sociological analysis, is the concept of the "ideal type." With this conceptualization, Weber attempts to construct a model by using the most stylistic and characteristic features of phenomena that change in time and place through observation (Weber, 1978, p. 20). In this context, the ideal type means demonstrating a complicated event in its most usual and representative ways, thus giving shape to the analysis based on the framework provided by them.[23]

To avoid any possible misunderstanding of the word "ideal," Weber explains that "ideal type" is not being used to express what should happen, but rather the ideal representation of the event. In this regard, the ideal type has a logical

---

23   According to Mommsen, in the article published in *Logos* in 1913, entitled "Über einige Kategorien der 'verstehenden' Soziologie" (Bd. IV, Heft 3, Tübingen, pp. 253–294), a change takes place in Weber's methodological approach. (This article was later developed and constituted the introduction to *Economy and Society.*) After this, according to Mommsen, (1977, p. 13) "the ideal type" stopped being a methodological tool and became the purpose of research itself. He argues that Weber starts dealing with building extremely complicated ideal type systems, regardless of whether this could be applied to empirical reality or not. It would be an extreme interpretation which suggests this was the main goal of his studies after this date, even though ideal type conceptualizations constantly appear.

use, not an ethical one.[24] Weber proposes that the ideal type logically searches for the perfect model and excludes all moral judgments. This is because ideal types clearly show that social events have different aspects and facets to them (Weber, 1978, p. 21).

In this context, Weber presents the ideal type approach as an alternative to historical materialism. It not only constitutes an alternative to historical generalizations, but also encompasses those of historical materialism. According to him, the never-ending disorder of social reality and the unrelenting flow of historical change make the discovery of universal laws almost impossible. The only meaningful duties social scientists can ultimately achieve is understanding and explaining socio-historical reality within its own characteristics. The impossibility of historical generalization based on limited empirical data can only be transcended with the understanding of historical events through the framework of ideal types.

Weber's own methodology using the empirical concept of type and socio-historical models was based upon the probable alternatives to the evolutionary deterministic developmental schema (Roth, 1979, p. 195). This happened at an important point in modern history, when disappointment in the evolutionary views of the three previous generations of deists and naturalists revealed a new methodological tendency. In this regard, Weber attempted to crystallize his stance against evolutionism and Hegelian progressive perspectives. Weber's criticism towards positivism and progressivism developed around their analysis of social events with causal explanations (Ringer, 2004, pp. 85–87). He thought that objective causal laws did not exist in the cultural field and that in their absence the general development of culture needed to be re-analyzed with subjective interests (Roth, 1987, p. 81). The articles he wrote on Roscher and Knies (Weber, 1975) and his work entitled *Critical Studies in the Logic of the Cultural Sciences,* in which he criticizes Meyer's methodology, are products of this viewpoint (Weber, 1949b, pp. 113–188). Thus, Weber adopts a comparative perspective in regards to social development. While according to the evolutionist perspective history is comprised of phases which necessarily and inescapably follow one upon the other, relatively independent various social developments exist for those looking from the comparative perspective (Schluchter, 1981, pp. 1–4). As for Weber, he examines these developments within the social phases that are formed by comparisons.

On the other hand, rationalism holds a central place in Weber's progressive model and the creation of its stages. His adaptation of Kant's historical perspective where values realize themselves in historical stages have an effect in this (Schluchter, 1981, pp. 14–15). Weber categorizes religions based on their levels of rationalism, placing Protestantism at the top, which is totally disenchanted. By

---

24 Weber's *ideal type* concept resembles Menger's *pure type*. In fact, Weber uses the "pure type" concept in his later work. However, both attach different meanings to the concept. While Weber intends to make abstractions to enable the creation of models, Menger means conceptualizations which have universal validity (Camic et al., 2005, p. 17).

doing this, he creates stages that affect all social events and leans towards finding an answer as to why the West is the most developed (or the most unique). Ultimately, in the *Prefatory Remarks to Collected Essays in the Sociology of Religion (Vorbemerkung)*[25] Weber (2009b, p. 205) speaks on behalf of Western civilization, even though he stated in another place that, "The question of stages of economic development will be considered only insofar as it is absolutely necessary, and then only incidentally" (Weber, 1978, pp. 117–118). He frequently applies the stages of cultural development in practice as basic factors in inter-civilization comparisons.[26] Here Weber (1978, p. 68) mentions primitive, backwards, undeveloped and uncivilized societies within a framework of comparison with the West .

As explained in detail above, there are three main pillars in Weber's intellectual development which were formed within the context of his political, scientific and civilizational membership. Weber's topics emerged within the conditions of his age, more particularly, the effects of the debates and problems of the period on his basic thesis that the roots of modern society can be understood and its properties can be determined via comparison. By the usage of the ideal type analysis of world views and organizational differences, Weber's developmental history makes it possible to make a rationalistic examination of social events. The basic framework of this analysis, which is formed around the comparison of civilizations, is a social staging and cultural classification based on rationalism.

Debates about Weber's Approach to Oriental Societies

As mentioned above, Weber made a major contribution to the formation of sub-branches of sociology, such as knowledge, religion, politics, economics, law and art. Thus, a massive literature has been created on these subjects. But this is not the situation with Weber's research on Oriental societies. In comparison to the other subjects, his research into Oriental societies has been a rather neglected subject. The most important result of this is that the matter is treated piece by

---

25   Weber puts forth the main issue in the clearest manner in this essay. Completed just seven days before his death (June 7, 1920), this article is the introduction to the three-volume book which contains his articles on the sociology of religion. In this article, which Benjamin Nelson (1974, p. 271) sees as the *master clue* to Weber's thought, Weber puts forward the purpose and aims of his own sociology of religion as well as the crux of his general sociology. Despite this position, it cannot be said that Parsons, who is the first translator, attached enough importance to the introduction. This situation is mostly related to the process of translation. More specifically, because Parsons places this article at the beginning of *Protestant Ethic* under the title of "Author's Introduction," despite writing in the translators introduction that this piece is the introduction to the collected works of sociology of religion, for many years it was perceived as the introduction to *Protestant Ethic*. In this piece, I used Kalberg's revised translation (Weber, 2009b, pp. 205–220).

26   Parsons (1971, p. 36) explains that the comparison also has the purpose of showing how Weber interpreted the nature of the West.

piece in Weber's analyses of India, China, Islam and Judaism, and thus integrated evaluations did not emerge.

Weber's approach to non-Western societies, in particular Islamic societies, was problematized for the first time in 1950s within the scope of the literature of modernization. The comparative studies that Weber carried out on rationalization and patrimonialism had a major effect on modernization theories (Coşkun, 1989, p. 295), which entailed the reproduction of nineteenth-century Orientalism in post-war period conditions.

In this context, Maxim Rodinson (1915–2004) was the first person to critically approach Weber's analysis on Oriental societies in line with his statements on Islamic societies. Rodinson tries to demonstrate the possibility of capitalist development in Islamic societies by criticizing Weber's thesis (Rodinson, 2007). Intended to be Marxist in orientation, (Rodinson, 2007, p. 19) Rodinson's analysis tries to demonstrate that the arguments Weber puts forward about the role of Protestantism in the development of the capitalist spirit are also present in Islamic societies. In this context, Rodinson states that in the Islamic world it was not religious, but political factors that played a role in the failure of capitalism to develop. Thus, Rodinson confirms some parts of Weber's thesis while rejecting other. However effective Rodinson's research may be in demonstrating the groundlessness of Weber's assessments about Islam and Islamic values, it is equally inefficient in making clear the significance of this application in a general sociological evaluation.

Another study of Weber's approach to Islamic societies was carried out by Wolfgang Schluchter and Toby E. Huff (1999). In this work, which was essentially complied to evaluate the position of the Islamic world in the context of modernization, the article by Schluchter, a prominent expert on Weber, is remarkable (Schluchter, 1999). It deals with Weber's connection between Islam and modernization, and indicates that there are deficient points in Weber's Islamic analysis. These flaws result from the fact that the primary objective of Weber's work is to emphasize the eccentric character of developments in the West and to demonstrate its exclusiveness and unique nature over a very wide area (Schluchter, 1999, p. 123). However, despite the fact that he expresses all these flaws and clearly explains that the main objective directing Weber's work is rationalization, Schluchter cannot go beyond repeating similar claims about the superiority of the West.

Another significant article in this collection, again concerning modernization, is the piece by Samuel Noah Eisenstadt (1999). Eisenstadt states that there are many points at which Weber mistakenly defines characteristics of Islamic civilization. Like Rodinson, Eisenstadt writes that the reason for these mistakes is his main focus on the West, and, in contrast to what Weber thought, he claims that the social and religious structures of non-Western societies are not in essence in contradiction to modernization. Like the other names mentioned above, Eisenstadt criticizes Weber but evaluates the world from a Western centric perspective (Eisenstadt, 1999, p. 282).

Sabri F. Ülgener is another name that can be given for those who criticize Weber's analysis. He undertakes an examination of capitalism's takeover in the Islamic world from a Weberian stance. Referred as the "Turkish Weber" (Türkdoğan, 1985, p. 108, Sayar, 1998, pp. 251–258, 2006, pp. 37–43), in his early works Ülgener (2006a, 2006b) emphasizes the determinative mentality by examining questions of economic history. The criticisms of Ülgener (2006c) towards Weber, was influenced by the literature that developed after the 1960s in particular by Rodinson and Turner.

Ülgener, acknowledging his fellow Turkish historians' irritation with Weberian works, made his first criticism of Weber from a methodological stance. He states that Weber presented events from different times, religions and societies in the same argument, keeping some affairs in the background, while exaggerating others. Ülgener finds Weber's comparison problematic (Ülgener, 2006c, pp. 51, 58). According to Ülgener, the main reason for this is that Weber had an eclectic attitude when dealing with the Islamic world, even at the expense of neglecting his own method (Ülgener, 2006c, pp. 57–58). Thus, "When the first step is rushed and erroneous, the following ones will exceed the bounds even more" (Ülgener, 2006c, p. 71). He states that this approach brings Weber's research into question (Ülgener, 2006c, pp. 167–168), and indicates that Weber's approach, particularly to Islamic societies, is "the weakest point in his analysis," with most of the conclusions being unstable, rushed and one sided.

Ülgener states that this attitude is not unique to Weber, but has many points in common with other Western historians and analysts working on the issue of Islam and he goes on to say that the main objective of this one-sided eclecticism is presenting Islam and the beliefs of the Far East as being in contradiction to the West in order to prove the uniqueness of Western civilization. Thus, Weber established a social model of rationalism, as opposed to mystical and insular society, "In order to make the contrast apparent, whatever color one side is, the other side should be presented in the color of the greatest contrast" (Ülgener, 2006c, pp. 56–57, 64).

Ülgener (2006c, p. 61), argues that these methodological problems are the result of Weber's non-rational and stagnant depiction of Islam. He states that, "Islam is a religion that quickly manages to adapt itself to the world" and that it "presents its adherents with an extensive approach to worldly blessings" (Ülgener, 2006c, p. 67). However, according to him, Weber did not rank "the economic ethics of Islam, and, in particular, Sufism as it deserved" (Ülgener, 2006c, p. 16). In this sense, Ülgener specifically emphasizes that "As a religion that was resolved to open to the world, Islam is greatly supported by those who gird themselves with the sword for the exaltation of God's Word (*I'la-yi kelimetullah*)." However, that is not to say that Islam is entirely a "warrior religion" or that it is "blindly adhered to the social structure (in particular, the feudal structure) that is present" (Ülgener, 2006c, pp. 71–72). Rather, Islam is, first and foremost, "an urban religion" (Ülgener, 2006c, pp. 79–80).

In fact, Ülgener makes his most authentic contribution to the criticisms of Weber by expressing that there is no need to wait for religious reformation in the

West "to see that working within certain dimensions was transformed from an inconvenience into the level of worship ordered by God" (Ülgener, 2006c, p. 83). Ülgener attempts to show by means of philological comparisons that Islam does not lack a work ethic. He examines the word "profession" in reference to Weber's analysis of the word *beruf*, the equivalent in German. Accordingly, *sülûk*, a mystic *tariqat* concept that expresses the maturation of the individual in their approaching God, and the word *meslek* (profession), a word derived from *sülûk*, also carries the same meaning implicitly (Ülgener, 2006c, p. 47, fn. 27). Hence, in this sense Weber's analysis of Islamic society is not valid.

Despite all this, and although being an expert on *weltenschouung*s, Ülgener does not make an analysis about what led Weber to make these errors and one-sided analyses. Rather, he attempts to find extenuating circumstances in order to pardon Weber on these points, stating that the latter did not live long enough (Ülgener, 2006c, p. 16). But even if we do not take his previous work into consideration, it is clear that Ülgener does not refrain from using a Weberian framework, and by resuming the analysis of underdevelopment in Islamic societies from where Weber left off, he ends up contradicting his previous remarks. The fundamental problem of Ülgener in criticizing Weber from a Weberian point of view and presenting his inner-contradictions and inconsistencies is that his basic frame of analysis is flawed.

Starting in the 1960s and further developing after the 1980s, the position and importance of Weber's approach to the Orient in the remodeling of new Orientalism have been expressed. Anuar Abdel-Malek (1963) mentions that there are three basic features of this discourse in Weber's work which presents a classical example of Orientalism. First of all, there is a view that the essence of Oriental societies is different from Western societies. However, this is both an approach that is historical, as such a perspective stretches back to the beginning of history, and it is at the same time non-historical, as the object appears in a fixed, ageless manner. Secondly, the work focuses on the past by examination from cultural and particularly religious aspects. Thirdly, the sources of this work were taken from colonialist administrators, missionaries and travelogues (Abdel-Malek, 1963, pp. 104–112). Although there are some intervening criticisms, it is not possible to say that Weber gave enough space to critical treatment of Orientalism. Hence, the regularly cited critic of Orientalism, Edward Said (1935–2003), mentions that "Weber's studies of Protestantism, Judaism, and Buddhism blew him (perhaps unwittingly) into the very territory originally charted and claimed by the Orientalists" (Said, 1977, p. 259). However, it is impossible to say that Said provides an analysis about the place and or meaning of this transition in Weber. An example of such an analysis can, though, be found in James M. Blaut (1927–2000). Stating that the main purpose of Weber's sociology is to demonstrate the uniqueness of the West and that it is therefore focused to demonstrate the unique nature of modern capitalism, Blaut (1993, p. 83, 2000, p. 25) emphasizes that Weber attempts to make sociologic explanations for the common belief in the miracle of Europe.

But none of the points mentioned above are as effective as Bryan S. Turner's handling of Weber's analyses of Oriental society. Turner's work, entitled *Weber and Islam,* (1974a) has an important place in identifying the main themes and concepts present in Weber's analysis of the Orient. He demonstrates that Weber's sociology is a continuance of classical Orientalism and burdened with all the same problems. Weber carried out his analyses of Oriental society in order to find a counter-point for analyses of Western society; all his sociology has been shaped around an Orientalist East-West dilemma (Turner, 1981, pp. 257–258, 277–278). Thus, Weber's main point is to give an account of Western dynamism, Oriental stagnation and the non-existence of rationalism and capitalism anywhere but in Europe (Turner, 1974b, p. 230).

Turner's work is a milestone in studies on Weber, as it determines in detail the logical and intellectual frame of Weber's Oriental analysis. In addition to this, these works, which took shape in the context of the contemporary problematic, remain far from dealing with the effect of Weber's analysis of Oriental society on the main points of his sociology. In the prologue of his later work, *Marx and the End of Orientalism,* Turner states that in his studies on Weber he unintentionally and naturally succumbed to the basic subjects of the ideological market (Turner, 1978, p. 9). Under this influence, his studies on Weber alternate between Weber's position in sociologic analysis of Islam and Islam's position in Weber's sociological analysis, and as a result, his analysis cannot put forward crucial points which will be made in this study.

In this chapter, the development of Weber's sociology and his analysis of the Oriental societies were discussed. Although he is one of the founders of modern sociology and his analysis on Oriental societies was very central to his theory, in the sociological literature it was not studied enough. As it is shown above, the widespread discussions on Orientalism, even Said's prominent analysis do not give necessary critical place for the Weber's analysis on Orient. This is especially related to the place of Weber in the mainstream American sociology. I will try to focus on the development of Weber's analysis of Oriental societies, and his basing himself on the Orientalist sources of his age.

Chapter 8
Weber's Sources on Oriental Societies

As discussed in seventh chapter, Weber completed his intellectual development in the last quarter of the nineteenth century when Europe was increasing its dominance across the globe and Germany had newly secured national unity and was trying to increase its share in this dominance. Moreover, this period is when the theoretical framework of academic disciplines became more pronounced, and the division of labor was substantially clarified in an academic sense. On the other hand, in this period the knowledge that had existed about Oriental societies took greater hold within Western thought and Oriental research became institutionalized.

In particular, this last phenomenon was the basis for Weber's analysis of Oriental societies. From the third quarter of the nineteenth century, Orientalism made rapid progress generally, and particularly in Germany; various sub-fields quickly grew and a great corpus was produced. In addition to this, with the strengthening of the West's position in world politics, the influence of Oriental analyses increased. Thus, the areas dealt with by Weber were examined in a more comprehensive and multi-dimensional way.

Using the ethnological material provided by the developing Orientalism,[1] Weber had the opportunity to use a number of resources for his research topics. His sources are mainly positioned at the intersection of the history of religions and Orientalism. Having a good command of several European languages,[2] Weber used many important European magazines, such as *Journal of the Royal Asiatic Society*, *Journal Asiatique* and *Zeitschrift der Deuszschen Morganlandischen Gesellschaft*. There is a great bibliographic variety in his works.[3] The study of comparative

---

1 As Weber later confessed, he could not make use of this improving ethnology himself. Here it seems that the tendency in Weber's work was the principle cause of this inability (Weber, 1988, p. 68, 2009b, p. 218). As mentioned by Coşkun (2008, pp. 11–26), there are some very important differences between handling the "settled other" and the "unsettled other" in the Western analyses of the other. While Orientalism works on the settled other, ethnology works on the new other. Weber takes Mesopotamia, Egypt, India, China and Islamic societies as the settled other, and therefore, maybe, Weber did not need ethnological information.

2 Weber easily used eight languages (French, English, Middle and modern Italian, Middle and modern Spanish, Russian, Hebrew, Latin, Greek) in addition to German. This granted him access to a range of different sources, as clearly evinced in the variety present in his work.

3 Weber discusses the sources he used in the first footnote except *Economy and Society*. Although this discussion is an important guide in the search of his sources, the dense usage of sources and Weber's writing style makes it hard to determine which source

history of religions has a special place in Weber's sources. Ernst Troeltsch (1865–1923) was a close friend of Weber and was the greatest influence on him in the matter of religion.[4] In addition, Julius Wellhausen (1844–1918), a Protestant theologian who influenced his turn to comparative studies, had a significant effect on Weber's understanding of the relation between ethics and prophethood. Weber also closely followed the schema derived from the formulation of Herman Siebeck's (1842–1921) "rejecting the world" (Kippenberg, 2005, pp. 170–171).

Sources on China

At the end of the nineteenth century in Germany, there was another lively intellectual debate about China. Especially after the eighteenth century, the intellectual inheritance left by the Jesuits who started the debate was constantly developed (Honigsheim, 2000, pp. 42–44).[5] Weber composed his own work by commenting on the underdeveloped knowledge of China's economic life, believing that the originality of his work would be found in these comments (see Table 8.1).[6]

Weber was able to attain a great variety of scientific works, including books and PhD dissertations about the religious, social, political and economic history of China. He used articles from magazines such as *Journal of the North China Branch of Royal Asiatic Society, Journal Asiatique, Mitteilungen des Seminars für Orientalische Sprachen, China Review, Journal of Peking Oriental Society, Revue e l'Histoire des Religions* and the *Journal of the Peking Royal Society.* Not having knowledge of the language like the experts, and having to use translation of the classical texts, Weber felt that he was at a disadvantage in using sources. In fact, many classical Chinese sources had been translated into Western languages at that time and Weber had the opportunity to attain them (Yang, 1968, pp. xxxviii–xxxix). He used a number of books on Chinese classics, some of which were part of *the Sacred Books of the East* series prepared under the editorship of Max Müller (1823–1900). Others were the works that had an explanatory and critical introduction by James Legge (1815–1897) in the series

---

he used and how. Unless otherwise stated, discussions about Weber's sources are shaped around his attributions.

4   Weber even had a mind to do some work following *Protestant Ethic* but he gave up on the idea after Troeltsch's *The School Teachings of the Christian Church* (Weber, 2009a, p. 551 fn. 143).

5   As Jones (2001) reports unlike nineteenth-century Jesuits, the German Protestant missionaries lead Weber's interest to China at the end of nineteenth century. Legge, Soothill and Groot, are more skeptical and judgmental about *Chinese Ethic*. About the history of development of Sinology at the end of nineteenth century, see Jones, 2001, pp. 99–119.

6   Yang (1968, p. xlii) states that although there are some deficiencies in Weber's writings on China, he was able to successfully handle the Chinese religious structure and its relation with the socio-economical system. For an analysis of Weber's usage of developing Sinology and his contributions to this literature, see Jones, 2001, pp. 119–122.

of *Chinese Classics*, and the collection prepared by von Wilhelm.[7] In addition
to these are Lu's *Spring and Autumn Annals*. Weber also used the translations in
the *Sacred Books of the East* series and Faber's *Mind of Mencius* for Mencius's
texts. Aware that there were many translations of the Taoist classic *Tao Teh Ching
(Book of Wisdom, Path of Virtue)*, Weber used the 1870 German translation by
Victor von Strauss (1809–99) and the 1913 English translation by Daisetsu Teitaro
Suzuki (1870–1966) and Paul Carus (1852–1919). He also mentions a beautiful
selection of Chinese mysticism and philosophy by Wilhelm. The work entitled
Yu Tsiuan Tung Kin Kang Mu (1865) which relates the history of Ming Dynasty
in a translation by Dellamare was also utilized. These works are the basis for
Weber's comments on Chinese religion and values. He used the collection of
ancient Imperial edicts, translated to English under the title of *Peking Gazette*
and Édouard Constant Biot's (1803–1850) *Bamboo-Annals* translations in *Journal
Asiatique* as a primary source. These official documents also shaped his basic
views about the political history and management of China.

Weber essentially bases his knowledge of Chinese religion, on Jan Jakob
Maria de Groot (1854–1921) a scholar on history of religions. At the end of
nineteenth century, after Schlegel Groot, one of the leading Sinologists of the
time, he thought, like many of his contemporaries, that a spiritual essence could
be found behind the various religious, philosophical and political expressions
from China. Formulating the Chinese religion along certain basics, Weber adopted
these views from Groot, in particular, the belief that Confucianism was the official
Chinese religion, ancestor cult, and astral belief. The ritualistic position of the
ruler, the religious position of the elders and tolerance in Chinese religion were
also taken from Groot. Weber used his works *Religion of the Chinese* (1910), *The
Religious System of China*, 6 volumes (1892–1910), *Sectarianism and Religious
Persecution in China: A Page in the History of Religions*, 2 volumes (1903–1904),
*Universismus, die Grundlage der Religion und Ethik, des Staatswesens und der
Wissenschaften Chinas* (1918) extensively, referring to them a total of 37 times.

Another person Weber consulted on Chinese religion was the French Sinologist,
Édouard Chavannes (1865–1918). Weber particularly turns to him in connection
with original texts. His translation of chapters of *Sima Qian*'s famous *Shiji* (*Les
Mémoires historiques de Se-ma Ts'ien*, 5 vol., 1895–1905) were frequently used
by Weber. In addition, the historical texts about the Turks of the Tang dynasty
ruler, *Documents sur les Tou-kiue (Turcs) occidentaux* (1900) and his work
about Chinese religion, *Le T'ai chan: essai de monographie d'un culte chinois:
appendice Le dieu du sol dans la Chine antique* (1910), were among the main texts
that he used. There are 39 references to Chavannes in Weber's work.

---

7   These works are *The Life and The Teachings of Confucius* (London, 1887),
Selections from Confucius (the views or attributed views of Confucius *Lun Yü*), *Ta Hsüeh
(The Great Learning)* and *Chung Yung (The Doctrine of the Mean)*.

Table 8.1   Weber's sources on China

Subject		Source
Main sources on Chinese Religion	Jan Jakob Maria de Groot	*Religion of the Chinese*, New York, 1910 *The Religious System of China*, 6 vol., Brill 1892–1910 *Sectarianism and Religious Persecution in China: A Page in the History of Religions* 2 Vol., Amsterdam 1903–1904 *Universismus, die Grundlage der Religion und Ethik, des Staatswesens und der Wissenschaften Chinas*, Berlin, 1918
	Édouard Chavannes	*Les Mémoires historiques de Se-ma Ts'ien* (5 vol.), Paris, Leroux, 1895–1905 *Documents sur les Tou-kiue (Turcs) occidentaux*, Paris, Librairie d'Amérique et d'Orient, 1900 *Le T'ai chan: essai de monographie d'un culte chinois*, Paris, E. Leroux, 1910
	Otto Franke	*Ostasiatische Neubildungen*, Hamburg: C. Boysen, 1911 *Die Rechtsverhältnisse am Grundeigentum in China*, Leipzig: Dieterich 1903 *Die Verfassung und Verwaltung Chinas*, Leipzig; Berlin, Teubner, 1911 (Die Kultur der Gegenwart, 2,2,1)
Confucianism and Taoism	Rudolf Dvořák	*Chinas Religionen 1: Conficius und seine Lehre*, Münster, Aschendorff, 1895 *Chinas Religionen 2: Lao-tsï und seine Lehre*, Münster, Aschendorff, 1903
Taoism	Wilhelm Grube	*Religion und Kultur der Chinesen*, Leipzig, R. Haupt, 1910 *Die Religion der alten Chinesen*, Tübingen, J.C.B. Mohr, 1911 [1908]
Totemism	Martin Wilhelm Chriestlieb Quistrop	*Maennergesellschaft und Alterklassen im alten China*, Mitteilungen des Seminars für Orientalische Sprachen, vol. XVIII, 1915
Development and characteristics of Chinese literati	P. Albert Tschepe	*Histoire du Royaume de Ou 1122–473*, Chang-Hai, *Librairie de la Mission catholique*, 1896 *Histories du Royaume de Tsin 777–207*, Chang-Hai, T'ou-Sè-Wè, 1909 *Histoire du Royaume de Han 423–225*, Chang-Hai, T'ou-Sè-Wè, 1910
Irrigation	Johann Heinrich Plath	*China vor 4,000 Jahren: Nach chinesischen Quellen bearbeitet*, Munich, F. Straub, 1869.
Service fiefs	Édouard Chavannes	"Les deux plus ancien spécimens de la cartographie chinoise," Bulletin de l'Ecole Française d'Extrême-Orient, Tome III/2, Avril-Juin 1903
Corvée organization by officers	Ernest Alabaster	*Notes and Commentaries on Chinese Criminal Law Cognate Topics*, London, Luzac & Co, 1899
Operation of corvee system	Ariel Stein / Édouard Chavannes	*Les Documents Chinois découverts par Aurel Stein dans le sables du Turkestan Oriental*, Oxford, Impr. de l'Université, 1913
Tax-in-kind	Edouard Biot	"Mémoire sur la condition de la propriété territoriale en Chine depuis les temps anciens", Journal Asiatique, 3rd serie, vol.6, 1838, pp. 255–335.
Land system based on fief as a part of financial system	N. J. Kochanovskuj	"Semljevladjenie i Semljedjelji w Kitaje," Isvjestija Vostotschnavo Instituta d.g. isd., 1907/8, vol. XXIII, 2,Vladivostok, 1909
	A. J. Iwanoff	*Wang-An-Schi I jevo reformy*, St. Petersburg, 1906

Subject		Source
Land ownership of sibs	Bumbailiff	"Land Tenure in China" The China Review, or notes & queries on the Far East, Vol. 9 No. 1, 1880, p. 58
	Wen Hsian Liu	*Die Vorteile des laendlichen Grund Bodens und seine Bewirtschaftung in China*, Berlin, 1920
Chinese city	Johann Heinrich Plath	*Über die Verfassung und Vewwaltung Chinas unter den drei ersten Dynastien," Abhandlungen der Koeniglichen Bayrichen Akademie der Wissenschaften*, 1865, I. Cl. X Abt. 2p. 453vs.
	Eugène Simon	*La Cité Chinoise*, Paris, Nouvelle revue, 1885.
Chinese guild	Hosea Ballou Morse	*The Gilds of China: With an Account of the Gild Merchant or Co-hong of Canton*, London: Longmans, Greens, and Co, 1909
	MacGawen	"Chinese Guilds," *Journal of the North China Branch of Royal Asiatic Society*, 1888/9
	William C. Hunter	*The "Fan kwae" at Canton Before Treaty Days 1821–44*, London, Keagen Paul Trench & Co., 1882
Economic life in a modern Chinese city	Nyok Ching Tsur	"Die gewerblichen Betreibsformen der Stadt Ningpo," *Zeitschrift fuer die Gesamte Staatswissenschaft*, Supplement 30, Tubingen, 1909
Chinese village	Arthur Henderson Smith	*Village Life in China*, Edinburg, Fleming H. Rewell Company, 1899
	Yü-kao Liang and Li Kung T'ao	*Village and Town Life in China*, London, George Allen & Unwin Ltd., 1915
Elder rule in sibs	A.J. Iwanoff	Wang-An-Shi i jevo reformy, St. Petersburg,1906
Social life in modern China	Ferdinand von Richthofen	Tagebücher aus China, Berlin, Dietrich Reimer (Ernst Vohsen),1907.
	Arthur von Rosthorn	Das soziale Leben der Chinesen, Leipzig, Der Neu Geist Verlag, 1919
	Robert Kennaway Douglas	*Society in China*, London, A.D. Innes & Co., 1895
	David J. Singer	*Über soziale Verhaltnisse in Ostasien*, Leipzig/Wien, Deuticke 1908
	Joseph Edkins	*Religion in China*, London, Trübner & Co, 1884
Money system	Hosea Ballou Morse	*The Trade and Administration of the Chinese Empire*, New York, Longman, Green, and Co., 1908
	Hosea Ballou Morse, Francis Lister Hawks Pott, A. Théophile Piry	*Trade and Administration of the Chinese Empire*, London, Longmans, Green and Co., 1908
	Joseph Edkins	*Banking and Prices in China*, Shanghai, Presbyterian Mission Press, 1905 *Chinese Currency*, Shanghai, Presbyterian Mission Press, 1890
	W.P. Wei	"The Currency Problem in China," *Studies in History, Economics*, etc. No. 59, 1914
	Edward Harper Parker	*China, Her History, Diplomacy and Commerce: From the Earliest Times to the Present Day*, London, John Murray, 1901
General history of China	August Conrady	"China," *Weltgeschichte*, edited by Julius von Pffugk-Harttung, vol. III, Berlin, 1911, pp. 459–567
	Edward Harper Parker	*Ancient China Simplified*, London, Chapman & Hall Co., 1908
	Friedrich Hirth	*The Ancient History of China to the End of the Chóu Dynasty*, New York, Columbia University Press, 1908

Otto Franke's (1863–1946) *Ostasiatische Neubildungen* (Hamburg: C. Boysen 1911), *Die Rechtsverhältnisse am Grundeigentum in China* (Leipzig: Dieterich 1903) and *Die Verfassung und Verwaltung Chinas*, (in *Allgemeine Verfassungs- und Verwaltungsgeschichte* l, Berlin, Leipzig: B.G. Teubner 1911) are important sources for Weber on the birth, development and official state patronage Confucianism, as well as the systematic functioning of the Chinese government.[8] Although Franke, an important name in German Sinology, produced his works for the most part after 1920s, Weber was aware of his stance, used him extensively.

The studies on the development and characteristics of the Chinese literati by Père Albert Tschepe (1844–1912) have importance as a theoretical basis of Weber's studies on Chinese social and political structure. He takes his basic ideas directly from a number of works by Tschepe, such as *Histoire du Royaume de Ou* (1891), *Histories du Royaume de Tsin, 777-207* (1909) and *Histoire du Royaume de Han* (1910), published in the *Variétés Sinologiques* series. There are 37 references to him in Weber's work.

In addition to these four basic sources, Weber bases his main ideas concerning a variety of important matters on Chinese religion on work from several different names. On religion and the ethics of Confucianism and Taoism Weber uses the Czech Sinologist, Rudolf Dvořák's (1860–1920) two analyses (*Chinas Religionen: Lao-tsï und seine Lehre*, 1903 and *Chinas Religionen: Conficius und seine Lehre*, 1895) and ideas about Taoism from the French Sinologist, Paul Pelliot (1878–1945). In addition, he turns to the expert on *Tungusic* and *Nivkh* languages, Wilhelm Grube's (1855–1908) *Religion und Kultur der Chinesen*, Leipzig (1910), and *Die Religion der alten Chinesen* (1911) for ideas about Taoism. Weber uses the doctoral thesis of August Conrady's (1864–1925) student, Martin Quistrop, *Maennergesellschaft und Alterklassen im alten China* (1915) for Totemism in China. He states that totemism vanished after the twelfth century based on Franke's articles in a variety of volumes from the journal *Mitteilungen des Seminars für Orientalische Sprachen.*

The source for irrigation and service fief that form the basis of Weber's patrimonial state analysis is the work entitled *China vor 4,000 Jahren: Nach chinesischen Quellen bearbeitet* (1869) by the elder generation Sinologist, Johann Heinrich Plath (1802–74). In addition, Weber used Plath as a source for the city and village. Weber took the functioning of the corvée system from *Les Documents Chinois découverts par Aurel Stein dans le sable du Turkestan Oriental* (Oxford, 1913), which Ariel Stein collated in Turkestan and which was published by Chavannes.

---

8 This unfinished master piece is published in three volumes under the title of *Geschichte des Chineschichen Reiches, Eine Darstellung seiner Entstentung, seines Wesen und seiner Entwicklung bis zur Neuesten Zeit.* The first two volumes include the birth of the Celestial Empire and establishment of Confucian government. The third volume includes additions and readjustments of these two volumes (Weber, 1968, p. 250).

Sources on India

India, like China, was a country in which European Orientalists showed great interest. During Weber's time, in Germany as in other European countries the spiritual and socio-economic life in India formed an important research topic. In particular, Herder, Hegel, Schelling, Schlegel and Schopenhauer were pioneers in research on India through the nineteenth century. There were many Indian experts among Weber's contemporaries. German Lutheran missionaries, who acted as primary sources to Orientalists, played a major role in reading the Sanskrit, Prakrit and Pali languages and in the transmission of religious texts of religions like Brahmanism, Jainism and Buddhism. As a result, although not familiar with the languages of the subcontinent, Weber could carry out research based on a number of translations of religious texts and on contemporary discussions (see Table 8.2).

Weber's work on India includes more intense usage of primary sources as compared to that on China. One of the reasons for this is that the written tradition had been developed in India and there were a variety of religious texts which had already been translated and widely used. Weber used texts such as *The Upanishad, The Dharma Sutra, The Sacred Laws of the Aryas, The Bhagavadgita, Buddhist Suttas, Vinaya Texts, The Laws of Manu, The Grihya-sutras, Vedic Hymns, The Vedanta-Sutras, The Questions of King Milinda, Hymns of the Atharva-Veda, The Satapatha-Brahmana, Gaina Sûtras, Buddhist Mahâyâna Texts* and *The Minor Law-Books: Brihaspati* from *The Sacred Books of the East* series, and for the *Mahabharata,* he used S.J. Dahlmann's translation (*Das Mahabharata als Epos und Rechtsbuch*). In addition, Weber makes reference to important journals of the time, such as *Journal of the Royal Asiatic Society, Journal Asiatique, Zeitschrift der Deutschen Morgenländischen Gesellschaft, Journal of the Asiatic Society of Bengal* and *Journal of the American Oriental Society.* To a large extent he used inscriptions that included information concerned with historical periods. Most of these had been published (45 quarter volumes) in a major archaeological magazine, *Indian Antiquary,* with the original versions and comments. It was also published in part in *Epigraphia Indica.* Both of these journals included monographs by Hultzsch, Fleet and, more particularly, Bühler.

Other works that Weber relied on extensively were British Census Reports and some of the special studies written on these reports.[9] In addition to, he used works that included pure statistical information published in Calcutta. Using these two sources, Weber particularly discusses the population structure, distribution of religions and the caste system in India.

In addition to these sources, from 1881 on, Weber used *The Imperial Gazeteer of India* (1908–1909). According to him, this was similar to an Indian encyclopedia, organized in alphabetical order by Sir William Wilson Hunter (1840–1900). This "encyclopedia," which was published as a new edition of four volumes after 1908 with an introduction providing information about the natural, historical and

---

9   The first census covering all of India started in 1901 and was completed in 1911.

Table 8.2   Weber's sources on India

Subject	Source	
General sources on India	William Wilson Hunter (Ed.)	*The Imperial Gazeteer of India*, Oxford, Clarendon Press, 1908–1909.
Indian religion and social system	Hermann Oldenberg	*Buddha: Sein Leben, seine Lehre, seine Gemeinde*, Berlin, W. Hertz, 1881. *Die Religion des Veda*, Berlin, Verlag von Wilhelm Hertz, 1894. *Aus Indien und Iran: Gesammelte Aufsätze*, Berlin, Verlag von Wilhelm Hertz,1899. *Aus dem alten Indien: Drei Aufsätze über den Buddhismus, altindische Dichtung und Geschichtschreibung*, Berlin, Gebrüder Paetel, 1910. *Die Lehre der Upanishaden und die Anfange des Buddhismus*, Gottingen: Vandenhoeck & Ruprecht, 1915.
	Albrecht Weber	*Indische Studien X*, Leipzig, F.A. Brockhaus, 1868.
	Horace Hayman Wilson	*Religious Sects of the Hindus*, London, Trübner, 1861.
	Edward Washburn Hopkins	*India Old and New: With a Memorial Address*, New York, Charles Scribner's Sons, 1901. *Religions of India* (Handbooks on the History of Religions, Vol.1, edited by Morris Jastrow), Boston and London, Edward Arnold, 1896. "The social and military position of the ruling castes in ancient India" Journal of the American Orientalist Society, XIII, p.57vd.
Development of patrimonialism and bureaucracy	Horace A. Rose	"The Khokhars And The Gakkhars In Pan Iab History" Indian Antiquary, Vol. XXXVI, Bombay, Bombay Education Press, September 1907. "Hinduism in Himalayas," Epiqraphia Indica, Part CDLIX Vol. XXXVI, Bombay, Bombay Education Press, September 1907, pp. 253–264. 'A Report on the Penjab Hill TribesHinduism in Himalayas', Epiqraphia Indica, Part CDLIX Vol XXXVI, Bombay, Bombay Education Press, September 1907, pp. 264–284.
	Vincent A. Smith	*Asoka: The Buddhist Emperor of India*, Oxford, Clarendon Press, 1901.
	Raymond West & Georg Bühler	*A Digest of the Hindu Law of Inheritance and Partition*, Bombay, Education Societies Press, 1867–69.
Roots and operation of caste system	Emile Senart	*Les Castes dans L'Inde: les faits et le système*, Paris, Ernest Leroux, 1896.
	Celéstin Bouglé	*Essai sur le Regime des Castes*, Paris, F. Alcan, 1908.
	John Collinson Nesfield	*Brief View of the Caste System of the Western Provinces and Oudh*, Allahabad, North-Western Provinces and Oudh Government Press, 1885.
	Jervoise Athelstane Baines	"Ethnography: Castes and Tribes," in Georg Bühler, *Grundriss der Indo-arischen Philologie und Altertumskunde* (II. Band 5. Heft) Strassburg, K. J. Trübner, 1912.
	Baden Henry Baden-Powell	*The Land Systems of India*, 3 vols, Oxford, Clarendon Press, 1892.

Subject	Source	
Social history of India	Richard Fick	Die soziale Gliederung im nordöstlichen Indien zu Buddhas Zeit. Mit besonderer Berücksichtigung der Kastenfrage. Vornehmlich auf Grund der Jātakas dargestellt, Kiel, C.F. Haeseler 1897.
History of India	Vincent A. Smith	*Early History of India from 600 B.C. to the Mohammedan Conquest*, Oxford, Clarendon Press, 1904.
	James Grant Duff	*History of the Mahrattas*, Calcutta, Cambray, London, 1911.
Contemporary military history	Paul Horn	*Das Heer-und Kriegswesen der Gross Moghuls*, Leiden, E. J. Brill, 1894.
Social structure of India	Richard Pischel and Karl Friedrich Geldner	*Vedische Studien*, Stuttgart, Verlag von W. Kohlhammer, 1889.
Indian law	Julius Jolly	"Recht und Sitte," in Georg Bühler, *Grundriss der Indo-arischen Philologie und Altertumskunde* (II. Band 8. Heft) Strassburg, K.J. Trübner, 1896.
	Raymond West & Georg Bühler	*A Digest of the Hindu Law of Inheritance and Partition*, Bombay, Education Societies Press, 1867–69.
Law system of great Mongol states	V. Kanakasabhai	*The Tamils 1800 Years Ago*, Madras, Higginbotham & Co, 1904.
Historical knowledge on Indian religion	Auguste Barth	*Les Religions de L'Inde*, Paris, Librairie Sandoz et fischbacher, 1897
	Monier Williams	*Religious Thought and Life in India*, Part I, New York, Macmillian and Co., 1891.
Rise of Brahmans	Maurice Bloomfield	"The Atharva Veda," in Georg Bühler, *Grundriss der Indo-arischen Philologie und Altertumskunde* (II. Band 5. Heft) Strassburg, K.J. Trübner, 1899.
Phenomenon of guests peoples	Shridar V. Ketkar	*An Essay in Hinduism: Its Formation and Future*, London, Luzac and Co., 1911.
Indian village	Baden Henry Baden-Powell	*The Land Systems of British India*, 3 vols, Oxford: Clarendon Press, 1892. *Indian Village Community*, London, Longmans, Geeen and Co., 1896.
	James Grant Duff	*History of the Mahrattas*, Calcutta, Cambray, London, 1911.
Guilds	Ananda K. Coomaraswamy	*The Indian Craftsman* (Prosthain Series), London, Probsthain & Co., 1909.
Public duties of artisans	Ananda K. Coomaraswamy	*The Indian Craftsman* (Prosthain Series), London, Probsthain & Co., 1909.
Land of Indian monasteries and its management	John Campbell Oman	*The Mystics, Ascetics and Saints of India*, London, T. Fisher, Unwin, 1903.
Indian science	Brajendra Nath Seal	Mechanical, Physical and Chemical theories of the Ancient Hindus, Calcutta, 1910.
	Thakore Sahib of Gondal	*History of Aryan Medical Science*, London, Macmillan and Co., 1896.
	August F. Hoernle	*Studies in the Medicine of Ancient India*, Oxford, Clarendon Press, 1907.
	Bruno Liebich	*Panini: ein beitrag zur kenntnis der indischen literatur und grammatik*, Leipzig, H. Haessel, 1891.

Subject	Source	
Indian science (cont/d)	Georg Bühler	"Presentation", in Georg Bühler (ed.), *Grundriss der Indo-arischen Philologie und Altertumskunde* (I. Band 1. Heft, A.), Strassburg, K.J. Trübner, 1899
	Narendra Nath Law	*Studies in Ancient Hindu Polity*, (Based on the Arthashastra of Kautilya), London, Longmans, Green and Co., 1914.
Indian philosophy	Paul Deussen	*Allgemeine Geschichte der Philosophie: mit besonderer berücksichtigung der religionen* (Erster Band, Zweite Abteilung: Die Philosophie der Upanishad's) Leipzig, F.A. Brockhaus: 1899.
	Richard Garbe	*Die Samkhya-Philosophie: eine Darstellung der indischen Rationalismus nach den Quellen*, Leipzig : H. Haessel, 1917.
	Archibald Edward Gough	*The Philosophy of the Upanishads and Ancient Indian Metaphysics*, Edinburgh, London, Ballantyn Press, 1882.
'Secret teachings' of Brahmanic wisdom	Ramkrishna G. Bhandakar	"Vaisnavism, Saivism and Minor Religious Systems" in Georg Bühler, *Grundriss der Indo-arischen Philologie und Altertumskunde* (III. Band 6. Heft) Strassburg, K.J. Trübner, 1913.
Jaynism	Sinclair Stevenson	*The Heart of Jainism*, London, New York, Oxford University Press, 1915.
	Armand Albert Guerinot	*Epigraphic Jaina*, Paris, Publications de l' Ecole francais de l'Extreme Orient, 1908.
	Edward Balfour	"Jain," Encyclopedia of India and of Eastern and Southern Asia II, Madras, 1857.
	President Hörnle	"Address 1898," Royal Asiatic Society of Bengal, 1898.
	John Campbell Oman	*The Mystics, Ascetics and Saints of India*, London, T. Fisher Unwin, 1903.
Buddhism	Caroline Rhys Davids	'Notes on the early economic conditions in N. India'. J.R.A.S. 1901, pp. 859*f.*
	Hermann Oldenberg	*Buddha: Sein Leben, seine Lehre, seine Gemeinde*, Berlin, W. Hertz, 1881.
	Alfred Roussel	*Le Bouddhisme primitive*, Paris, Téqui, 1911.
	Louis Étienne Joseph Marie de La Vallée Poussin	*Bouddhisme: Opinions sur l'histoire de la dogmatique*, Paris, G. Beauchesne,1909.
	Heinrich Friedrich Hackmann	*Der Buddhismus*, Tubingen, Gebauer Scbweifcbke Druckerei und Verlag, 1906.
	Emile Senart	*Origines Bouddhiques*, Paris, E. Leroux, 1907.
	Ananda Maitreya	*The Four Noble Truths*, Rangoon, Publication of the Buddhasana Samayana, 1903.
	Vincent A. Smith	*Asoka: The Buddhist emperor of India*, Oxford, Clarendon Press, 1901.
	Léon de Milloué	'Annals du Musée Guimet,' Bibl. de Vulgarisation, Conference v. 18, XII, 1904.
Re-dominance of Hinduism in India	Rudolph Otto Franke	*Pali und Sanskrit*, Straszburg, Karl J. Trübner, 1902.
General literature on India	Moritz Wintemitz	*Geschichte der Indischen Literatur*, Leipzig, B.G. Teubner, 1908.

cultural situation in India, consists of 20 volumes with a geographical dictionary of place names, statistical data and summarized information.

This variety of references attributed to primary sources demonstrates that Weber thoroughly scanned the literature which existed in the West and utilized them in his work. In addition to these, Weber's work was benefited from the writings of the famous German Indologist, Hermann Oldenberg (1854–1920), an important name in Hindologue studies. Oldenberg, whose philological work created a basis for analyses on Indian religion, affected Weber's view in many important areas, such as mystical character, theological dimensions, and the social effects of Hindu religion. Oldenberg's ideas about the position of mysticism and sacrifice in religion are taken by Weber to be the basic cosmologic elements of Hinduism. Moreover, for the appearance of Jainism and Buddhism as religions that renounce the world, Weber relies on Oldenberg again. All in all, he gives reference to Oldenberg's *Buddha* (1881), *Aus Indien und Iran* (1899), *Die Religion des Veda* (1894), *Aus dem alten Indien* (1910), *Die Lehre der Upanishaden und die Anfange des Buddhismus* (1915) a total of 13 times in his work.

Another important source for Weber on India was the American Sanskrit expert, Edward Washburn Hopkins (1857–1932). Completing his doctorate in the important Sinology center of Leipzig in 1881, and occupying an important place in the development of Sinology in the USA, Hopkins provided evidential support to Weber, particularly in reference to the structure of Indian cities as the location for priests and noblemen, Indian guilds, Indian religious sects, the rise of Jainism, the nature of sacred Hindu wars and the structure of the priesthood. Weber consults Hopkins's *The Religions of India* (1895) and *India Old and New* (1901)13 times in his work.

Sources on Islam

The fact that Weber did not produce a distinct work on Islam makes it hard to trace his sources in this area. The final edition of *Economy and Society,* where analyses of Islam are numerous, was not compiled by Weber, with the result being that unlike his other works there is not a great deal of citations (except on matters dealing with the Sociology of Law). The late development of Islamic studies in German Orientalism also contributed to the weakness in Weber's usage of sources (see Table 8.3). However, according to researchers such as Turner, Schluchter and Kippenberg, by questioning Weber's analyses of Islamic societies and working from his partial references and general ideas, it is possible to determine the general sources (Kippenberg, 2005, p. 170; Schluchter, 1999, p. 59; Turner, 1981, pp. 269–270).

Islamists such as Alfred von Kramer (1828–89), Theodor Nöldeke (1836–1930), Ignaz Goldziher (1850–1921), Carl Heinrich Becker (1876–1933), Joseph Kohler (1849–1919) and Christian Snouck Hurgronje (1857–1936); historians such as Leopold von Ranke (1795–1886) and Jacob Burckhardt (1818–97); and religious historians such as Wellhausen, all helped to shape Weber's basic view about Islam. Thus, in general, his sources portray the standard Orientalist view of Islam, according to which, Islam shares an inheritance with Judaism, but developed with its own rules and institutions. The general understanding was that as Prophet Muhammad could not impose his prophethood on the Jews, he established his own religion. Here, psychological analyses of Prophet Muhammad's personality and speculations about his private life are both significant. In these analyses, Islam is characterized as a martial religion. Right after its birth, it transformed into a religion of warriors and the pursuit of territory that destroyed the spiritual piety it fostered. Therefore, Islam, with its all social and political structure, reflects the patrimonial political structure of ancient Mesopotamia. Although the military success initially helped the rapid extension of Islam, in the long run it created a break in its social structure and prevented the necessary development from occurring.

It is only possible to determine Weber's sources for Islamic societies by analyzing his ideas. Kippenberg presents Ignaz Goldziher (1850–1921) as Weber's main authority on the history of Islam (Kippenberg, 2005, p. 170). Although it is not possible to find direct evidence in the texts, Weber's assessments about Islamic societies run parallel to those in *Muhammedanische Studien* (2 Volumes) (1889–90) and *Vorlesungen über den Islam* (1910) by Goldziher, contained in the Hinneberg series. When the intensive usage of other texts from this series is taken into consideration, it is possible to state with some confidence that Weber makes use of Goldziher. At the same time, the parallel between Goldziher's and Wellhausen's explanations about the characteristics of Islam supports this thesis. According to them, establishing its own character by competing with Judaism and Christianity, Islam adopted Christian ascetic ideals at the beginning, but later on turned to a religion of conquest and the Christian ideals became defunct.[10] In general, Weber makes similar statements to these. His thesis about Islam's makeup, that is, imitating Judaism and Christianity, coincides with Goldziher's evaluation of Islam's faith in God, fasting and *Qibla* (direction of prayer) practices.

Similarly, the Dutch Orientalist Hurgronje's work mentioned in Weber's sources includes the portrayal. Hurgronje argues that as a political religion, Islam's universal importance is based on the combination of religion and politics, which are theoretically incompatible (Djait, 1985, p. 121). Weber also takes up the characteristics of Islamic cities, from Hurgronje in particular. In order to demonstrate that Islamic cities have been unable to shake off tribal restrictions and give rise to a bourgeoisie community, Weber consults the work of Hurgronje entitled *Mekka, vol 1: Die Stadt und ihre Herren* (1888).

---

10 For an analysis of Goldziher's studies on Islam, see Görgün, 1996, pp. 105–111.

Table 8.3   Weber's sources on Islam

Subject	Source	
Social, political and religious structure of Islamic Societies	Ignaz Goldziher	*Vorlesungen Über den Islam*, Heidelberg, Carl Winter's Universitatsbuchhandlung, 1910 *Muhammedanische Studien*, 1,2 Halle, Niemeyer, 1889–1890
	Julius Wellhausen	*Reste arabischen Heidentums, gesammelt und erliiutert*, 2nd ed., Berlin, De Gruyter, 1897 *Das arabische Reich und sein Sturz*, Berlin, Reimer, 1902
	Carl Heinrich Becker	*Beitrage zur Geschichte Agyptens unter dem Islam*, 2 vols, Strassburg, Trübner, 1902–1903
	Theodor Nöldeke	*Aufsatze zur persischen Geschichte*, Leipzig, Weigel, 1887
	Henri Lammens	*Le berceau de l'Islam*, Roma, Sumptibus Pontificii Instituti Biblici, 1914
Islamic law	Joseph Kohler	"Zum Islamrecht," *Zeitschrift für vergleichende Rechtswissenschaft* 17 (1905), 194–216;
	Richard Schmidt	---
Islamic cities	Christian Snouck Hurgronje	Mekka, vol. I, Die Stadt und ihre Herren, The Hague, Nijhoff, 1888.

Another author that is directly mentioned and used by Weber is one of the key writers of the important *Encyclopedia of Islam*, that is, the Prussian minister of education, Becker. Being an important figure in German Orientalism, Weber directly refers to his articles from the journal *Der Islam* (1913) and to his work entitled *Beitrage zur Geschiche Agyptens unter dem Islam* (1902). His assessments of the social, political and economic structure of Islamic societies are substantially similar to Becker's. While describing the feudal system in the Near East, Weber (1978, pp. 261, 380) consults Becker, who he describes as the first person to have understood the difference between the Near East feudal system and the European system. Moreover, Weber uses him as a source in the matter of the stagnant economic structure which is affiliated with the political system in Islamic societies. In particular, Weber depends on him for the thesis that, as the political structure does not guarantee ownership and as accumulative property in Islamic *waqfs* are illiquid, there is no capital to help realize a capitalistic transformation and thus, the *waqfs* have an important role in the economic backwardness of the Orient (Weber, 1978, pp. 1096–1097).

Another person Weber used as a source is his friend from Freiburg University, Richard Schmidt (1862–1944). Weber takes the term "*qadi* justice," a kind of "irrational" judgment from Schmidt's 1908 work on law (Crone, 1999, p. 266, fn. 14). Weber uses this term to characterize the legal system in Oriental societies in general, and Islamic societies in particular (Weber, 1978, p. 819).

As mentioned above, Weber was aware of and used Wellhausen's research extensively. In addition, Turner states that there are valid reasons for considering that Weber knew about Theodor Nöldeke's (1836–1930) *Aufsatze zur persischen Geschichte* (1887) and Henri Lammens's (1862–1937) *Le berceau de l'Islam* (1914) (Turner, 1981, pp. 269–270).

The research of Orientalism, which was used by sociologists to explain the social form of Europe and turned the Orient into an explanatory tool, started to become institutionalized at the beginning of the nineteenth century. Due to the consequent widening and deepening of the discipline by the time of Weber's writing, although not an expert on the Orient lacking command of the original languages, he notes that he was able to carry out sociological analyses on Oriental societies using this knowledge and the translations. Carrying out his research without realizing the problems inherent in Orientalist analyses, Weber could not avoid repeating their mistakes and generalizing from their narrow findings. He transformed the knowledge in his sources into a sociological explanation and established general explanatory models. By going a step ahead of his sources Weber used this knowledge to analyze Europe's identity. In the end he created an Orientalist sociology. It is this subject matter that I will discuss in the next chapter.

Chapter 9

Same Old Differences: Differentiating Between the Orient and the Occident

In its most general form, Weber uses the Orient as the opposite of the West, that is, to mean non-Western. In a number of places, he (1967a, pp. 331–332, 1978, p. 553) uses terms such as Asiatic and Oriental interchangeably when making generalizations regarding Oriental societies. Weber generally uses Asia to refer to India, China, and the Far East, excluding the Near East—or the Middle East—and Egypt. However this is not his only usage. From time to time, Weber also uses the term Asia as a means of generalization. Similarly, Weber generally uses the terms Mesopotamia, Near East, Middle East and West Asia interchangeably (Weber, 2003, p. 321), while he refrains from approaching Africa (excluding Egypt) and Oceanic islands including Polynesia within the Orient (Weber, 1978, p. 1092). In sum, Weber uses the term Orient to refer to an expansive geography that begins from Egypt, extends to China and Japan and which includes Russia.

Weber's Orient–Occident definition represents two poles that have been separated from one another. Thus, Weber tries to show that while the West has entered a route to development, the Orient occupies a dormant state. In Western societies there is dynamism rotating on the axis of rationalism, while in Oriental societies there is passive inertia, fixed on the axis of patrimonialism. Here, two bases, that of Ancient Greece and Hebrew societies, are important points of distinction in this eternal differentiation of the Orient and Occident for Weber.

"Only in the West": The Rationalism and Unique Nature of the Occident

In Weber's works, while dealing with a number of issues, Weber uses the phrase "only in the West" many times and mentions that the rational and rationalism are unique to the West.[1] According to Weber, professional management, expert officials,

---

1 Rationalism is commonly held to be Weber's main theme in presenting the importance of the modern West in world history. Karl Löwith, (1993) who made an important analysis of Weber at the beginning of 1930s, had an important role in giving rise to this view. Although at the end of the 1930s, Talcott Parsons (1968[1937]) argued that the term "social action" was central in Weber, rationalism was placed into the center once again by developing studies on Weber in the 1960s under the leadership of Reinhard Bendix (1960), Raymond Aron (1965) and Julien Freund (1968, p. 143). Rationalism, as Weber's main thesis, is strongly stated by Friedrich Tenbruck (1980, pp. 316–351), a follower of Bendix

citizenship, a monetarized economy, monetary policies, rational accounting, rational law, rational government, political parties, demagogues, cities, rational science, rational historiography, experimentation, rational religion, rational ethics, rational individuals and rational music, factories, rational organization of labor and ultimately, rational capitalism, etc. only exist in the West. And the list is not limited to these. In fact, if the factors that Weber considers as unique to the West were to be listed here, it would be many times longer. Whatever is the opposite of that listed here inevitably belongs to the Orient.[2] Starting from Ancient Greece, Weber believes that the West was open to improvement at every historical period, with rationalism being the differentiating principle in history.

Weber's definition of rationalism can be found at the beginning of *Economy and Society* where he gives four ways to *define (bestimmt)* an action: (1) *Traditional* action through existing habits; (2) *affectional* action through strong feelings; (3) *value-rational (wertrational)* action through a conscious belief in the value of acting in a certain way, with no thought of the consequences and (4) *instrumentally rational (zweckrational)* action, actions which are determined by the appropriate tools to attain calculated results (Weber, 1978, pp. 24–25). Handling each type of action in detail, Weber proposes that there is no one social action that can be described with only one of these types, rather, every social action has a number of different directions. However, a social action can still be included under one of the types in a determinative way. In his later analyses, we can see that Weber's traditional and value rational actions are mostly identified with Oriental societies, whereas his goal-instrumental rational actions are mostly identified with Western societies.

Evaluating each field of social life in a sense of rationality, Weber uses the word rational in a variety of adjective meanings: systematical, calculable, impersonal,

---

and Freund. In his work, he problematizes the thematic unity of Weber's texts. Subsequent to this, Wolfgang Schluchter (1981, p. 9) and Rogers Brubaker's (1984) works made great contributions to the discussions. Hennis (1983, p. 138) states that Weber's key issue is considered to be the "development of rationalism" in general, but from Weber's answers to criticisms on *Protestant Ethic* and methodological texts, we can deduce that his central question is "the development of humanity." However, this is not presented consistently. For rationalism as Weber's central theme, see Blaut, 2000, pp. 19, 102; Boucock, 2000, p. 4; Collins, 1986, p. 62; Ferrarotti, 1982; Kalberg, 2005, p. 27; Love, 2000, p. 173; Marshall, 1982, pp. 56–57; Parkin, 1982, p. 65; Poggi, 2006, p. 53; Roth, 1987, p. 86; Turner, 1974a, p. 151; Wrong, 1970, p. 25; Zimmerman, 2006, p. 71.

2 In *Prefatory Remarks [Vorbemerkung] to Collected Essays in the Sociology of Religion* we find this perspective in its clearest form. Here Weber makes evident the universal historical perspective that gives his entire corpus harmony. In particular, he emphasizes two points in connection with the aim of his work: (1) Western civilization is distinct from others due to its particular and special rationalism; (2) the central objective of universal history is to explain this unique rationalism and to characterize it (Weber, 2009). Similarly, Weber gives this type of summarizing general comparisons in his work from time to time (Weber, 2003, pp. 313–314).

pure, instrumental, accurate, quantitative, rule orientated, predictable, farsighted, consistent, effective, understandable, methodological, moderate, precise and goal oriented (Brubaker, 1984, pp. 1–2; Eisen, 1978, pp. 57–70).[3] Yet these different usages do not violate but support one another and present different aspects of the social institutions in Western civilization. At the same time, rationalism functions as an explanatory principle that connects Weber's empirical and methodological research to political and ethical thoughts (Brubaker, 1984, pp. 1–2, 36).

According to Weber, there are three important sources of the unique and superior rationalism of the West. First of all, there is the prophethood of ancient Judaism, which is the basis for modern science and technology as it purifies magic and the searches for irrational salvation. Secondly, there is the institutional heritage of Rome, with the creation of standardization and formalization of law in the Canonical tradition of the Church. And finally there is the mentality and institutional structure imposed by the Western monastery system based on asceticsm. In this sense, Weber uses the term rationalization to define three inter-related groups of facts: procedural achievement of aimed goals via calculation; the *intellectualization* of the world in a positive sense, *disenchantment* in a negative sense (iron cage is the negatives result of this); and the formation of an ethic that systematically leads to definite goals.

According to Weber, the basic indication of rationalization is calculability. He thinks that calculability, parallel to rationalism, has a central role in the appearance of modern civilization. Accordingly, the point where modern civilization differs from others is in the placing of means-oriented calculability at the center of economic decisions while eliminating traditional values and their restrictions. In addition, alongside capitalism, Protestant asceticism and the fact that all aspects of life are used as objects of calculation combine to make rationalism dominant throughout life (Weber, 2009, p. 214).

Weber thinks that the most important obstacles standing in the way of rationalism are traditionalism and the perception of the world as a kind of magical garden (Weber, 1978, p. 30). In this sense, with secularization in the West, the obstacles in front of rationalism, that is, traditional life styles and religious beliefs, were removed. According to him, it is here that Christianity and Judaism are unique among world religions. As Christianity continued the tradition of prophethood, it maintained a dynamism that is not present in Oriental religions. The values of Hinduism, Buddhism and Confucianism are too imbued in daily life, unlike Christianity where religious institutions differ from the general structure of society. In the absence of a central authority like the Church to explain religious values to the public in these religions, these values become intellectually stratified. The intellectual values which were associated with a specific group departed from the values held by the public. Thus, the effects of these values are traditional and

---

3   Weber lists the six meanings of rationalism as follows: purpose, calculability, control, rational harmony, universality and system. For the different usage of rationality by Weber, see Bendix, 1960, pp. 278–279 note 33.

conservative. Experts and interpreters of these religions head towards in-depth expertise in the sacred texts or ethereal forms of communication with the sacred rather than externalizing religion in daily life in spiritual and ceremonial forms. According to Weber, such religious experiences are of course present in Christianity, but because of the tradition of prophethood the latter also tries to overcome the tension between the divine and the worldly via a militant transformation of the world. What is more, the advanced organized institutions of the Church and the monasteries, due to their separation from the general social order are able to have an independent effect on the social order.

As stated by Marianne Weber, using a conceptualization from Friedrich Schiller while working on world religions, Weber discovered the disenchantment in the course of the development of religion (Marianne Weber, 2008, p. 333). "Religion, according to Weber, arises out of magic and is originally indistinguishable from it" but as religion becomes rationalized, it changes from magic to doctrine such that "rationalization creates and progressively intensifies tensions between religious and 'worldly' values and obligations" (Brubaker, 1984, p. 75). As a result of these tensions, the world becomes disenchanted and ultimately becomes a machine fully controlled by men (Freund, 1968, pp. 143–144). This discomfiture of magic leads to the belief that, as the result of technological developments and inventions, the human being is the master of nature. According to Weber, only Protestantism was able to succeed in totally cleansing religion of magic. Confucianism and Hinduism, at their very outset, and indeed, all Asian religions, have been unable to rid themselves of magic, and thus lacked the ability to rationalize the world.

Weber is not the only person to have emphasized the particular rationalism of the Western social order. But there are differences between the role Weber assigns to rationalism and the role assigned by the Enlightenment and nineteenth-century progressive thought. According to Weber, rather than being an inner logic that leads from the beginning to the end by realizing itself in a Hegelian manner, rationalization in the history of the West appears as a result of "elective affinities" of circumstances and unintended consequences.[4] Rationalization in Weber is rather the result of the expertise and technical differentiation that is particular to Western culture. In this sense, rationalization is formulized as calculability, a system of open rules, systematical technology and rationally planned institutions. Weber's view is not progressive (Collins, 1986, p. 94; Giddens, 1972, p. 43; Hindess, 1987, p. 144), but rather, developmental (Schluchter, 1981, p. 22, 1987, p. 92) and neo-evolutionist (Roth, 1987, p. 76). However, in the subjects that he studied, his statement about the superior position of West as a result of rationalism leads him to a similar position with progressive and positivist thinkers from the nineteenth century (Ferrarotti, 1987, p. 105). In this sense, Weber's arguments about Western rationalism are fundamentally teleological (Allen, 2004, p. 130). When Western civilization is defined as requiring the appearance of rationalism

---

4   According to Weber (1978, pp. 882–883), although it is present in every part of the world, the degrees of rationalization are not the same everywhere.

for its development, other civilizations can only be understood due to their lack of the same (Hindess, 1987, pp. 144–146).

On the other hand, Weber's mentioning partial rationalism in other civilizations and the relativity of rationality[5] has led some Weberians to judge him as not Eurocentric. Nevertheless, when his rationalization analyses are thoroughly examined, it can be seen that he perceives Oriental rationalism as an obstacle standing in the way of genuine (Western) rationalization. For example, according to Weber, rationalism in Confucian ideology and management types has contributed to the lengthy survival of the imperial system in China, a system that is not rational or open to development (Weber, 1968, p. 249). Thus, in terms of historical development, the existence and development of rationalization in the Western form is essential for Weber, but, according to him, it emerges empirically from the combination of current circumstances in the West. "If this development took place only in the Occident the reason is to be found in the special features of it, a general cultural evolution which are peculiar to it" (Weber, 2003, pp. 313–314).

The Determinant Element in Oriental Societies: Patrimonialism Based on Water

Weber's analyses of Oriental societies are clearly influenced by his analyses on the originality of the West (Freund, 1968, pp. 143–144). However, in order to attain a clear-cut Orient–Occident distinction, he needed to develop a terminology and typology that could deal with the variety of societies that have existed for over 2,500 years. Weber (1978, p. 357) followed the previous generations of Orientalist tradition and saw climatic differences explanatory and sufficient for his scientific analysis. He analyzed the Orient in the context of patrimonialism shaped by irrigation under certain climatic and geographical circumstances.[6]

According to Weber, the basic reason that led to the difference between the Orient and the Occident was the need for an irrigation-based agriculture located near water. As a consequence, the great civilizations in the Orient emerged based on solving the problems concerned with water in fertile river basins. The Nile in Egypt, the Euphrates and Tigris in Mesopotamia, the Ganges and Indus in India, the Yellow River in China; all these were the cradles of the first settled areas, the first cities and civilized life. Thus, for Weber, the Orient consists of civilizations based along watercourses, whereas Ancient Greece and Rome were shore civilizations. This difference resulted in two different characteristics, with

---

5   Something may be seen as rational from a certain perspective, and can seem irrational if viewed from the perspective of the other realms of life (Weber, 2009, pp. 215–216).

6   In his letter to the conservative historian Georg von Below in June 21, 1914, about *Economy and Society*, Weber states that patrimonialism is at the heart of his work (Von Below, 1925, p. xxv).

the two types of civilization becoming alienated from one another and progressing in different directions (Weber, 2003, pp. 321–322).

According to Weber, this differentiation led the rise of the patrimonial system in the Orient, as the construction of irrigation canals for agriculture and the need for their protection led to the rise of a strong central bureaucratic structure. For large-scaled public affairs in the Orient, such as constructing canals, roads and castles and irrigation, there was the imposition of labor duty known as corvée. Although the situation changed depending on the needs and location, corvée was present in all Oriental societies. Another aspect that requires a central patrimonial government is defense against nomadic tribes from the surrounding mountains and deserts.[7] Thus, the military arena was a determining factor. The patrimonial army is not only a defensive mechanism, it is a power that controls society at the same time.

According to Weber, battle systems and the social position of the soldier were different in the Orient from the West, and the difference depended on the position of the government. In Europe, the paramount power was the cavalry, which had to provide their own weapons and training, whereas in the Orient, the infantry, equipped, fed and trained by the ruler, fulfilled the primary role (Weber, 1967a, p. 71). At the same time, the fact that the army was directly organized by the ruler prevented the appearance of independent military forces as seen in the West and ensured the ultimate dominance of the patrimonial will. In contrast to this, the independent feudal forces in Europe were able to collaborate and force the ruler to accept their requests. Thus, while estates appeared in the West, there were no such thing in the Orient due to the structure of the military and political system (Weber, 1978, p. 1028). All these became factors that could be referenced to explain the appearance of modern rational capitalism in the West and the lack of the same in the Orient.

Like other Orientalists before him, Weber reinforced the Orient–Occident comparison via the study of different types of land property.[8] According to Weber, the Orient was not as developed as the West in terms of private property on land. In the Orient, land was allocated by the ruler in return for a tax-in-kind.[9] In reference to Europe Weber writes, "in Asia, on the contrary, there was a shift from extensive, and hence nomadic, agriculture to horticulture without milk-cattle breeding" (Weber, 1988, p. 37). In Weber's view, even though it is possible that such

---

7   In Mesopotamia the people had to defend themselves against the people of Arabia and Iran, while China had the same problem with the people of Turkestan and the northern mountain regions. Owing to natural obstacles, Egypt was partially exempt from such a situation (Weber, 1988, p. 157).

8   Weber (1988) deals with the different types of agriculture associated with geographical circumstances at the beginning of his work, *The Agrarian Sociology of Ancient Civilizations*. Here he also examines the formation of land property dependent on these circumstances.

9   For a wide discussion of the property relations in agriculture and industry, see Weber, 1978, pp. 149–150.

comparison may not be applicable to pre-historic times, it was important enough to have created basic divisions. Thus, while the appearance of private property on land is connected to the division of pasture land into smaller groups among the people in European society with private property appearing with the final division and allocation, there is no such development among Oriental societies.[10] In this way, by adding to the Oriental despotism thesis which was popular in Europe, Weber explains how the land in the Orient belonged to the king or the state, and that the lords who appeared to own the land were in fact not the true owners and could only use what had been granted to them by the king or state on a temporary basis. In contrast, feudal lords in the West often owned their own land, and they formed the basis for free, enterprising and plentiful production.

When describing Oriental societies, Weber states that artificial irrigation was seen in some European societies. However, according to him, the existence of these irrigation systems did not lead to the consequent systems in the Orient. Just as Marx states that in Italy and Flanders artificial irrigation systems did not cause the same effects that were seen in the Orient because they were carried out with an independent social organization, Weber provides the same explanation for the Ancient Greek irrigation systems. Comparing it to those of the Orient, he writes that in Greece "irrigation was important from early times, but with this difference: no centralized, bureaucratic control of it was needed" (Weber, 1988, p. 148). Because of the organization of society, that of the irrigation system did not require any bureaucratic channels regardless of the political authority. However, it can be said that here Weber resorts to some question-begging explanations in order to make his case. He saw irrigation systems as the main and unquestioned source for society's dependence on the government in the Orient. But the same irrigation systems are not seen to have had the same effect in Greece because of social and cultural factors that affected their organization before the advent of irrigation. Weber never asks why these factors did not appear in the Orient, and, as a result, pushes the Orient into a geographically determined category, while characterizing the West as controller and determiner of the same geographic factors.

Historical Roots of the Differentiation: Greek and Hebrew Societies

Weber attributes the final difference between the Orient and the West to the way that the two ancient bases of the Western civilization that are Greek and Hebrew societies. They realized their social order in a way that was different from those in the Orient. More specifically, according to Weber, the social and political development of these two bases progressed in a different way from Oriental societies, eventually creating gaps between their respective social and political structures which could not be closed.

---

10   For comparative usage of land and distribution in Mesopotamia and Rome, see Weber, 1988, p. 97.

Weber gave special importance to determining the difference between Greek and Near Eastern societies.[11] According to him, at the very beginning, Greek civilization was a product of dynamism. In contrast to the bureaucracies of the Near East which developed towards a *world monarchy* such as Assyria, in Greece there was a central role for the type of military city that later lead to the creation of the *polis*. Weber thinks that the existence of irrigation-based agriculture, a bureaucracy to organize public affairs, as well as the dominance of religious tradition, the political power of the priests, and the conquests of river-based societies by foreign nomadic invaders from Arabia and Iran enforced the obedience of the individual to society in Mesopotamia. As opposed to what occurred in Greek societies, these developments brought about ultimate obedience and weakness in Near East societies (Weber, 1988, pp. 157–158).

These differences first appeared in the characteristics of the army. In the Near East, while the army became a royal legion that was nourished, equipped and controlled by the king's bureaucracy, the subordinates of the Greek kings increased in power relative to the monarch, and, as a result, a yeoman army who provided their own weapons emerged (Weber, 1988, pp. 157–158). Weber uses this difference between independent military classes (knights) who provided their own weapons and a dependent military fed and equipped by the king as the basis for the explanation of many developments.[12] Most importantly perhaps, he takes it to be at the root of the formation of democracy in the West, and despotism in the Orient. In this way, Greek civilization is supposed to have been permanently and irrevocably differentiated from the Near East (Weber, 1988, p. 159).

According to Weber, the major consequence of this phenomenon was the creation of a city-state civilization in Greece based on democracy. In Ancient Greece, political development followed a typical progress along the line of the aristocratic *polis, hoplite*[13] *polis,* culminating in *radical democracy* (Weber, 1988, pp. 175–176). In contrast, Near Eastern societies were formed under tyranny, and although it can be seen in Ancient Greece and other parts of Europe which fell under the influence of the Orient in some periods of history, tyranny was not a permanent feature of Western civilization.[14]

---

11 As mentioned by Bernal (1987), from the end of the eighteenth century until the beginning of the nineteenth, over a relatively short span of time, European thinkers raised Ancient Greece to the position of cradle of European civilization and Weber continues in this mindset (Hobson, 2004, p. 295).

12 For the effects of an independent self-equipped yeomanry and bourgeois army on socio-political order, see Weber, 1988, pp. 174–175.

13 The word Hoplite comes from the word "Hoplon" in Greek. Hoplits are noble and armed Greek spear-bearers. Having the same advantages and disadvantages as the spear-bearers, they have greater abilities to defend. However, due to their armor and the positions they adopted, they moved much slower than other spear-bearing infantry.

14 As Weber was speaking of tyranny, in this context in which he emphasizes the similarity with the Near East, the dilemma of the Persian tyranny against the classic Greek democracy is once again brought onto the agenda.

Weber claims that the basis for the tendency towards tyranny in the Orient and to democracy in the West was the fact that the Orient was theocratic and Greece was secular. "[P]urely secular civilization" and capitalist development of Greece arose as a result of lack of a Near Eastern type of bureaucratization (Weber, 1988, pp. 157–158). Weber states that "the real reason why religion was so much less dominant in the Occident was that the priestly order there was not organized, ranked and unified" (Weber, 1988, p. 186). Working from Eduard Meyer, Weber here states that the "Persian Wars can be regarded ... as a decisive struggle between these trends, supported by the Persians in Greece as elsewhere, and the secularism of Hellenic civilization" (Weber, 1988, pp. 187–188). The victory of Greek democracy and secularism in this struggle determined the destiny of the West. As the priests were no longer powerful in Greece, theocracy could not develop and thus a Near Eastern patrimonial despotism did not appear. This is what made Greece the cradle of democracy.

But there is a problem that must be solved at this point. There has to be an explanation for Mycenaean society, which is seen to be a basic part of Greek civilization and a society that bequeathed to Western civilization many characteristics, including the name "Europe" (Weber, 1978, pp. 1282–1283).[15] Mycenaean society consisted of exactly what Weber attributed to Near East civilizations, that is, a central bureaucracy, irrigation systems, extensive public affairs, corvée, artisans working in the management of palace and a theocratic order of priests (Weber, 1988, pp. 155, 162). Weber gets by this by stating that Mycenaean civilization was under the influence of Near East societies and that these features came from there. However, with the removal of the supporting external bases, the system came to an end. In this sense, Weber thinks that, like the central patrimonial kingdom in Ancient Israel of King Solomon and King David, which had Near Eastern characteristics, the undertakings to develop a patrimonial government in Mycenaean civilizations failed because it went against the inherent culture that existed.

Attempts to separate the basis of the Occident from the Orient are also present in Weber's evaluations of Ancient Israel. By abstracting Hebrew society from its cultural context and by centering geographical/climatic explanations, he makes this society unique and provides the required viewpoint from which to differentiate European civilization from others. Departing from these geographical circumstances via the religious–ethical system, Weber examines Hebrew society not as a kind of Oriental despotism, but rather how this system and its thought constitute a foundation of Western society. Weber starts by differentiating the basis of geographical circumstances of river-side civilizations and Palestinian settlers with a "climatic opposition" (Weber, 1967b, p. 8). According to him, Palestine's

---

15   Weber tries to offer an analysis of Sparta in this sense. According to him, the city of Sparta was like Near Eastern city castles, but "In contrast to the position in the Near East, this castle is not controlled by the king, but by the warriors" (Weber, 1988, p. 163). A similar case exists for Cyprus (Weber, 1978, p. 1282).

separation from the two great civilizations surrounding it was due to geography—the mountains, valleys and deserts, all of which stalled the development of its political and social systems (Weber, 1967b, pp. 5–10). These terms of comparison can be seen most particularly in Palestine's relations with Egypt: "The Egyptian corvée state, developing out of the necessity for water regulation and the construction works of the kings, appeared to the inhabitants of Palestine as a profoundly alien way of life" (Weber, 1967b, p. 8).[16] Here an important explanation for this separation is the assumption of a special relationship between Jewish society and their God (Jehovah). According to Weber, the definition of the wells of the Jehovah Mountains in the Old Testament presents an important difference between Israel and Egypt in their relationship with God. While God sends rain to the Palestinian mountains and meadows, producing crops, the Egyptians had to cultivate and water the land "like a vegetable garden" as it is phrased in Torah (11:10) (Weber, 1967b, p. 66). Jehovah shows to his folks that providing product does not depend on the artificial watering in Israel. "It is not a product of bureaucratic administration, of the king on earth and the work of the peasant, but it is the result of the rain given by Yahweh according to his free grace" (Weber, 1967b, p. 129).

Thus, social life in ancient Israel gained a totally different characteristic from the surrounding civilizations of Mesopotamia and Egypt. At this point, the independent character of the warrior tribes, the tradition of the nobles versus the palace prevented the development of the centralized kingdom that was seen in Near East societies (Weber, 1967b, p. 118). According to Weber, the most important obstacle in the development of a patrimonial central kingdom in ancient Israel was the tradition of prophethood. Presenting themselves as the leaders of society, representatives of ancient Jewish traditions and followers of the implementation of Jehovah's religion, the prophets considered any kind of tendency to central bureaucracy as an Egyptian innovation, thus refusing to implement anything of its kind (Weber, 1967b, pp. 109–111). Stating that in the Ancient West this was paramount to a remonstrance delivered by the plebeian class against the nobility, Weber transformed this into a differentiating feature of East and West. Later, he mentions a number of times how the charismatic Jewish prophethood, which came to the West via Christianity, introduced a distinguishing characteristic to these societies (Weber, 1967b, p. 117).

However, despite such geographical obstacles, ancient Jewish society was affected to a degree by those great patrimonial civilizations (Weber, 1967b, p. 7). We find Weber writing in particular about King Solomon's attempt to establish an Egyptian-style central bureaucratic kingdom and the spreading of the Baal belief of the Canaan in Philistine territory. He claims that as a result of Solomon's imitation of Egypt and Babylon and his attempts to establish a despotic government, Israel took on the features typical of the great warrior forces of the Orient. In this process,

---

16   In this sense, as a determiner of Old Israel's identity, "the antagonism toward Egypt was, in the last analysis, based on natural and social differences between the two realms" (Weber, 1967b, p. 8).

The standing army, the royal bodyguards and mercenary troops gained in importance at the expense of the old peasant summons. ... Finally there were also corvées in the Egyptian manner. A regular harem appeared with kinship ties and alliances with the rulers of the great powers, above all, with Egypt and Phoenicia, affording opportunity to engage in world politics. This led to the import of foreign cults, in part only in the form of court chapels for the strange princesses; in part, however, it also led to the incorporation of strange gods into the home cult. Such were the prompt ramifications of kingly power. Thus kingship acquired the typical features of the great warpowers of the Orient. (Weber, 1967b, pp. 100–101, see also 1988, pp. 140–142)

As a result, chariots were adapted for the Israel army and warrior tribes and villager knights came under the dominance of the city monarchy. In this way, the knight with his independently acquired weaponry started to lose his importance and a patrician society emerged established around Solomon's palace. As in the Near East, within King Solomon's kingdom were moves to give the judicatory power to the bureaucracy while theocracy developed and the bureaucracy improved. In this sense, the fact that the kind of measures typical of a theocratic city state arose, such as the installment of a poor tax amounting to one-third of the tithe to help establish grain silos, seems unsurprising.

But according to Weber, the system that developed based on Solomon's military organization was not accepted by the Israelites (Weber, 1988, pp. 140–142) and it did not continue due to its incongruity with the geographic circumstances of ancient Israeli society (Weber, 1967b, p. 18). The economic basis needed to develop a despotic bureaucratic government, a land surrounded by mountains, valleys, steppes and deserts with only small rivers, was not present (Weber, 1967b, pp. 5–10). The independent tradition of prophethood played an important role in the failure of the corvée system's establishment in Egypt, the place remembered as the "land of slavery" in Jewish exile memoirs (Weber, 1967b, pp. 200, 254). This was because Solomon's attempts to combine religious institutions with the palace through a king-prophethood system around the temple failed, in turn making the rise of the prophet- or god-king impossible (Weber, 1967b, p. 104). In connection with this failing, later politically and socially independent prophets began to appear (Weber, 1967b, p. 18).

Whereas the court's prophets who promised long life, many children and political success to the ruling dynasties, the success of independent prophets lay on the re-emergence of villagers as professional warriors. Yet the independent and true prophets who defended, lived for and stood against the kings and the masses in support of Jehovah's religion, were to determine the characteristic of Israeli society (Weber, 1967b, pp. 109–111, 280). The prophets of the Holy Books, from Amos to Jeremiah and Ezra removed magic and ethically elevated Judaism, defending obedience to God rather than the people, thus saving people from the pitfalls of magic. "The prophets were supported by Yahwistic families among the rural gentry that oriental despotism in Palestine had not been able to suppress. The prophets kept alive anti-royalist attitudes, voiced the needs of the economically exploited, legally oppressed, socially descending demilitarized peasants and husbandmen." They elaborated the glorious memories of the old: King David the mountaineering boy who slew the Philistine knight; the ass riding—not charioteering—popular king of the peasant militia; the charismatic leader; Moses the liberator who struck down the Egyptian slave master and led the oppressed out of the house of bondage. These were counter images to the pomp and glory of despotic kings, marrying foreign wives, honoring foreign deities, establishing harems, forsaking the ways of the fathers, entering into alliances with hated Egypt (Gerth and Martindale, 1952, pp. xxii–xxiii). These prophets, who could not be suppressed by Oriental despotism, but were supported by Yahwistic families, kept alive the opposition to the kingdom by the villagers who had been economically exploited, legally oppressed, disarmed and lived in social collapse, thus providing the society, which faced political and social problems, with an exit and new direction. The view of these prophets was in complete contrast to the splendor and magnificence of despot kings who established alliances with Egypt and abandoned the path of their ancestors, that is, the rulers who built harems, honored foreign gods and married foreign women.[17] In the end, instead of a central bureaucratic patrimonial kingdom, the idea of cooperation among the public around a *contract* was established. According to Weber, "[t]his was connected with the peculiarity of the political and religious constitution of Israel" (Weber, 1967b, pp. 303–304).

In conclusion, Weber bases his account on a differentiation of Orient and Occident, clarifying the characteristics of the West with his analysis of rationalism, and those of the Orient with his analysis of the patrimonialism. By analyzing how Greek and Hebrew society contrasted with their neighbors, he suggests that the difference between the Occident and the Orient existed from the very start in reference to these civilizations that were seen as the foundations of the West. By securing the foundations of Western civilization, Weber creates two separate directions in the historical process. As a result, while the West has a chain of development culminating in modern society, the Orient is forced into a never-ending cycle of stagnation. In this way, Weber clarifies the basic points of differentiation he uses in the discussion to demonstrate the unique nature of Western civilization. What is more, it is in this context that he analyzes Oriental societies and presents them as the complete opposite of the West.

---

17   The expressions used to determine the features of those kings who opposed the prophets completely coincide with the Oriental king and palace image that was created by Orientalist studies. In addition, for the comparison of the vision of these prophets and Hellenistic political vision, see Weber, 1967b, pp. 267, 275.

Chapter 10
Divergences: Religion, Politics and Economics

Based on the economic ethics of world religions a very comprehensive scope frames Weber's approach to Oriental societies. As shown above, according to him the political system determines the entire social formation in the Orient. Weber continues with the Orient–Occident comparison at each and every point in order to reach a holistic analysis of the Orient that is in opposition to the West.

The Differentiation of Religious Thought and Mentality

Weber carried out his studies to demonstrate the impact of *Weltanschauung* on social life, and differentiation in mentality was the first point used in his Orient–Occident analysis. This is why it was important for Weber to determine the basic character of world religions, and to reveal the fundamental differences between Oriental and Occidental religions. Combining research from the history of religion with analysis of modern Western culture was a common practice during Weber's lifetime. With the influence of the Protestant theologians who were carrying out comparative religious studies, Weber's objective was to demonstrate the unique development of Western civilization via the comparative study of world religions.[1]

Weber's study concerning world religions contains the assumption that there is a direct and fundamentally interrelation between the beliefs and social structures of a society. For instance, Weber proposes the existence of a relation between Egyptian gods and bureaucracy; the particular gods of every occupational group with the level of Indian economic development (Weber, 1978, p. 415); as well as the astral gods with bureaucratization in Babylon and China (Weber, 1978, pp. 417–418). Similarly, there is a close link between a personal, transcendent, and ethical god, which is a Near Eastern concept, and a king who establishes dominance through bureaucracy. Not only does religion influence the social order, but the social order also influences religion. For instance, Weber (1978, pp. 448–449) says that in the Near East, the control of irrigation in deserts and semi-arid regions became the source of the notion of a god that created human

---

1 Weber (1946b, p. 267) refers to religions such as Confucianism, Hinduism, Buddhism, Christianity and Islam, where believers focus on a central religious thought or ethic. In spite of Jews being a minority at all times and frequently pariahs, he adds Judaism to the list due to its influence on the other two Abrahamic faiths.

beings from nothing, contrary to belief of a god who gave birth to the earth and humans through fertilization as found elsewhere. "In the Middle East the old centralized bureaucratic administration undoubtedly promoted the concept of the supreme deity as a King of Heavens who had 'created' man and the world from nothing" (Weber, 1968, pp. 21–22). Likewise, the emergence of the astral belief in China is related to the political and social order, and, according to Weber (1968, p. 28), the difference between the Western personal hero gods such as the Homeric Greek gods in Olympus or the Christian god and China's animistic faith and the chthonian cult are as antithetical as the Western and Chinese social orders .

The dual contrasts that shaped the different scholarly views of the Orient and Occident and including their opposing social structures played important roles in the exposition of the unique and inimitable Western image that Weber was trying to build on sociological grounds.[2] These contrasts were made using the supposed "passive Oriental," and "active Occidental" of Western perception formed throughout the nineteenth century by the Orientalists. Weber adopted this frame in claiming that prophethood emerged in its true sense only in the West, while only priests and sorcerers arose in the Orient, thus, making the West ascetic and the Orient mystical (King, 1999, pp. 7–35).[3] Western religious thought directs one to this world, while religious thought in the Orient isolates one from the world. While religious thought in the West has been rationalized, with the latter's absence traditionalism dominated the East.

The first of these dual contrasts is the theory of purifying religious thought from magic and rationalizing it. For Weber, the rationalization of a system of religious creed includes the elimination of magic and sophistry in favor of rational faith and ethic norms. Accordingly, in the West religion has been purified from magic and rationalized at an advanced level. In explaining the foundations of this development via the influence of ancient Judaism and Hellenic–Roman thought on Christianity, Weber holds that an event such as this did not grace the Orient (For detailed discussions see Gane, 2002, pp. 17–18; Schluchter, 1979, pp. 32–33). The institution of prophethood in ancient Judaism (Weber, 2003a, p. 322)[4] and other social forces made a fundamental contribution to the progress of rationalization in the West (Weber, 2009a, pp. 114–115). The Jewish image of a transcendent god that is different from human beings is the most important element in breaking the hold of magic, for separating the direct link of God to humanity eliminates the importance of magic in religion.

Another development Weber thought equally important is the idea of predestination in Calvinism. According to this idea, the individual is a tool for

---

2   In fact, here Weber believes that Oriental Christianity, which is not open to such influences, has not been able to develop rationalism like Western Christianity.

3   Regarding the foundations of the mystical category in Western thought see King, 1999, pp. 96–118. For the creation of Hinduism and the discovery of Buddhism as a mystic religion, see King, 1999, pp. 143–161.

4   For the age of prophets in world history, see Weber, 1978, pp. 441–443.

the realization of God's goals in the world. Questions such as, "Am I amongst the predestined who have been saved? How can *I* become certain of my status as one of the chosen?" (Weber, 2009a, p. 110) take on unique significance being allied to the transformation of the human pursuit of salvation into an active operation and a process of world transformation (Weber, 2009a, p. 119). At a practical level, the teaching basically denotes "God helps those who help themselves" and, thus, that "the Calvinist *himself creates* his salvation" (Weber, 2009a, p. 113). Contrary to the Catholic belief, in Calvinism there is no certainty regarding salvation. Hence, the Calvinist must grant his or her life in its entirety a methodical organization with *"systematic self-control"* (Weber, 2009a, pp. 114–115). This led to the rise of an individual always active and who transforms the world in the process, perhaps, of working for the mercy of God.

In this context, Weber's most important contradiction is the extreme similarity between the understanding of predestination in Islam and that he tries to ascribe to Protestantism and Calvinism. Later, Weber states that the Islamic understanding of predestination prior to being transformed into the Sufi understanding of *kismet* (fate, predestination) is similar to Protestantism. However, while the Protestant understanding of predestination produces rationally planned processes for ethical strictness, legalism, and the shaping of life, Weber writes that the Islamic *kismet* leads to carelessness towards oneself and the world. Islam, the religion of war, does not have a rational system of ascetic control to govern everyday life, and, what is more, its understanding of forgiveness, allied to the doctrine of Islamic predestination, prevents the individual from striving for salvation due to the continued magical characteristics it still holds and the belief that forgiveness is the prerogative of the God alone upon those destined for hell. Thus, "the doctrine produced no planned procedure for the control of the workaday world, as did the Puritan doctrine of predestination" (Weber, 1978, pp. 573–575).

Weber indicates the change in the Calvinist understanding of predestination by tracing the transformation of the term *Beruf* (occupation or calling) in translations of the Bible (2009a, p. 89). According to him, in traditional societies nobody highly valued or respected work.[5] While worship, reflection, and other full-time religious tasks were worthy of respect in society, all "worldly" works were seen negatively. For the nobles, work was considered to be an indication of lower class membership; only slaves, serfs, and those who were born into the lower strata would work on a continuous basis. Weber believes that the term *Beruf* as used by Luther in view of the Bible has an important place in a reversal social thought, for

5   With his analysis of the term "vocation," Ülgener shows the error of this claim, and that it is at least invalid for traditional Islamic societies. Accordingly, the term "vocation," which comes from the same root as suluk (constant occupation of oneself, body and heart, in the obedience to the Creator) has a certain prestige. This is why suluk, which means getting closer to God step by step, also encodes working in the mind as a tool for getting closer to God (Ülgener, 2006, p. 47 fn. 27). For occupational and sectoral expertise in cities in medieval Islam, see Rodinson, 2007, pp. 60–61.

prior to the Luther's translation, the worldly use of the term *Beruf* does not exist in any Western language in the worldly sense (Weber, 2009a, p. 89, 476 fn. 3). Weber writes, "this moral legitimization of vocational life was one of the Reformation's most influential achievements, and in particular the achievement of Luther" (Weber, 2009a, p. 90).[6] In the final link in this process, the Puritans regard magic as the field of Satan and their rejection of it rationalized the relationship of God and the world (Weber, 1978, p. 544). Contrary to this, Confucianism, Hinduism, Buddhism and other Asiatic religions turned the world into a magical garden both in theory and in practice, and, as a result, made the basic pattern of behavior a matter of either compliance with the world or escape from it. Although in these religions, rationalization was effected in some areas of life, its general evolution is impossible in this magical garden.

According to Weber, throughout history there have been two main principled and consistent ways of avoiding the tension between religion and the world. They are asceticism and mysticism (Weber, 1946a, pp. 323–363). The asceticism which leads one to seek salvation in worldly tasks is held by Weber to be specific to the West alone, while mysticism, which leads one to avoid the world, is specific to the Orient (Weber, 1978, p. 544). Similarly, Western rationalism appears in a form of controlling and gaining dominance over the world, while the Oriental irrational pursuit of magical salvation leads one to either acquiesce to the world or deny it.[7] In this sense, the Jewish idea of a God and Creator transcending the world, taken up by Christianity and confirmed by Protestantism, is particularly important for the active and ascetic orientation associated with the search for salvation. Such an ethereal positioning of divine power along with the depersonalization of God prevents any pursuit for mystical integration with the Divine. Thus, according to Weber, while the idea of God in Europe leads to a legally definable relationship of servitude and the formation of a methodical technique to reach salvation, in Asia no such technique was formed (Weber, 1978, pp. 552–556). With reference to Troeltsch, Weber states that this close relationship between an ethereal God and active asceticism is not inherited; it excludes the other two monotheistic faiths and makes the Western one unique:

---

6   According to Weber, Luther used the term *Beruf* in opposition to the church and monastery. Exalting work and working against priests and men of the cloth who continue their lives through the labor of others, and the feudal aristocrats who made up other fundamental element in the social system, he defined worldly work as a tool of the grace of God and undoubtedly threatened the church order. Accordingly, Luther transformed working into a tool of salvation (Weber, 2009a, p. 90).

7   A general comparison between mysticism as the Orient's rejection of the world and asceticism as the West's rejection of the world can be found in Weber's Religious Rejections of the World and Their Directions (Weber, 1946a, pp. 323–359). Weber wrote this text between his articles on Chinese and Indian religions. Hence, the word *Zwischenbetrachtung* (Intermediary Observations) is noted above the original title. However, this word has not been used in the English translation.

The Christian Trinity, with its incarnate Savior and the saints, represented a conception of God which fundamentally was rather less supra-mundane than was the God of Jewry, especially of later Jewry, or the Allah of Islamism. Jewry developed mysticism, but it developed hardly any asceticism of the Occidental type.[8] And early Islamism directly repudiated asceticism. The peculiarity of Dervish religiosity stemmed from quite different sources than from the relation to a supra-mundane God and Creator. It stemmed from mystic, ecstatic sources and in its inner essence it was remote from Occidental asceticism. (Weber, 1946a, pp. 324–325).

Devoid of a monotheistic, deist, ethereal view of God despite being aware of worldliness and asceticism, according to Weber the Asian tradition is unable to have any concept of a cultural combination with the religions of salvation. At first glance, he approaches this through studying worldly Confucianism and ascetic Jainism which have features arguably similar to ascetic Protestantism. Accordingly, the religious ethics of Confucianism provide a motive for the rational transformation of the world. In fact, Jainism encourages a trade-focused capitalism. Unlike Confucianist worldliness which has no connection to asceticism, the asceticism of Jainism directs one outside the social order. Confucianism encourages compliance with the world while Jainism encourages a certain apathy and aversion towards the world in a way that is applicable to all Asian religions.

While an ascetic implements positive and divine solutions in which definitive meanings are hidden as part of creation and predestined by God, mystical salvation is merely turning to attain the completely irrational through religious experience (Weber, 1946a, p. 326). An ascetic life with a worldly incentive leads to the absolutizing of religion and gaining some formal perspective. This leads to the destruction of a mystic's introverted existence and the formalization and rationalization of life (Weber, 1978, pp. 549–551). This is because the salvation of an ascetic is only possible through what he does in the world. Hence, the ascetic clings to it and acts with worldly motive. Contrary to this, avoiding this world through reflection is, Weber says, to a degree the character of all Asiatic and Near East religions of salvation.

Here, the main characteristic of the process of the acquisition of knowledge is significant. Contrary to that which is required in Western science and expertise, knowledge in Asiatic religions is more concerned with the meaning of "existence" than matters of this world, nature, and the nature of social life. According to Weber, Oriental knowledge does not reveal the features characteristic of the empirical sciences that make it possible to dominate nature and humans in a rational way.

---

8 According to Weber, although Judaism and Protestantism are progressively similar in terms of their rational characteristics, there is no asceticism in Judaism. Hence the economic rational practices there did not lead to capitalism. Here it should be noted that Weber's discussions concerning the relationship of Judaism and capitalism mostly target Sombart's theses (Weber, 1978, pp. 621, 1200–1201).

Rather, it leads one to assume a mystical and magical dominance (gnosis) over the individual and world.[9] Thus, in these religions the idea of mystical integration with the Divine and through reflection directs the believer to a specific type of knowledge. Thus social passivity became a phenomenon since an area of knowledge that is not socially objective came to the fore. (Weber, 1946a, p. 340, 1978, pp. 544–545). While knowledge for an ascetic means to take the world under greater control, to dominate it more, and hence to further guarantee one's salvation, the knowledge of a mystic distances him from the world and causes him to despise that which is worldly (Weber, 1946a, p. 328).

This structure of knowledge and connection with God also determines the social position of religion. According to Weber, the great religious doctrines of Asia are the products of intellectuals and reforms in these religions can only be made by intellectuals. Yet, the intellectualism they house is not of a pariah or bourgeois kind, it is rather aristocratic. This type of intellectualism also determines the abstemious character of these religions (Weber, 1978, pp. 502, 506, 508). Establishing a contrast between Asiatic intellectualism and prophethood, Weber states that ethical prophethood does not exist in Asian religions and that the most frequent examples of prophetic teachings in this region are found in activity of "model prophets". That is, religion is continued in the life-model of the prophet; there is no tradition of rational interpretation. Oriental religions continue as intellectual religions in the aristocratic form. In harmony with Weber's claim that prophethood changed the foundations of patrimonial ruling, he holds that patrimonialism is also related to the absence of prophethood as well as resulting from the above mentioned Oriental religious characteristics. In addition, Western monasticism has a key role in the rise of ascetism.[10] Weber states, "[t]he organisation of life in Western monasticism was emancipated from all random flight from this world and all heroic self-torture. ... This organised life, which was systematised, thoroughly shaped, and methodical-rational, had the goal of overcoming the *status naturea*" (Weber, 2009a, p. 116). Monastery life in the West includes meditation,

---

9   For Weber, mystical knowledge "becomes more incommunicable the more it is specifically mystical, it is nevertheless recognized as knowledge" (Weber, 1978, p. 545).

10   According to Weber, theoretically the foundation of Western rational capitalism is predestination, and practically the idea is the monastery system. Although the church hierarchy and bureaucracy may not be worldly in the West, during the emergence of rational bureaucratic organization and the manner of rule, monasteries were the first estates in which the rational methods of economic businesses were discovered and managed (Weber, 1978, p. 1169). Despite its own interests, the rational Western hierocracy developed a rational adjudication procedure along with the rational canonic law, and has placed all emphasis on adopting a rational law, the Roman law (Weber, 1978, p. 1186). In this context, the Occidental church developed a "continuous lawmaking on the basis of rational jurisprudence ... [and] on the model of Roman law, or encouraged through its example" (Weber, 1978, p. 1192). Similarly, "the fact that the Occident alone developed canonic music, as well as the distinctiveness of its scientific thought can be ascribed in large measure to Benedictine, Franciscan and Dominican monasticism" (Weber, 1978, p. 1169).

and asceticism, while that in the Orient includes only meditation. Consequently, the monastery gave birth to stagnation in the Orient and to active worldliness in the West.[11]

Weber states that the mystical characteristic of Oriental religions has an important place in the formation of the passive individual, stagnant society, an economic life distanced from the possibility of improvement, and a political order closed to rationalization. According to Weber, the rational action of the West against the pure ritualism of the Orient becomes tangible in the active individual (Weber, 1978, p. 531). The efforts of an active individual in dominating the world and the formation of systematic, methodological behavior patterns are closely related. Yet in the Orient seclusion instead of activity and dissipation instead of method are dominant.

Weber compares world religions within the scope of these parameters where four dimensions appear: the formal relationship of world dominance in the study of Protestantism, the compliance to the world in the study of Confucianism, the escape from the world in the study of Hinduism, and the overcoming the world in the study of Judaism and his comments on early Islam. His characterization is revealed in the most explicit form in his account of the representatives of the strata that were true spreaders and bearers of the world religions:

> If one wishes to characterise succinctly, a formula so to speak, the types representative of the various strata that were the primary Carriers or propagators of the so-called world religions, they would be the following: In Confucianism, the world-organizing bureaucrat; in Hinduism, the world-ordering magician; in Buddhism, the mendicant monk wandering through the world; in Islam, the warrior seeking to conquer the world; in Judaism, the wandering trader; and in Christianity, the itinerant journeyman. To be sure, all these types must not be taken as exponents of their own occupational or material "class interests," but rather as the ideological carrier of the kind of ethical or salvation doctrine which rather readily conformed to their social position. (Weber, 1978, p. 512)

As a result, Weber differentiates the Western and Oriental mentalities within the context of the active and passive in his study of religion. He secures the unique nature of the Western mentality by depicting the Orient's world view as an irrational, mystical, and passive in contrast to the rational, active, world-transforming, world-dominating creed found in the West. This leads him to set up an opposition between established dualities. By taking as his basis the historical role of worldview and ideas over actions, Weber sees such a differentiation of world views fundamentally important. Indeed, it is the result of these differentiations

---

11 Believing that the powerful influence of Western monastery rationalism over the essential contents of culture can only be clarified through comparison with the Near East and Asia, Weber wrote that all of these qualities are unique to the West and did not emerge anywhere else (Weber, 1978, p. 513).

in mentality that Weber holds a systemization and rationalization have taken place in every area of life in the West. In the following pages his ideas about the development of the rational capitalism on these foundations.

The Birth of Modern Private Enterprise: The Spirit of Capitalism and Economic Rationalization

Weber's definition of capitalism contains two fundamental elements: the spirit of capitalism[12] and economic rationalization. He emphasizes the place and significance of the spirit of capitalism in the emergence of modern capitalism, and notes the spirit of capitalism and capitalist organization of work alone cannot adequately explain the emergence of capitalism (Weber, 2009a, p. 80).[13] According to him, Protestantism determined the direction of society much like a switchman changing the route of trains. However, it is not the single factor in the development of modern capitalism. While the capitalist spirit constitutes a dimension of the capitalist mentality, rationalization ensures its social, political, and economical formation.

The spirit of capitalism, according to Weber, acted as a catalyst in the development of modern rationalism and rational capitalism, given its containing the most important components for transforming the world into a tool for salvation. The emphasis in Protestantism on working and earning, and the breaking down of the patterns of economical traditionalism, is the first manifestation of this phenomenon.[14] Weber brings to the fore the direct connection between Calvinism's pursuit of salvation with work in the world. Yet, although this *work ethic* encourages the transformation of the world, Weber (2009a, p. 68) is aware that it is not applicable to the first generation leaders of Protestantism, such as Luther, Calvin, Knox, or Voet. Their views in fact oppose many central elements of modernity. The qualities required for capitalism to succeed are to be found in

---

12   In his text, Weber uses many concepts in quotation marks to indicate that he is aware the meanings of these concepts are questionable or that they are used in a way opposed to their general use. He also continuously uses *spirit (geist)*, which is a central concept to the study, in quotation marks. Weber does this to indicate that he is aware of the ambiguity of the concept, and more importantly, to differentiate himself from the German idealist use of the concept particularly in Hegelian tradition (Weber, 2009a, p. 463 Stephan Kalberg's note).

13   On this point Weber was widely misjudged. He has no claim that Protestantism is the only cause of modern capitalism. When he realized that his analyses were misunderstood in this way, he expressly stated his position in a sentence which he added to the text in 1920: "We shall not defend here two foolish and doctrinaire theses in any form: (1) that the capitalist spirit (in the still provisional use of this term utilized here) *could* have originated *only* as an expression of certain influences of Reformation, and (2) that the capitalism as an *economic system* was a creation of Reformation." (Weber, 2009a, p. 97).

14   For Weber's work on economic traditionalism, see Weber, 2009a, pp. 76–77.

emergence a couple of generations later, in connection with *unintended results* of Protestantism (Weber, 2009a, pp. 71–72). In this context, Weber views Benjamin Franklin and Richard Baxter as the representatives of this transformation.[15]

Weber explains the role of the capitalist spirit created by the Protestant Ethic within the context of "elective affinities" (Weber, 2009a, p. 97). This term generally refers to the aggregation of singular conditions that give rise to certain historical states under specific circumstances and processes, in particular, the connections between religious ethics, professional morals and working life. In a sense, it addresses the role of mentality in shaping financial conditions, and the process of this formation. In this context, the spirit of capitalism has a very important role in the selection and aggregation of the singular conditions that existed in the Middle Ages. Despite there being many conditions deemed necessary for the emergence of capitalism in the Orient, the fact that it did not appear there is due to the lack of the capitalist spirit (Weber, 1967a, p. 4, 2009a, p. 75).[16]

According to Weber, being rational is what separates modern capitalism from various others of its type, such as adventure capitalism and commercial capitalism which existed prior to its emergence. Despite being aware that rationalism in *no way* follows a *parallel developmental line* in all areas of life, Weber (2009a, p. 87) believes that modern rational capitalism is realized within *a series of rationalizing parallel improvements*. The primary events in this process are the disassociation of the home and work place, and the completion of the capital accounting system. As

---

15   Soon after its publication, Weber's *Protestant Ethic* fired a heated debate. These discussions, in which Weber gave responses, developed around the claim that his thesis could be easily rejected based on clearly opposing empirical data. The criticisms directed can be categorized under four basic headings: (1) Weber's interpretation of Calvinism is incorrect; (2) the religious texts that are referred to are not representative; (3) businessmen behaved in a capitalist manner long before the Reformation; and (4) the assumed relationship between Protestantism and capitalist development is not effective in Scotland, Hungary, or the Netherlands for a number of reasons. The most important of these criticisms, perhaps, is the one regarding Weber's selection of texts. More specifically, it is claimed that he only selected texts that would confirm his theses and ignored the others. Another criticism comes generally from historians who considered Weber to be an idealist in a manner similar to Hegel. According to them, Weber attributed the emergence of capitalism only to religious ideas and ruled out the significance of materialist factors. One more criticism directed at Weber is that a couple of works he selected, *Baxter's Christian Directory* (1673) and *Franklin's Advice to a Young Tradesman* (1748), belong to a period that was too early to indicate the influence of Protestantism. There is an inexplicable time-span of almost a century. Among these criticisms, Weber responded only to those of Karl Fischer and Felix Rachfahl. For criticisms aimed at Weber and his responses, see Weber, 2001.

While Weber reviewed his text in 1920, he included his responses to the criticisms, as well as amendments to a couple of points. However, the debate around his thesis continued even after his death. Ephraim Fischoff (1944) emphasizes how current the subject still is when giving the date of the discussions.

16   In his account of the opposite to the spirit of capitalism in *Protestant Ethic*, Weber directly refers to examples from Oriental societies (Weber, 2009a, pp. 74–75).

a result, rational accounting and bookkeeping system, which developed alongside the company structures, were formed. What followed this was the emergence of the rational entrepreneur type, which completed this entire process. In parallel to these developments, modern industry was established on the foundations of ancient craftsmanship, and free labor emerged. These developments were combined as a whole in the modern state system, which was formed with the development of the modern formal legal system and administration, thus constituting the rational capitalist system.

According to Weber, the disassociation of the home and work place was a major point in the development of business partnerships and the emergence of the modern rational business structure. This not only covers a spatial disassociation, but also a disassociation in terms of management and accounting,[17] and, hence, operational capital and personal wealth. Such separations include aspects relating to business and the entrepreneur to the same degree that they do relating to the political and legal systems. The development of the Law of Bankruptcy and Law of Obligations in Europe, which declared that no compensation shall be given to businesses for loss of personal wealth, and the formation of the formal management of modern bureaucracy respectively constituted the foundations of this divorce (Weber, 1978, pp. 379–380). Thus, modern business gained its legal status, and, from Weber's view (2009a, p. 212), the modern rational organization of the capitalist industrial company could not have emerged without the establishment of this disassociation. According to Weber, all these developments are specific to the West, and exist in other places only in the form of an undeveloped seed. There are no business partnerships in Oriental societies. In Islamic cities in particular, the spatial disassociation of home and work is insufficient as the legal system and laws also necessary have not emerged to ensure capitalism's complete fruition.[18]

For Weber (2009a, pp. 212–213), although it is possible to come across homes that are separate from the business in the ancient world or the Orient, the disassociation of personal welfare and business capital within an accounting system is specific only to the modern West. The development of calculability provided the most important technical tool of capitalism, and the discovery of the *double-entry accounting system* is a major development in this respect.[19] According to Weber (2009b, p. 209), in spite of the rationalization of capital bookkeeping to a moderate level in all world civilizations, a rational profit–loss calculation and capital accounting was unique to the modern West. This is because the aforementioned terms necessary to achieve a fully developed capitalist

---

17 The history of commercial corporations in Europe was Weber's first academic area of study. In his doctoral thesis entitled, he (2003b) studies the emergence of business partnerships in late Middle Age Italy.

18 For a discussion about this in contemporary Turkish business life, see Sunar, 2012.

19 For his account of the fundamental conditions necessary for capital accounting in production enterprises to reach the most advanced degree of formal rationalism, see Weber, 1978, pp. 161–162.

business and rational accounting system never emerged in Oriental societies. Weber believes that a calculation-based system cannot survive in a patrimonial society where everything is determined by politics.[20]

Thus, Weber believes that the modern business formed within the scope of a rational accounting system shaped both modern economic accumulation and the structure of capital. He writes, "[w]herever capitalist acquisition is rationally pursued, action is oriented to *calculation* in terms of capital" (Weber, 2009b, p. 209). In this respect, Weber distinguishes modern capital from primeval accumulation. According to him, while "a 'capitalist' economic act involves first of all an expectation of profit based on the utilization of opportunities for *exchange*; that is, of (formally) *peaceful* opportunities for acquisition," primeval accumulation acts "through violence" and "follows its own special laws" (Weber, 2009b, p. 208). In light of the disassociation noted above, Weber states that only a primeval accumulation based on tyranny or politics is possible in Oriental societies, and that modern capital can only occur in the West with its antecedents.

Weber believes that another factor determining modern capitalism is the emergence of free labor. According to him, as the foundations of rational capitalism were created side by side within adventure capitalism, they were also legitimately laid by the rational–capitalist organization of free labor (Weber, 2003a, pp. 312–313). The free trading of labor as though it were a commodity is compulsory for the completion of rationalization and calculation. The grounds of such a legitimate relationship between labor and investor emerged only during the modern era in Europe. In ancient and mediaeval times, only some degree of labor's rational organization could be attained in the West. And "[o]utside the West, free labor has been found only occasionally" (Weber, 2009b, p. 211).

Weber adds the advancement of craftsmanship to the list of factors which contributed to the special development of the city in the West. Similarly, he adds the emergence of modern industry from this foundation to the conditions constitutive of modern capitalism. In this context, "the possession of the work place, tools, and raw materials by a single owner" for the picture of a modern factory can only be drawn in relation to the realization of capital accumulation which is "the first stage of capitalism" (Weber, 2003a, p. 167). Neither capital accumulation nor the emergence of the aforementioned free labor was possible anywhere else. The transformation of workshop productions into the modern factory was prevented by the exclusion inherent in India's caste system, and the clan economy of China (Weber, 2003a, p. 176). In the West, however, the factory emerged in relation to the organization of craftsmanship (Weber, 2003a, pp. 158–159).

---

20 Later studies have revealed that many of the factors which Weber confidently claims had emerged in the West primarily existed previously in the Orient, and were taken and used from the Orient. One of these is business partnerships based upon a legal and administrative outline. In this sense, Çizakça (1996) draws an excellent picture of business partnerships (*mudaraba*) in Islamic societies.

In Weber's view (2003a, p. 333), the formation of a democratic demand mechanism and mass market is vital for the development of industry in this way. The court and social circle around it, which was the home of craftsmanship in the Orient (through India, China, Egypt and Mesopotamia), as well as the luxurious consumption of the bureaucrats and tenants, not only prevented the development of industry but also failed to encourage it (Weber, 2003a, p. 310,126). A class of independent craftsman did not emerge in the Orient since production functioned under the supervision of the state. Hence, the transition from craftsmanship to industry did not take place. Another factor lies in the significance that the distinction between quantity and quality had in Oriental craftsmanship. Often the quality of an item was determined by the specific orders of the customer (Weber, 1988, p. 200). Such differences as these also prevented the foundations being laid for the emergence of capitalist mass production in the Orient.

Weber states that another condition for the development of modern capitalism was the monetary economy. The development of a monetary economy during the modern era supported the development of the rational accounting and bookkeeping techniques required by capitalism. In this context, the invention of banknotes, the most perfect and subtle tool of exchange, and its transformation into a single value medium through the elimination of all other varieties of money, was a major development in the improvement of the monetary economy. Accordingly, the foundations of a monetary economy existed only in the West (Weber, 1978, p. 113), and Oriental societies, despite the discovery of money and partial monetarization in the economy,[21] failed to transform from a natural economy to monetary one (Weber, 1988, pp. 310, 46, 105).[22]

All these developments, according to Weber, are related to the development of the modern state as a result of the emergence of rational bureaucracy and predictable law. There are many reasons for the emergence of a rational formal law, however amongst these the demand of the bourgeoisie for self-assurance is crucial. The formation of a predictable legal system, which is essential for the development of capitalism, is only possible through the implementation of written laws in individual cases, and independent and impartial executive adjudicators. According to Weber, such developments took place upon Roman and Canonic legal foundations during the development of the city and the security of property and freedom, both which were vital for the bourgeoisie. However, as will be discussed later, Weber claims that there was no such demand for development outside the West. Alongside the progression of Western law stands the development of rational bureaucracy as another entity that was shaped by the

---

21   For Weber's analyses regarding the formation of a partial monetary economy in Egypt see Weber, 1988, pp. 125–129; in relation to India see Weber, 1967a, pp. 78–79; in relation to Ancient Greece see Weber, 1988, p. 163.

22   Weber (1968, p. 53) attempts to prove this conclusion with his thesis on the Orient's taxation and payment system, taxes-in-kind and payments-in-kind, which has been repeated by all Western political economists since Smith.

exclusive demands that emerged in the West. Nevertheless, the bourgeoisie turned towards ensuring the predictability of administrative operations for self-serving stability. Thus, work needed to be carried out according to certain written rules, and a rational bureaucracy is required, not only for a rational state system, but also for the organization of modern business. Formality in modern business can only be ensured by the technical tools of a rational bureaucracy.

Consequently, there is a close connection between the development of the modern state and capitalism. According to Weber, capitalism is intimately related to the birth of the modern state as the latter had to have the virtue of making the bourgeoisie feel secure. In such a state system, the bourgeoisie were able to gain prior knowledge regarding the results of their actions, and consequently were able to invest comfortably as entrepreneurs. Beyond this, Weber says, the state not only cleared the way for capitalism but also supported it. Similar to the example of England, the support of the state makes it possible for the bourgeoisie to ensure their fundamental accumulation. Nevertheless, in modern Germany, Weber identifies how the state supported the formation of the bourgeoisie with commercial laws. In this context, he claims that the fundamental conditions of capitalism, that is, a professional management and professional civil service, as well as a state system that has a contractual relation with its citizens, existed only in the Western world (Weber, 1978, pp. 1192–1193, 313–314, 338).

As a result, Weber explains the development of capitalism by reference to a series of unique conditions that emerged in Europe under the influence of a capitalist spirit that was inspired by Protestant ethic. The developments of infrastructure that saw the emergence of modern cities and rationalization were finalized with the later development of business and the emergence of rational business techniques. The rationalization reached its climax when it filtered into all areas of life and brought about emergence of modernity. However, none of these developments existed in the Orient, either partially or fully. Consequently, rational capitalism emerged only in the West.

The Differentiation of Political Systems: Rational Authority and Patrimonial Sovereignty

For Weber, the development and nature of bureaucratic systems is one of the most dividing features of Oriental and Western civilizations. He classifies political authorities according to the main impetus they have behind them, and in this context he defines three types of authority. These are the legal, traditional and charismatic authorities based on rational, traditional and charismatic foundations respectively. Weber (1978, pp. 310, 217–218) indicates that the pure type of legal authority is established on ideas like legality, the abstraction of law, the impersonalization of authority, membership-based obedience and the impersonalization of obedience to authority. According to this view, in rational legal authority, certain legal norms, determined either forcibly or in conciliation, compose the basis of the organization of the members. Thus, there is a legal order established by the implementation of abstract legal rules to individual cases. The persons who compose the authority are also part of the impersonal order and their authority continues through this order. Membership-based obedience exists for the service of laws; obedience to authority is not obedience to the person, but to the impersonal order. The conditions of such rational legal authority are the rule-based continuity of the form of official affairs. They are as follows: The existence of a special field of judgment, the hierarchical organization of offices, the existence of technical rules and norms that determine the conditions of the office, the obligation upon all members of the administration to refrain from appropriating the means of production or administration, the necessity that official posts should not be appropriated, the necessity that administrative actions, decisions and rules be formulated and written, and, finally, that officials should have a fixed wage paid in cash according to their hierarchical position (Weber, 1978, pp. 218–219, 310). The organization and operation of the bureaucracy in rational legal authority is an important distinction for Weber since he thinks that these foundations form a distinguishing point of the rational West.

Weber defines three main types of traditional authority that he considers to be opposed to rational legal authority: gerontocracy, patriarchy and patrimonialism. Gerontocracy is the administration of the elder; this is usually seen in religious societies. Patriarchy is the implementation of a group organized administration on the basis of kinship by one person who has been selected according to hereditary rules. Neither of these two has any economic basis. In Patrimonialism, the third type on which Weber focuses the most, the authority first emerges as the right of an elite group, and later transforms into a personal right appropriated by the "master." According to Weber, (1978, p. 232) "in principle," the patrimonial master "can exploit his right like any economic-asset—sell it, pledge it as security, or divide it by inheritance." The most extreme situation of this authority is *sultanism* wherein administration and military power emerge as the personal tools of the master.[23]

In patrimonialism, the main element of bureaucracy is that the relationship between the administrator and the official is based on personal loyalty:

> The person exercising authority is not a "superior," but a personal master, his administrative staff does not consist mainly of officials but of personal retainers, and the ruled are not "members" of an association hut are either his traditional 'comrades' or his 'subjects.' Personal loyalty, not the official's impersonal duty, determines the relations of the administrative staff to the master. (Weber, 1978, pp. 226–227)

In this situation, it is not the task or legitimacy which determines the relationship between the officials and the masters, but personal loyalty. Weber writes that so far as his action follows principles at all, these are governed by considerations of

---

23   For an evaluation of Weber's ideas on sultanism from the viewpoint of the Ottoman system, see Inalcik, 1992.

ethical common sense, of equity or of utilitarian expediency. "They are not formal principles, as in the case of legal authority" (Weber, 1978, p. 227). In the pure type of traditional authority, no fields of skills are clearly defined in compliance with impersonal rules, rational hierarchy, free contract or a regular appointment system based on regular promotion of technical education and fixed wages paid normally in cash, all of which existed in the pure type of rational legal authority (Weber, 1978, pp. 221, 229 and 956–958). In this way, Weber defines traditional authority as that which is not legal (modern rational).

There are two main principles that Weber refers to while separating modern rational bureaucracy from patrimonial bureaucracy: specialization and formalization. According to Weber, in contrast to the ancient *skilled man*, the *specialist* is the type found in modern rational legal bureaucracy. This type has to be educated specifically in order to undertake tasks in particular posts in which the specifications and requirements have been pre-defined. This situation leads to specialization in every field of modern life (Weber, 1978, p. 1002). Here, "the purely bureaucratic type of administrative organization ... is, from a purely technical point of view, capable of attaining the highest degree of efficiency." Thus it is, "in this sense formally the most rational known means of exercising authority over human beings" and "superior to any other form" (Weber, 1978, p. 223). Another principle is formalization. In modern rational bureaucracy, unlike patrimonial bureaucracy, officials are subject to impersonal formal relations. Decisions are not taken *ad hoc* by administrators, but are taken or amended within the framework of predetermined rules (Weber, 1978, pp. 1029, 1030–1031). The factors that raised the strictly bureaucratic administration to the optimum point are "precision, speed, unambiguity, knowledge of the files, continuity, discretion, unity, strict subordination, reduction of friction and of material and personal costs. ... As compared with all collegiate, honorific, and vocational forms of administration, trained bureaucracy is superior on all these points" (Weber, 1978, p. 973).

According to him "the spirit of bureaucratic work differed widely in the East and in the West" (Weber, 1968, p. 50). Likewise, even though its pioneers had emerged outside the West, the stratum of specialized *civil servants*, which is the cornerstone of the modern state and modern economy, emerged only in the West, whereas the precursors outside the West were not determinative for the social order. Hence, "No nation and no epoch has come to know state civil servants in the way that they are known in the modern West, namely as persons trained in technical, commercial, and, above all, legal areas of knowledge who are the social carriers of the most important everyday function of social life" (Weber, 2009b, p. 207). For, "the "state," in fact, as a political institution (*Ansalt*) operated according to a rationally enacted "constitution" and rationally enacted laws, and administered by civil servants possessing *specialized* arenas of competence and oriented to rules and "laws," has existed with these distinguishing features in the West..." (Weber, 2009b, pp. 207–208, see also Weber, 2003, p. 338)

Establishing a close and direct connection between traditional sovereignty and economic traditionalism (Weber, 1978, p. 237), Weber (1978, p. 998) also sets up a connection between capitalism and rational legal authority and bureaucracy (Weber, 2003a, p. 339), while at the same time maintaining that there is an inverse correlation between patrimonial centralism and the conditions of capitalism (Weber, 1968, p. 84). The more centralism increases the more the conditions for capitalism weaken. For this reason, the applications in a patrimonial system, for example, coerced labor, corvée, taxes-in-kind and fiefs, prevented the development of modern capitalism (Weber, 1978, p. 199). The most significant drive behind modern capitalism is that it requires a fast, controllable, continuing public administration. Thus, not only the state administration but all fields of life were bureaucratized (Weber, 1978, p. 974).

The Development of Patrimonial Bureaucracy and Its Character

Patrimonial bureaucracy, which Weber identifies as irrational as it does not include a division of labor based on professional specialization or skill, owes its existence to the fact that the rational elements in administration have not emerged. In this context, due to geographical and historical conditions, patrimonial bureaucracy, which was the only way to establish and maintain an empire in the Orient (Weber, 1968, p. 271 endnote 1, 1988, pp. 84, 97, 106, 157), is one of main characteristics of Oriental societies (Weber, 1978, p. 371).[24]

According to Weber, in Oriental civilization the need for the organization of large-scale public affairs engendered patrimonial bureaucracy, which prevented the formation of a rational administration. Weber (1978, pp. 971–972) thinks that water-side administration and the distribution of water in the Orient determined the functioning of the state. In Egypt, the oldest model of bureaucratic state administration, bureaucratization was a technical necessity to ensure the public regulation of the hydraulic economy. Carrying out agriculture in the lands along the narrow coastline of Nile, was possible only by calculating the annual flooding and taking measures to make the movement of flood waters predictable and controllable. The need of constructing systems for evaluating, channeling, orienting and distributing the water of the Nile necessitated an administrative structure that would organize these affairs from a center (Weber, 1988, p. 107). However, facing few invasion threats due to its geographical position, the bureaucracy in Egypt was mainly composed of officials related to the Pharaoh's court (Weber, 1978, pp. 967, 1044). As a consequence of this, clerks and officials emerged and the military was activated in order to organize large-scale public affairs (Weber, 1978, pp. 971–972). According to Weber (1988, p. 84), Sumerian, Acadian and Assyrian scriptures from the north, that is, the most ancient centers of civilization, have taught us that the channel and irrigation systems formed the basis of bureaucracy in Mesopotamia as well. In order to construct and maintain channels and trenches in these places, forced labor in various forms was enforced upon the population and carried out at the discretion of the imperial guardians.

---

24 For the emergence and functions of the state in Orient, see Coşkun, 1991, pp. 79–80.

Another area in which patrimonial bureaucracy reached a high level was China, although essentially of a different type. Weber (1968, p. 20) thinks that more than irrigation, China needed the construction of channels for preventing floods and transportation purposes in addition to the construction of roads and ramparts for defense.[25] Again here, the power of patrimonial officials depended on the development of a central bureaucracy for the implementation of large-scale public works (Weber, 1978, p. 1047). The case of India is more similar to Mesopotamia than China. "In India, as in the Orient generally, a characteristic seigniory developed rather out of tax farming and the military and tax prebends of a far more bureaucratic state" [26] (Weber, 1967a, p. 71). In ancient Israel, even though a patrimonial bureaucracy developed under the administration of King Solomon, the arrival of prophets supported by ancient, powerful families believing in Jehovah and as well as a decline in the standing of the peasantry eliminated this bureaucracy.[27]

According to Weber, in Egypt, China, Mesopotamia and India, where a *hydraulic* bureaucracy developed, the organization of corvée for public service was a bureaucratic function (Weber, 1967a, p. 107, 1978, p. 198, 1988, p. 118). In these places, where agricultural activities ceased for long periods of time, the systematically centralized regulation of rivers and large-scale construction projects required the introduction of corvée (Weber, 1978, p. 1045). While in Egypt and the Near East, the personal affairs of the sovereign such as the construction of palaces, temples and monumental works, could require coerced labor;[28] in China such labor was sustained in an integrated way with the tax system (Weber, 1968, pp. 52–53). In Egypt, the general rule in the functioning of forced labor was that all the land-owners and craftsmen were obliged to pay some taxes, with the peasants having to pay land taxes and craftsmen for license tax and a percentage of their products. Those who did not fulfill these obligations would have themselves and their families liable to pay via *debt slavery* to the Pharaoh and would work for him under the surveillance of bureaucrats. However, in contrast, "all who owed payments to the state were just as dependent as simple workers" (Weber, 1988, pp. 117, 127–128). Weber once again emphasizes the general

---

25 The word *chich*, which means "governing" in Chinese, denotes the *regulation of waters* in ancient terminology and the concept *fa*, which means law, means *distribution of waters* (Weber, 1968, p. 16). For the development of a bureaucratic system based upon irrigation in China, see Weber, 1968, p. 51.

26 Weber is aware that irrigation is not prevalent across all of India but only in some parts. For instance, he mentions an agricultural and political system based on irrigation in Ceylon, but nothing for southern India. However, Weber (1967a, p. 242) generalizes the political administrative form (patrimonialism) and the social structure which he thinks emerged due to irrigation.

27 For the relationship between the patrimonial kingdom and bureaucracy in Ancient Israel, see Weber, 1967b, p. 117.

28 Because in patrimonial administration almost all the country is seen as a household of the king (Weber, 1978, p. 1047).

slavery in the Orient and indicates that all were the subjects of the patrimonial ruler (Weber, 2003a, p. 57).

Weber (1978, p. 1055) indicates that the establishment of new cities in the Orient, considered to be one of the ways in which the ruler can increase his income,[29] were built at the will of the sovereign through this widespread public service and corvée. These cities, where the sovereign and his subordinates lived, were established on forced labor and tax-in-kind. The bureaucratic character of the city—as will be dealt with below—determines the general operation of the military and political structures. The Oriental city is established by the bureaucracy and this fact determines its character; here neither an independent civic stratum nor a guild of craftsmen emerges. Thus, the character of the Oriental city is the subject of the imperial bureaucratic ramifications (Weber, 1968, p. 16).

Weber thinks that one of the main issues of patrimonial sovereignty is the continuity of legitimacy. In the patrimonial state, which is characteristically inclined to prosperity, the legitimacy of the sovereign is dependent on the continuity of the people's wellbeing (Weber, 1978, p. 240, 1988, p. 121). Explaining the relationship between political legitimacy and religion,[30] Weber indicates that situations like famine and invasion led to general discontent because of their adverse effects upon the people's welfare (Weber, 1967a, p. 18). For instance, the emperor in China required great charisma, for example, via achieving military successes or, at least, by avoiding great failures in order to maintain his administration. In this way, the emperor had to maintain a relatively high level of general happiness and domestic order in the country to sustain effective governance. If this order was subverted and an abundant harvest was not obtained, it was thought that the emperor failed to realize the heavens' expectations and thus, the legitimacy of his rule ceased to exist (Weber, 1967a, p. 31). For this reason, in China there was a close connection between rational government and salvation by the world of spirits (Weber, 1968, p. 110).

Against such a loss of legitimacy, emergency storage depots are provided and maintained by the patrimonial sovereigns to maintain central public affairs efficiently, ensure defense against foreign invasions and to be used during times of famine (Weber, 1988, p. 121). Weber states that for this reason an overall change in Oriental society depends on external factors like climate change, which can cause famine and invasion, but there is no possibility for the society to change from

---

29   According to Weber, since the crucial element in the usage of land in the Orient was irrigation, every new settlement required the construction of new canals. This task, which required a large-scale collective social organization, was relatively different from the clearing of untouched forests in the West (Weber, 1988, p. 84, 2003a, p. 57).

30   In the patrimonial system, the king was perceived as the god who provided the crops, thus engendering the system of God-King. In Egypt the Pharaoh, and in China the son of the Sun, were the most well-known examples of this. Contrarily, in a system in which the king was only a political administrator, an omnipotent monotheism and tradition of Hebrew prophets emerged (Weber, 1968, pp. 21–22).

within. If a revolution takes place, which would be caused by the aforementioned external factors or out of the general stagnancy stemming from the bureaucracy and its religious bases of that legitimacy, the change would not be a change of the order but a change of sovereign (Weber, 1978, p. 227). For this reason, foreign invasions in the Orient (at least in China, Egypt and India) were considered to be *legitimate* if they were in compliance with the required rituals of the administration (Weber, 1968, p. 40).[31]

According to Weber (1978, p. 964), there is a close relationship between bureaucratization within patrimonial states and the non-monetarization of the economy. In a natural economy in which the patrimonial bureaucracy maintains its existence, the taxes are collected in-kind as the wages are also paid in kind. Accordingly, the administrative stratum attains surplus product in return for the organization of public affairs and public safety; it gathers the tax-in-kind in warehouses and wherefrom the subordinates of the sovereign also benefit. In this way, a personal connection between the officials and the sovereign emerges. What was in the beginning a household system of the sovereign over time transformed into the establishment of a land-grant system. Here the sovereign allocates certain lands and incomes in return for duties. With the emergence of this system, the character of land property, agriculture and military in the Orient gained a central character. According to Weber, over time the formation of this system brought about some significant contrasts between the Oriental patrimonial state and the European feudalism of the Middle Ages. Weber basically dealt with these contrasts by comparing the feudal fief system and the prebendal benefice system.

The Differences between Feudalism and Prebendalism

Indicating that feudalism is not unique to Mediaeval Europe (Weber, 1988, p. 38), Weber separates two types of feudalism based on manor (fief) and benefices (*timar*). In this context, he generally refers to the first as feudalism and the latter as prebendalism.[32] Weber describes fief feudalism as an ideal type wherein no land granted in return for a certain service (usually military) (Weber, 1978, p. 255).[33] It emerged in the West as a consequence of a series of historical developments related to each other after Rome (Weber, 2003a, pp. 51–56). As an outcome of these developments, lords who had gained power "composed of three elements,

---

31 The issue of administration in India and Egypt by foreigners is an issue that has always been kept alive in order to legitimatize colonialism.

32 Actually, Weber differentiates between prebendalism and feudalism, land tenure and fief in terms of their definitions and outcomes. Weber indicates that in some places land tenure in the West existed and feudalism existed in the Orient. However, they differed greatly from one another in terms of their features and functioning within the general system with consequently varying outcomes. (Weber, 1968, p. 58)

33 In another place Feudalism is defined as "estate-type patrimonialism, a marginal case that contrasts with patriarchal patrimonialism" (Weber, 1978, p. 1086).

first, land holding (territorial power) second, appropriation of men (slavery) and third, appropriation of political rights, through usurpation or through enfeoffment." When the lords seized more lands, it would more often become available to agriculture than the weaker members of society, and so the latter survived by becoming subordinated serfs (Weber, 2003a, p. 65).[34] Oriental prebendalism, however, emerged more on the basis of tax collection. Land grants entailed no permanent individual rights, and were rather recognized as an extension of the military administration (Weber, 2003a, pp. 59–60, 62–63).[35] According to Weber, even though there were some tendencies towards fief feudalism, the latter's ideal type could never emerge and prebendalism was always dominant.

In China prebendalism was never fully implemented. The occasional move[36] towards "the emergence of feudal status and thus the emancipation of officials from central authority was prevented under Chinese patrimonialism by world-famous and highly efficient means" (Weber, 1968, p. 50). The most influential of these means were the amelioration of the examination system and the implementation of the assignment of civil service posts according to education, rather than affinity or class. Even though these systems gave birth to a permanent struggle between the educated and feudal nobles, with every tax and administrative system, the power of the educated in the form of imperial authority was re-established. In this way, "typical Oriental patrimonialism" was repeatedly re-founded (Weber, 1968, pp. 44–45).[37]

In Japanese feudalism, which is the most developed example of Oriental feudalism, the transfer of the benefice via inheritance was made possible. However, an autonomous feudal lord did not emerge as in the West (Weber, 1978, p. 1075). In Russia, where the manors were allocated by the tsar in return for certain service and tax obligations, the feudal system is closer to that of the European system (Weber, 2003a, pp. 62–63). Nevertheless, Weber thinks that in all these examples, prebendalism remains more dominant than fief feudalism, and it was in

---

34   There is in particular an important role for agricultural and military techniques here. Yet, the discontinuity of slave agriculture in the West after the collapse of the Roman Empire is also significant. Weber discusses this issue in detail in his *habilitation* (Weber, 2008).

35   Weber states that there were three types of *timar* (*benefice*) that developed: *benefices in kind* (*Deputatpfründe*), *fee benefice* (*Sportelpfründe*), *landed benefice* (*Amts-oder Dienstland*) (Weber, 1978, p. 1032).

36   For the tendencies toward feudalization in China and the distribution of land see Weber, 1968, pp. 73–74.

37   After the age of belligerent states, with the political union provided by Pren Ch and the elimination of feudalism in 221 political centralism and a skill-based educated class emerged, as did bureaucratization of the state (Weber, 1968, pp. 42–43). To compare this with the feudal noble class in the West see Weber, 1968, p. 44.

such a manner that *Standestaat*, which he deems the most developed form of fief feudalism, developed in Europe (Weber, 1978, p. 1087).[38]

Attributing the emergence of fief feudalism in the West to specific conditions related to the collapse of the Roman Empire, Weber ascribes the emergence of Oriental prebendalism to the particular position of the patrimonial bureaucracy.[39] The allocation of land grants to patrimonial servants composes the foundations of this system, though "[o]riginally the patrimonial officials are typically maintained at the ruler's table and from his supplies, as is every other household member" (Weber, 1978, pp. 1031). At earlier times the *timar* were received in-kind from the administrator's grain warehouses and stocks on the condition of being *registered for lifetime* in Egypt, Assyria and China. However, later this was transformed into a system based on the allocation of certain lands with financial foundations (Weber, 1978, pp. 1031–1032). Weber explains the bias of the patrimonial state to the *timar* system as the transfer of a variable income risk to the entrepreneur in a tax-like form of agriculture. In this way, the needs of the patrimonial administration are guaranteed. Through this system the patrimonial state ensured the procurement of warriors and arms by providing the government with power to be used to a certain extent and for a certain span of time. This helped meet the costs of civil administration and guaranteed the tax payments made to the budget (Weber, 1978, pp. 259–261). Thus prebendalism has significant functions in sustaining the principles on which the patrimonial administration is established and provides for the continuity of the state (Weber, 1967a, p. 71).

In this context, the fact that feudalism and prebendalism emerged historically from different backgrounds transformed them into the main factors of two opposing political structures. The main issue that forms many differences between the Orient and Occident is the foundations of fiefdom and *timar* as well as the ways they were obtained and their outcomes. According to Weber (1968, p. 35), the fief system, which was founded on hereditary rights, granted certain autonomy to the feudal lord. On the other hand, in the *timar* system, the land grants do not have a hereditary character but are in repayment for certain services or taxes. Thus, the lord has no power vis-à-vis the sovereign, and thus, the patrimonial government sustains its existence with an abundance of power (Weber, 1978, pp. 235–236, 1073–1074). The patrimonial sovereign was able to change officials as he desired due to his military power (Weber, 1978, p. 1028), and since there were no hereditary rights on the *timar*, there was no autonomous power to prevent this. On the contrary, the free vassal who did not obey any patrimonial sovereign would be subject to a code of honor and duty. In the most advanced form of relationship under feudal administration, the most opposite elements are combined, such as a strict personal loyalty and a contractual commitment of tasks and rights, or depersonalization of

---

38   For transformation of manors into *timar* in Near East, see Weber, 1988, pp. 76, 93–94.

39   For the differences in usage and distribution of land in Mesopotamia and Rome in a comparative manner, see Weber, 1988, p. 97.

rights and duties by virtue of rental agreement and the final hereditary control over property (Weber, 1978, pp. 1073–1074). Thus, manorial economy, which limited the powers of the sovereign in the West, emerged (Weber, 1968, p. 65).

According to Weber, both feudalism and patrimonialism had negative influences on the development of capitalism. Traditionalism and tyranny, two factors of these two systems, and the ones that caused stagnancy in the economy, seriously influenced the ability of capitalist development due to the fact that these two factors caused unpredictability and instability. However, according to Weber, there is a significant differentiation between the economic consequences of prebendalism and feudalism. In feudalism, the existence of different economic actors and the decentralization of the economic systems are more inclined to engender conflicting interests and thus economic rationalism (Weber, 1978, p. 1091). Contrary to this, tax-in-kind and wage-in-kind, some of the main characteristics of the Oriental natural economy upon which prebendalism is based, creates economic stagnation (Weber, 1978, p. 101).[40] The reason for this halt is the lack of production for the market within the framework of this natural economy and no commercial life formed within the framework of this production.

The division between the autonomous and powerful feudal lord as opposed to the sovereign and the dependency of the feudal subject to the sovereign manifests itself within military systems. According to Weber, the most important factor determining whether a military is patrimonial or not is to what extent it is composed of the personal forces of the sovereign. In the cases where the sovereign is most patrimonial, the military is sustained directly thorough the sovereign's income and resources. The more this rule is maintained the more the power of the sovereign increases (Weber, 1988, p. 90). In prebendalism, which is the extended version of this system, fostering, training and equipping a certain number of soldiers is demanded in return for a certain amount of land (Weber, 1978, pp. 1015–1020). The vassals who tend these military lands and fulfill their individual services cannot convey or bequeath the lands that they obtain in return for service (Weber, 1988, p. 89). The opposite of this system is found with the feudal military forces in the West who equipped themselves and professionally used weapons (Weber, 1978, p. 1078). The fact that the feudal lords obtained their own arms and that they possessed permanent propriety rights on their land gave them autonomy. As these feudal lords, who had their own individual independent forces, united and attained some concessions from the patrimonial patron, the democratic structure of the Western administration began to form (Weber, 1978, p. 1086).

Weber considers feudalism to be a significant progressive dynamic, as it possesses an autonomous and competitive character that can oust the patrimonial sovereign through the unity of lords against the king. For Weber, while there is centralization of power due to the official limitation of Oriental prebendalism

---

40   For payment-in-kind and tax-in-kind in Oriental economies, see Weber, 1978, p. 124. However, contrary to his principle observations, Weber indicates that in another place specifically in Greece, payment-in-kind existed as well (Weber, 1988, p. 203).

over the autonomy of the noble, in feudalism chivalry possesses a remarkable hierarchical organization. While in feudalism the knights enforce the king to accept that he is only one among equals when among the lords; in prebendalism the knights aspire to transform their land tenure into permanent feudal rights and create their own peripheral sub-empires and small kingdoms and, thus, continue to obey a patrimonial patron (Turner, 1981, p. 286). In feudal Europe, the cavalry was the militarily superior force, while in the Orient the military was dependent on the infantry (Weber, 1967a, p. 71). The technique of knightly combat apparently led to an individualist social order in the Homeric Hellas and the Occidental Middle Ages (Weber, 1968, pp. 24–25). In this way, the existence of a power which provided its own arms and training formed the boundaries of patrimonial absolutism.[41]

In conclusion, by separating the patrimonial bureaucracy in the Orient from the historical conditions where rational bureaucracy developed, Weber attempts to demonstrate the unique nature of the Western political system. Trying to explain the differences in the development of the patrimonial system in the Orient from that of the feudal system in the West in historical terms, he depicts the foundations of the distinct nature of developmental history in the West. Weber tends to explain the reason why a Western formal, rationalized and specialized bureaucracy did not emerge in the Orient via geographical and historical conditions, which he takes to have engendered patrimonial authority. Separating feudalism and prebendalism from one another in detail, Weber then highlights rational representation, which together with a parliament founded on this historical background, is unique to the West: "Even in the Middle Ages the seeds of these phenomena were present in the Western World, and only there. It is only in the Western World that "cities" and "estates" (rex et regnum) "bourgeois" and "proletarians" have existed." (Weber, 1978, p. 298)

---

41   The distinction which Weber formed on the basis of providing arms and military power emerges most clearly in his analysis of Ancient Israel. With the commencement of patrimonial bureaucracy under the administration of Solomon, the military based on the chariot emerged leading the free peasant chevaliers to lose their power and assured absolute sovereignty of patrimonialism (Weber, 1967b, pp. 101–102).

Chapter 11
Disengagements: Basic Elements of Weber's Study on Oriental Societies

In his famous *Prefatory Remarks* (known as *Author's Introduction* or *Vorbemerkung*) Weber draws a unique depiction of Western civilization. In this highly effective text Weber lists many areas that Occidental civilization disengages from the Orient. After creating a divergent Orient and Occident on the basis of religion, politics and economics, Weber tries to show the different development of societies. As a scholar believing in the uniqueness of the Western modernity he is seeking to show its distinguishing character in every field of life. Among those fields he gives a special place to the cities, law and art. Weber gives a central place to the Western cities in the development of capitalism. Then, he discusses the importance of law in the development of a rational capitalism in those cities. By labeling the Oriental law as *qadi* justice, he creates a clear-cut differentiation between the Orient and Occident. Finally, he examines the development of Western music in a comparative way. With this examination he completes his perfect comparison chart and covers all fields. In the following paragraphs I will discuss cities, law and music respectively.

The Western City as a Location for Capitalism and the City in Oriental Societies

The city for Weber is an important theme for differentiating between the Orient and the West. Weber, mentions the city in particular in the final chapter of *Economy and Society* (*The City*) and in other works. He differentiates the Orient from the West by emphasizing the relative underdevelopment of the city in the Orient.[1] Thus, he interprets the appearance of cities in the West as a characteristic that demonstrates its superiority.

Weber approaches the distinction of the city on the basis of patrimonialism and rationalism. Taking the city as the location for the formation of rational capitalism, he places a special emphasis on the appearance of the bourgeoisie and a social structure unique to Western societies. He brings the special place of the bourgeoisie in the city to the fore, making a connection between the construction of a contractual society and the development of the city. In the context of this kind

---

1 Engin Isin (2003, p. 324) states that Orientalists used the Oriental city for demonstrating the peculiarity of Western cities.

of participatory characteristics found in relation to the Western city are determined in subsections, such as guilds, citizenship and political autonomy.

According to Weber, the reason why the true city appeared not in Asia but in the Mediterranean basin is that the organization of water distribution is at the center of life in the Orient, which creates patrimonial bureaucracies. Patrimonial rulers organize major bureaucracies as the bases of their power, establishing massive armies to maintain it. Accordingly, as the cities are under the control of the patrimonial bureaucracy, no *city* communities that are independent from the royal forces emerge. For this reason, the cities of the Orient were not able to take on the qualities of a real city. According to Weber, the presence of autonomous military units composed of farmers who provide their own arms, knights or *bürger* militants ensured that city dwellers were able to avoid the feudal and legal dependency on non-urban authorities (Weber, 1988, pp. 343–344).

Weber establishes a basis for the Oriental–Occidental comparison of the city and develops explanations about its beginning to demonstrate the unique nature of Europe. For the purposes of this comparison, the two early examples of Ancient Greece and Israel have great importance. Weber is aware that the first cities were established in the Near East, but working around the description of the city above, he proposes that the development of the ideal type of a city was first accomplished in Greece. The establishment of the city in Greece seems to be connected with the arrival of cultural elements from the Near East via the participation of coastal areas in overseas trading. But according to Weber, the appearance of a city that converted cultural elements into a communal life, which had its own power and ruled itself, is an honor that should be accorded to Greece. Similarly, the cities of Israel differ from other patrimonial societies (Weber, 1967b, p. 43). Open to trade and financial development, the Palestinian land has been interspersed with cities from the beginning. However, even though a monetary economy was developed in ancient Israel, a patrimonial bureaucracy that condemned the city to the vice of bureaucracy did not develop (Weber, 1988, p. 146). In addition to these explanations, Weber (1978, pp. 472, 481) emphasizes the urban character of early Christianity. According to him rising in urbanized Palestine, Christianity has been the religion of the urban and artisans since the beginning. It is a religion that is associated with the urban middle class, and the upper and lower classes. Owing to the ethical elements of Christianity, it was easier to create a basis for a rational economical life. Yet, when compared to villagers, urban petit bourgeoisie (artisans and traders) are less connected to nature and more inclined to rationalism. For this reason, it was easier for them to detach themselves from mysticism and the irrational powers of the nature (Weber, 1978, pp. 481–483).

Foundation and Development of Cities

In this context Weber states that, "[e]verywhere outside the West the development of the city was prevented by the fact that the army of the prince is older than the city" (Weber, 2003a, p. 320). He thought that in the Orient cities were established mandatorily for the rulers to raise their income by opening new areas to farming and irrigation under the custody of patrimonial armies. Besides, patrimonial governments established cities as a special way of creating a new regional executive tool (Weber, 1978, p. 1055).[2] For these reasons, the city had always been under the control of central bureaucracy, and their prosperity depended on that of their patrimonial governments.[3] When the government changed, the patrimonial rules changed, and thus, so did the cities. (Weber, 1968, p. 16). In contrast to this, the European city from an earlier date was transformed into collocations that had advanced prerogatives and stable rights. Cities in the West appeared independently from the ruler's palace and the ruler's prerogatives (Weber, 1978, p. 1214). The master of the city had no technical bureaucratic tools to rule it, and thus, over time, cities managed to create a military unit which could successfully close their gates to an army (Weber, 1968, p. 16). Weber (1978, p. 1285) considers that the geographical characteristics of the ancient cities were important for this development in the West.[4] In contrast to the territorial cities of the Orient, "The polis of Antiquity originated as an overseas trading city" (Weber, 1968, p. 15, see also 1988, pp. 64–65),[5] being a coastal city from the beginning.

Weber is of the opinion that the dilemma and tensions that existed around the garrison and the castle had a vital role in the history of the cities. Here, Weber holds that the cities are castle cities in the Orient, while in the West the majority are based on market. According to him although in some periods, market dominant cities appeared in the Orient, these were under patrimonial dominance (Weber, 1967a, p. 87). In this sense, the *polis* of the West is not only a political, but also an economical center, a market; it is for this reason that other laws were legislated at such early times to arrange trade and the basic prerogatives applied to the city (Weber, 1988, p. 163). Ultimately, "[t]he Oriental city was not a "polis" in the sense of Antiquity, and it knew nothing of the "city law" of the Middle Ages, for it was not a "commune" with political privileges of its own" (Weber, 1968, pp. 13–14).

---

2   While portraying the Pharaohs, Weber states that they built cities (Weber, 1967b, p. 18). Besides, while explaining the exile of Israelites to Babel, he states that they worked in the desert to make channels for building new cities, then that they were forced to live there (Weber, 1967b, p. 346).

3   In this context, for the evaluation on the Arabic coastal cities at the time of the prophet Muhammad, see Weber, 1978, p. 1231.

4   Although Weber states that land cities do not mean cities with no foreign trade, he does state that the combination of the terrestrial character of the Oriental city with other factors resulted in the withdrawal of the city (Weber, 1988, p. 339).

5   Like Marx, Weber thinks cities of Antiquity ruralized after the decline of Rome. "In the Roman Empire, the final phase of Antiquity, the centres of culture and population (the latter being of military significance) shifted inland in the West away from the coast." (Weber, 1988, p. 77) The results of these changes over economic and imperial spheres signaled the transition to the Medieval Age.

As opposed to the Western city's commercial and extrovert characteristics, the Oriental cities constituted merely royal headquarters. Although Weber thinks some in India were, at least for a period, in some way reflective of city development to the West, according to him, India consists of villages. The city is a larger village, a combination of these little villages (Weber, 1967a, p. 111). Similarly, the city in China is an organic combination of tribal areas, and there is no relation or interaction between these tribal zones. From this point, Weber (1967a, pp. 15, 91, 93) states that the Orient consists of essentially a village, not a city.

Features of Western Cities and Comparison with Oriental Cities

According to Weber, what differentiates Middle Age cities in the West are (1) the *autonomy* of the city due to its own armed forces, (2) the *autocephaly* of this autonomous city from any authority, (3) the legislation and application of the *city's own legal system*, (4) possession of an autonomous *market rights* and *economic policies*, (5) an independent *taxation* system, (7) and independent *citizenship*. However, the Oriental cities have only a few or none of these aspects (Weber, 1978, p. 1226). Weber relates all these qualities of Western cities to the appearance of the bourgeoisie. Accordingly, the demand of the Western Medieval *bürger* for a kind of political legitimacy based on a contractual system and their insistence on taking active participation within it pressured the traditional lords. As mentioned above, Weber thinks that for the city to have autonomy, it must achieve a communal character and that such cities have only appeared in the West. Oriental cities were not able to establish an independent class or city community like the bourgeoisie. Yet, while there was a substation of blood groups in the organization of guilds in the Western city, in the Orient such kinds of union could not appear since some taboos prevented the *confraternization* of citizens, thus continued tribal organizations:

> [In the Orient] existed no association which could represent the commune of burghers as such. The very concept of an urban burgher and, in particular, a specific status qualification of the burgher was completely lacking. It can be found neither in China nor in Japan or India, and only in abortive beginnings in the Near East. ... In China the city was a fortress and official seat of the imperial agencies; in Japan the "city" in this sense was completely unknown. In India the cities were royal seats or official centers of the royal administration as well as fortresses and market centers.... Neither politically autonomous cities and a burgher stratum of the Occidental type nor a special urban law alongside the royal law can be found in Mesopotamia. ... The Arab cities—Mecca, for instance—were typical clan towns all through the Middle Ages and almost up to the present. (Weber, 1978, pp. 1228–1232, see also 1248)

According to Weber (1978, pp. 1251–1260), in Italy the *coniurationes* (conspiracy unions) took the power of the city lord, while *confraternities* (brotherhoods) in Germany provided the bourgeoisie with political superiority in the cities, allowing them to seize power and declare the city autonomous, establishing their own legal system. The development of autonomous city law meant the disintegration of feudal unions and patrimonialism (Weber, 1978, p. 1254). However, the fact that these cities had their own law destroyed the centralization necessary for the latter. In this sense there is a close relationship between the rationalization of the law subsequent to city independence and the development of capitalism. "[T]he legal institutions adaptable to capitalism had their origin precisely in the urban law systems" (Weber, 1978, p. 1325, see also 2003b). Such a political autonomy for the city and participation of bourgeoisie in the local administration were only seen in the West (Weber, 1978, p. 1228). It is not possible to speak of autonomy in a Chinese city, which from the beginning was a city of the emperor's pavilion or the residence of the governor or other nobles, nor in a ruler's city like Moscow or in Egypt, where the only city is the capital (Weber, 1968, pp. 13–14). Although the religious issues were considered to be autonomous, there was no political autonomy of the city in the bureaucratic city-kingdoms in the Near East such as Assyria, where despotic government was dominant (Weber, 1988, pp. 72–74). In this sense, according to Weber, Oriental cities were under the strict supervision and control of the patrimonial lord who was affiliated with the emperor.

The city creates its own laws due to having its own administrative body through the bourgeois consuls. In order to establish these autonomous bodies, the city needs armed forces to maintain unity and defend its borders. According to Weber, until the Roman era, the main body of the forces, formed either from conscripted villagers and knights or bourgeois unions, continued to equip themselves in the West, where the individual responsible for participating in these forces had *autonomy*. If the sector under the lord's control was to unite against him, the lord would be unable to continue his reign without negotiating with these militarily and economically independent *leaders*. Therefore, the presence of an autonomous city unity and independent bourgeoisie unit with accompanying armed forces formed the basis of the autonomy of the Western city. As for the Orient, the patrimonial bureaucracy held the entire city under its control and it was not possible for the city to maintain its own power (Weber, 1978, pp. 1260–1262).[6]

According to Weber, although cities did not have full independence in the West, they were *independent* from political and religious authority. Having their own law and administrative instruments, European cities could enter into contracts

---

6   Within the context of this relationship established between the development of rationalized law through the autonomy of the city, Weber has difficulty in explaining the case of an exception in England, which was the first place in which capitalism developed. "Under the tight organization of the central administration, the individual English cities had never developed separate and individual political ambitions because they defended their interests in Parliament as a group. They had formed trade cartels, but not political town leagues as on the Continent." (Weber, 1978, p. 1324)

and form alliances. With their own legal system and judicial formats controlled by representatives who had been chosen from among the bourgeoisie, the cities could be independent. The main factor behind this independence was that the lord was economically dependent on the bourgeoisie, and this financial power ensured that the city had rights and protection (Weber, 1978, pp. 1326–1327). Thus, the city avoided the feudal and church ties that had prevented its advancement, and, in time, established its own government.[7]

Such self-government was first seen in the existence of autonomous economic policies and taxation. Being independent, the city was not totally free from the taxation system of external powers, but had autonomous taxation power over its own bourgeoisie (Weber, 1978, p. 1327). Similarly, the city gained the right to organize markets, autonomous trading, and artisan activities as well as establishing an exclusive monopoly. The market was a part of every medieval city and was taken from the hands of the lord by a directorship consul. In later times, the city lord was basically excluded from the organization of trade and production, and such arrangements in the local power structure came under the control of either government authorities or artisan unions. In contrast to this, Oriental cities had no autonomy in economic policy, taxation or regulations for artisanship.

According to Weber, the internal development of a rich and autonomous guild and community life in the city related to being freed from the legal and political interference of patrimonial or feudal civil servants. Beside the coastal cities of Western Antiquity, "inland towns arose which became the seats of craft groups locally specialized and producing for a local market" (Weber, 2003a, p. 146). This allowed the guilds of independent artisans to occupy a special position in the city.[8] However, as mentioned in earlier pages, in the Orient the organization of artisans was fashioned by the government, and the guilds were shaped as bureaucratically dependent structures. In India, however, "[d]uring the period of flowering of the cities" in the West, "the position of the guilds was quite comparable to that occupied by guilds in the cities of mediaeval Occident" (Weber, 1968, pp. 35–36). Yet because of obstacles set by the caste system "these beginnings of guild organization in the cities led neither to the city autonomy of the Occidental type nor, after the development of the great patrimonial states, to a social and economic organization of the territories corresponding to the "territorial economy" of the Occident" (Weber, 1967a, p. 33). Moreover, these independent artisans were the basis for the industrial revolution in the West; the dependence of the artisans in the Orient played a major role in the failure of the industrial revolution to appear.

According to Weber (1978, p. 1331), the inhabitants of the city that armed and trained its own army and was economically self-sufficient, had rights of citizenship within a formal equality. With the formation of a framework that determined procedures for both insiders and outsiders, a city unity shaped around ties of

---

7 For the position of church and clergy in the cities, see Weber, 1978, pp. 1331, 1334.

8 For the functions of guilds in the West, see Weber, 2003a, pp. 140–141; For the functions of guilds in the China, see Weber, 1968, p. 18.

citizenship appeared exclusively in Western cities (Weber, 2003a, pp. 313–314). Oriental cities, on the other hand, did not have martial or religious autonomy, and the individual's right to citizenship was not recognized (Weber, 2003a, p. 316). In the Near East and Ancient Egypt, martial princes had ultimate control over the cities. In China, the educated classes defined the assimilated city. In Japan, where one or several civilian administrative agencies may be found, "a special status of the town dweller as a "citizen," in the ancient and medieval sense, did not exist and a corporate character of the city was unknown" (Weber, 1978, pp. 1227–1228).

As a result, Weber (2003a, pp. 316–317) thinks the city introduced many of its characteristics to the West. The development of independent guilds via independent craftsmanship was the basis for modern industry. As the city developed its own law with the establishment of Canonic law, the basis of modern rational law in the West took shape. Citizenship, political representation, and political organization all played a major role in forming the modern state (Weber, 2003a, p. 316). Above all, the city was the location of capitalism. Many factors in the development of capitalism in the West took root there. Defining the position of the city in the history of Western civilization, Weber notes all these characteristics, comparing them with the Orient. Without this comparison to Oriental cities, it would be almost impossible to demonstrate these qualities in Western cities. And what is more, Weber focuses on the impossibility of the Orient to give birth to the Western type city from out of the bureaucratic structure of patrimonialism and the conditions that established it.

Rational Formal Law versus *Qadi* Justice

In Weber's sociology, a major role is played by the sociological analysis of law. Starting from his doctoral study, Weber's analysis of legislation is directed at the appearance of rational economic, political and social institutions in the West, that is, the rationalization of judicial thought and the legalization of social power from the earliest times. Weber thinks that the West is unique in the development of legal thought, law making and the operation of the legal system. There are a number of reasons why others were unable to form a rational and formal legal system, but the combination of those circumstances that appeared in the West caused the rationalization of the law in the historical process, and these circumstances and a structure like that in the West did not exist in the Orient.

Weber sees a close relationship between the development of formal judicial rationalism, which has advanced control and predictability, and the appearance of the bourgeois political and economic demands over the social processes that enabled individuals to control their own lives and follow their goals for themselves according to a plan. Yet, according to Weber, as modern rational Capitalism requires calculable technical devices, it needs a calculable law and administration in order to operate according to formal rules. This is the basis that whereupon the differentiation between modern capitalism and adventure capitalism, speculative trading-based capitalism and the other types are determined politically. Yet, other types are more effective without a calculable law or management, even if they are only present under these circumstances, as "a rational industrial firm—with fixed capital and reliable *calculation* and operating in a private economy—is not possible without this type of law and administration" (Weber, 2009, pp. 214–215). Moreover, in such political and social conditions the rational mentality of the bourgeoisie also seriously affected the development of the modern law.

An important step was taken in this sense once the cities, whose independence and autonomy were reinforced by the bourgeoisie in the Middle Ages, established their own laws. As mentioned in detail in the previous section, according to Weber, the city has its own law and this is what enabled it to divorce the law from patrimonial and feudal connections. Moreover, via the city councils, the existence of an autonomous government in the city enabled it to adopt a formal legal structure. Yet, an institution that is open to public supervision has to be transparent and neutral. Thus, around the institutional basis that dates from Rome, under the demands of rationalization and formalization by the bourgeoisie, the establishment of their own laws by the city was an important stage in the development of modern law in the West.

The basis of Weber's insistence on autonomy and rational law for the city is that these developments appeared around the idea of a contract and also the active participation in social political developments, thus leading to the establishment of law in society. Weber puts the freedom to make contracts in a central position in "the main process of the development." Here it can be claimed that Weber follows his close colleague Tönnies, however, he (1978, p. 647) also thinks that modern rational society is a contractual society foreign to other societies in terms of the obligations included in the contract. Examining the contribution of the idea of a union that is bound by a pledge in Western history to the judicial character of the contract, Weber attaches great importance to the contributions of the Hebrew and Greek experiences to Western civilization. Moreover, Roman law has an important position in the idea of the development of social and political relations in the context of a contract (Weber, 1978, pp. 669–675).

Thinking that the contract elevates the position of the individual in a rational legal system, Weber (1978, p. 811) thinks the basic effect of this is to guarantee private property and freedom. According to him, the judicial formalism that enables the process of the legal system to function correctly guarantees the highest freedom to individuals and groups and increases the possibility of predicting the judicial results of actions. He claims that such a development of a legal system is only present in the West and such guarantees do not exist anywhere else. According to him, "[t]he very word "liberty" was foreign to the [non-Western] language. This can readily be explained from the nature of the patrimonial state and from historical vestiges" (Weber, 1968, p. 147). The conflict as the basic nature of politics in the West, the stratified structure of the society, the unique position of the development of the city and the requirements of the economic system are guaranteed under the law and lead to the development of the idea of individual rights.

According to Weber, the fundamental degree in the development of the idea of guaranteed rights and the development of a contractual social life must be intellectually associated with the birth and development of natural law, institutionally an inheritance from Roman and canonic law. Weber (1978, p. 869) thinks, from the view of natural law, that two important standards, "nature" and "mind," are unique to the cultural inheritance of the West. According to him, the source of this thought comes from the Roman and Greek roots of Western civilization, where the idea of natural law emerged and was developed by Christianity, causing a contradiction and conflict between the sacred and the secular. This conflict created the basis for secularization and rationalization, as well as for the development of rational law. Such an idea of natural law, with its antecedents and consequences, is not present in any other religion than Christianity (Weber, 1978, p. 599). However, the social frame and religious thought of these religions did not form the basis for the formation of the idea of natural law. Outside of the West, there is no "'natural' order of people or objects against the positive social order" and thus, against *natural law.* The problems that lead to the appearance of the concept of *natural law* are not present in India, because "There simply was no "natural" equality of man before any authority, least of all before a super-worldly god" (Weber, 1967a, p. 144). In China, no doctrine of natural law as it appeared in Western Antiquity, particularly among the Stoics and in the Middle Ages, ever formed. Yet, there is no tension between the sacred and the secular (Weber, 1968, pp. 148–150). In this sense, according to Weber, although close to Christianity to a degree, due to the imposition of Roman law and common origins, Islam does not have any other social or political developments that would accelerate the development of natural law.

Weber thinks that Roman law played an important role in the development of rational and formal law in the West (Weber, 1968, p. 148). However, beyond the idea of law, its effect appears more clearly in legal institutions. Weber states that Roman law was established upon three basic components: autonomous city work life that requires a complaint diagram; the rationalization of judicial techniques by nobles; and the rationalization of the bureaucracy of the Eastern Roman Empire (Weber, 1968, pp. 148–150). These features compose its most important qualities and advanced analytical nature. On the other hand, another basic quality of Roman law was that as a result of the increasing needs of *urban* work activities through contracts, in connection with both the rules related to the essence and their procedural application, it became formal and rational at an advanced level (Weber, 1978, p. 797). Moreover, the modern systematization style is built upon the analytical nature of Roman law.

When it comes to the effect of Roman law on modern rational law, Weber pays extra attention in examining the development of Islamic law in comparison with that of the Western. Although according to him, in the development of Islamic law, Roman law played a significant role, Weber acknowledges that many applications, for example, record keeping, notary offices, promissory notes, which were taken from Oriental societies and developed within Roman law, were transferred to

Europe only after their application in Islamic societies (Weber, 1978, pp. 682–683). However, according to Weber, there is a basic contradiction between Roman and Islamic law in regards to the complete secularization of the administration of law. According to him, in any field of life in Islam, secular law is independent from sacred norms (Weber, 1978, pp. 818–819). This basic contradiction is that while European law is detached from the basic values of European civilization, Islamic law, in contrast, represents Islamic values. Thus, while European law is applied in its entirety by the government, Islamic law is completely free from governmental control.[9]

While problematizing the religious source of Islamic law, Weber suggests that Christian Canonical law had a basic role in the development of modern rational formal law. According to him, in contrast to the general belief, many capitalistic legal institutions "are of medieval rather than Roman origin, although Roman law was much more rationalized in a logical sense than medieval law" (Weber, 1978, pp. 687–688). According to him, with the help of the conceptualization of Stoic *natural law*, the formal components of Germanic law established the first systematic legal system within the frame of the rational Roman traditions, which implemented independent control of the law's management. This was taken as the model by the Church and through this, Christian Canonical law was shaped. Thus, a more rational and formal law than other sacred examples was born. In addition to these qualities, in the Middle Ages, both theological and secular legal education were separated from Canonical legal education in Western universities. Therefore, the complex theocratic structures that developed in other places did not appear, and a strict logical and professional law technique was developed through both ancient philosophy and ancient legal sciences. The action of collating legal sources and the decisions taken by the Church created sources that were not to be found in other "churches." Eventually, and above all, after the ending of the charismatic age of the early Church, the characteristic of Church law came under the influence of the rational bureaucratic positions of members of the Church (Weber, 1978, pp. 828–829). One of the reasons for this unique development in Canonical law was that it had a secular rival which had attained an extraordinary formal degree, that is, Roman law, which, historically, went on to become the international law (Weber, 1978, p. 830). Not having such a rival, the Oriental Canonical law remained in its original field without any effect on economic life, continuing its presence in a totally stable form (Weber, 1978, p. 831). Therefore, while Canonical law in the West was a guide for secular law in the rationalization process, in the Orient this was not the case.

According to Weber, it is not possible to find a phenomenon similar to Christian Canonical law outside the West. Non-Western religious factors combined with the patrimonial monarchy and prevented the formalization of law. Dependent

---

9   Weber's knowledge about the sources of Islamic law and the application of the law are erroneous, at least technically. For instance, he describes fiqh as the source of Islamic law. Actually fiqh is the actual name for Islamic law (Weber, 1978, p. 819)

on the royal individual, these authoritative forces generally created an informal legal system. However, formal justice introduces an area of rights and freedoms for the individual and reduces the need for mercy and the power of authority. In non-Western societies, groups that demanded the guarantee of autonomy for individual rights and freedom gave great importance to the stability and predictability of the legal procedure; economic and social organizations which demanded stability did not exist. In India, the mystical character of the law and the control by the priesthood in all fields of life, the patrimonial factors in China and the indisputable religious character of Islamic law prevented formalization (Weber, 1978, pp. 811–819). Similar to canonical law, the judicial interpretation of sacred texts in the Islamic and Hindu legal systems was guaranteed. But neither in Islam nor in Hinduism did this canonic interpretation of sacred sources create a rational legal establishment as was the case in the Western Christian church councils (Weber, 1978, pp. 790–792). In contrast to this, the combination of the legal rules for religious and ritual regulations being no different from secular rules meant that the characteristic theocratic system invariably operated, and in this case, an *informal* form of law maintained its presence.

For Weber, one of the important bases for the formalization of the law is the secularization of legal education in medieval universities and the legal establishment and application that was formed around it. There are two ways that professional legal education can develop: education of judges through empirical observation based on a mentor system or their education in a formal system. Both systems have social reasons and effects. In a system where the judges are empirically educated, the judiciary is under the monopoly of certain classes and families, and, in terms of profession, it operates like a craft. In this case, it is hard for a rational legal education or theory to emerge. When the control of legal education is in the hands of practitioners, the economic benefits of the attorney guilds are clarified not only in the standardization of official law, but also in its empirical adaptation to change. But this at the same time also prevents the rationalization of the law through legislation and legal science. In contrast to this, modern legal education in universities represents the pure form of the second method (Weber, 1978, pp. 784–789). The system where only judges who have received a secular legal education at university alone attend to the administration of the law is very important in the latter's formation and application. Accordingly, "scientific, artistic and economic development, as well as state-building, were not directed in China and India into those tracks of *rationalization* specific to the West" (Weber, 2009, p. 215). In China, judges were subject to typical patrimonial methods of appointment and dismissal, and there was no appointment autonomy. Moreover, "as he [judge] was given leeway by sacred tradition" (Weber, 1968, p. 149), there were no principles of equality or neutralism in front of the law. A similar situation can be seen in the Anglo-Saxon law, but wherever "formal law created by a class of lawyers whose mode of legal thought was conditioned by Roman and Canonical law," a formal legal system developed (Weber, 1968, pp. 148–150).

With the effect of such formalization via university education and judicial thought, the creation of general norms and rules, which means the accommodation of the rules created around these norms (*lawfinding*) to specific cases, was developed in the West. In contrast to this is the law-making system that evaluates a case without consistency, with the judgment being made according to the individual case (Weber, 1978, p. 654). Weber aims to show the unique nature of modern Western law in the context of a comparison with the irrational and unpredictable legal system shaped by *qadi* justice *(Kadijustiz)*. According to him, the modern legal law-finding system enables the prediction of judicial results of individual actions, the standardization of management and equality in front of the law.

Weber takes the term '*qadi* justice' *from* R. Schmidt who was the first to use it in a 1908 text about the structure of the legal system in the Orient (Crone, 1999, p. 266). Weber uses this term not for the Islamic law system in particular, or even the entire Oriental legal system that contains established rules of a formal rational law in general (Weber, 1978, p. 819). Rather, he uses it for a legal system that is inclined to the suitable postulates of religion, morality, politics or particular rational law (Weber, 1978, p. 806 Rheinstein's note 40) as a kind of *irrational* judgment. According to Weber (1978, pp. 819–820), in *qadi* justice formal judgments are not an extension of rational conceptualizations but depend on the interpretation of past cases by analogy (*qiyas*). Defining this system as 'empirical justice', Weber has to provide an explanation (more of an interpretation) for why the British legal system possesses such an empirical justice system. Almost every provision mentioned above by Weber for the rational formal law appeared in Britain.[10] But despite that, British empirical law satisfied the need of calculable law for the bourgeoisie. Therefore, the inverse proportion Weber established between empirical justice and the development of capitalism does not work in England where capitalism developed first and at the highest rank.

According to Weber, despite the empirical system, the main factor that enabled the development of capitalism in England was the application of the law by a class of judges. The presence of such a class caused the partial application of the law to economically weaken groups in the judgment process. Thus, the first capital accumulation opened a limitless area for the bourgeoisie and in this way capitalism in England was brought about by this empirical judgment system. On the other hand, Weber says that such laws that were shaped by the stable effects of the parties which have benefitted from the system created a calculable and extensive contractual autonomy (Weber, 1968, p. 102). In addition to this explanation, Weber emphasizes the variation of the inner character of the judgment, based on the denominational structure and benefits of the judges. According to him, although there is empirical justice in Anglo-Saxon law, earlier judgments and rules were strictly recorded and collated, and therefore there existed standardization

---

10   British law has never gained the formal normative character of Roman law. Rather, there was class control over the law and in universities Roman law was not taught. Besides that, Canonic law was not taken into consideration (Weber, 2003a, p. 339).

in the legal applications. However, these were never seen in the patrimonial and theocratic systems of the Orient.

As a result, proposing that the legal systems were rationalized at different levels, according to Weber, Western law represents the highest level of rationalization, depending on the interaction of various factors. First among these factors is the systematizing effect of Roman law. The formation of the law was realized on the basis of Roman analytical principles. In addition, the ancient idea of natural law formed the intellectual basis of the modern contract and rights-based law. Moreover, the main factor in the development of modern law was the applications created by the Christian canonical law. On this foundation, a need for education at universities arose in order to develop secular law and provide instruction in rational law, as well as apply former rulings. Thus, the law was implemented by independent judges who had a secular legal education, thus enabling the neutral application of the law. In addition to this, the development of the city, its autonomy and formal, systematic, predictable guarantee of rights and property ensured that the demands of the bourgeoisie system would be fulfilled. This also played a determining role in the combination of existing foundations and the appearance of a legal system that would eventually form the basis of modern rational capitalism.

However, according to Weber, these circumstances did not appear in the Orient. The Oriental legal system was centered around the dominant patrimonial ruler and did not transform into an independent system. Oriental societies had no ancient systematic source of laws, no concept of natural law or a system equivalent to the canonical law of the Church. Nor was there a class like the bourgeoisie demanding rights and freedom, and, finally, there was no predictable and formal judicial system. There everything was characterized with the absolute being of theocracy and variations in the law depending on the individual.

But in the mystical differentiation of the discourse, Weber falls into a dilemma. In the cradle of modern capitalism, England, the Anglo-Saxon empirical law reflected the Oriental system. Despite this similarity, because of the mentality of the British legal system and the denominational position of the judges, Weber claims that they attained the same results as the continent. Defining the Oriental legal system as *qadi* justice and emphasizing its inconsistencies, it is interesting to see how Weber explains the character of the British empirical justice system, without a reasonable or satisfying factual explanation with a vague reference to mentality.

The Rational Foundations of Modern Music

In a number of texts, Weber touches upon the subject of how Western art differs from other arts within the framework of rationalism. In the text *The Rational and Social Foundations of Music*,[11] written in 1911, Weber takes on the topic of the

---

11 Whether or not the text is a part of Economy and Society is debatable. It was not published during Weber's lifetime, and was first published as a separate book with an

paradigmatic relationship between music and rationalism. In this article, as in most of his work, Weber researches the foundations of Western culture on the basis of rational, technical and social conditions, and moves towards emphasizing the difference between Western culture and others. By comparing Western music with other musical traditions, and by emphasizing its individualistic foundations, Weber claims that Western music is uniquely rational and open to development.[12] According to him, it reaches the highest possible level in rationalism.[13]

In the *Prefatory Remarks*, Weber puts forth his thoughts on rationalism in the shape of (the most) general explanatory formulations. He maintains that in parallel with other fields, an unprecedented and advanced level of rationalism in art was also reached in the West. He explains that the primary point here is not to reach advanced rationalism in each individual field separately, but to obtain it through the combination of factors:

> The musical ear, apparently, was developed to a more refined degree among peoples outside the West than in the West to this day; or, at any rate, not less so. The most diverse sorts of polyphonic music have expanded across the globe, as did also the simultaneous playing of a number of instruments and singing in the higher pitches. All of the West's rational tone intervals were also widely calculated and known elsewhere. However, unique to the West were many musical innovations. Among them were rational, harmonic music (both counterpoint and harmony); formation of tone on the basis of three triads and the major third; and the understanding of chromatics and enharmonics since the Renaissance harmonically and in rational form (rather than by reference to distance). Others were the orchestra with the string quartet as its core and the organization of ensembles of wind instruments; the bass accompaniment; and the system of musical notation (which made possible the composition and rehearsal of modern works of music and their very survival over time). Still other innovations were sonatas, symphonies, and operas (although organised music, onomatopoeia, chromatics, and alteration of tones have existed in the most diverse music as modes of expression). Finally, the West's basic instruments were the means for all this: the organ, piano, and violin. (Weber, 2009, p. 206)

In this regard Weber analyzes the development of rational music around the question, "Why did polyphonic as well as harmonic-homophonic music and

---

introduction by Theodor Kroyer in 1921. It was published again in 1921 as an addendum to Economy and Society. Moreover, it was featured in the second (1924) and fourth (1956) German editions, but was not a part of the English editions.

12   For Weber's detachment of modern from pre-modern music on rationalist foundations, see Feher, 1987, pp. 149–154.

13   After mentioning primitive types of music, Weber gives examples from Oriental musical styles, such as Chinese, Javanese, Indian, and Japanese music, and classifies these as primitive music (Weber, 1958, p. 15).

the modern tone system develop out of the widely diffused preconditions of polyvocality only in the Occident?" (Weber, 1958, p. 83) Weber answers this question with the aid of musical theory and experts who researched Oriental music at the same period, such as Hermann L.F. Helmholtz, Raphael Georg Kiesewetter, Guillaume André Villoteau, Père Collangettes, A.H. Fox Strangways, Max Wertheimer, Frederick William Verney and Percival R. Kirby. According to him, the preconditions expressed in the above-mentioned question existed to an equal degree in Ancient Greece, Japan and other places, but that the rationalism that permeated all areas of life did not exist in other place but the West.

Based on this basic thesis, Weber analyzes the rationalist foundations of Western music around six points: (1) harmony in its relation to melody, (2) measures, (3) the problem of polyphony, (4) notation as a means in the rationalism of music, (5) the role of musical instruments, (6) and the place of individual composing in the competitive development of music.

Weber analyzes the social and technical factors that shape rationalism by dealing with the rationalism in Western music in an analytical and comparative manner. He writes that the development of Western music is based on the tension between rational and emotional components. The value of rationalism in music is the ability to calculate the process of musical creation through intelligible rules, known meanings and effective instruments. Honigsheim states that some people claim this was made possible through the effect of a musical theory developed by those around Weber. According to this theory, Christianity is the only religion which does not have dance because it detests the human body, and this is taken as the reason why its music was based on melody and not rhythm (Honigsheim, 2000, p. 215). We have no real proof as to whether or not Weber was influenced by this theory. However, he thinks that Western music evolved from being melodic to harmonic through the process of rationalization.[14]

Weber thinks that melodic music is less developed (more backwards). Because in Arabic and Indian music fourths were originally divided by one interval, each was movable and eventually irrational in terms of melodic motion. This melodic music was more emotional and less rational (Weber, 1958, p. 22). While the shift towards expressiveness in modern music left behind the harmonic elements in Ancient Greece, the same orientation in Western music, from the Middle Ages onwards, led to different results, chord harmony being among them. This is because the demand for expressiveness came into being alongside contemporary polyphony, and as a result followed the path of polyphonic music. But as Weber states, polyphonic music does not only exist in the West, and so there must

---

14   Weber repeats the famous dilemma between rationalism and loss of meaning by stating that these technical advancements, from the melodic to the harmonic, reduce flexible musical expression and emotional intensity. Weber is concerned about music evolving into mathematical equations and breaking away from feelings and melodic components as it becomes more harmonical. Yet despite these concerns, he takes rationalism to be an inescapable process in the development of music.

have been other factors besides polyphonism in the shift from melodic music to harmonic music (Weber, 1958, p. 65).

In this regard, Weber stresses the role of the pure diatonic scale. According to him "[h]ence no evolution toward harmonic music could have begun with the organum of the Occident, if other conditions, especially pure diatonicism as a basis of the tone system of art music, had not already existed" (Weber, 1958, p. 82). But the diatonic scale did not develop in Oriental music.

> All Oriental music contains the irrational third, which probably originated from the old bagpipe, a primitive instrument known to all cattle breeders and Bedouins. It is evidently permanently attached to the peculiar ethos of this very irrationality. ... The diffusion of Arabic music over the whole of Asia Minor restricted any development toward harmony or, even, pure diatonicism. Only the Jewish synagogue song was unaffected. (Weber, 1958, p. 93)

This later carried over into church music, with the synagogue music being an important starting point in the development.

In addition to the effect of diatonicism, the development of the principle of chords is also important in harmonic music, and chorded music attained final development in Western orchestras. Although it "is very close to music oriented primarily toward intervallic melodicism," temperament did not develop in the Oriental melodic music (Weber, 1958, p. 98). In this sense, the actors in all modern orchestral harmonic music appeared as a direct result of the chord (Weber, 1958, p. 101).

According to Weber, (1958, p. 44) the major and minor chords in Western music, which were rationalized harmonically, do not exist in any other kind of music. Weber states that modern chromatism is fairly new as compared to diatonicism and harmonism. He writes, "[d]uring the Renaissance new chromatic split tones were harmonically formed through third and fifth derivations" (Weber, 1958, p. 25). Weber (1958, p. 28) also states that even though Arabic musical theory is successful in dividing the octave into 24 quarter tones and accomplishes the mathematical analysis of music, these theoretical developments were disconnected to the application of music, and as a result were not transferred to practical use (Weber, 1958, p. 94). The Arabic musical system continued the Hellenic speculations related to absolute mathematical intervals developed under Greek and Persian influences, but these foundations were lost after the Mongol invasions, never to be rediscovered. The fact that the success of the Arabic musical system remained theoretical, significantly reduces its importance, since the modern tone system cannot be theoretically understood without examining its actual effects (Weber, 1958, p. 103).

According to Weber, the tonal development in harmonic music and the modern shaping of scale is a success achieved only in Western music. Even though tonality exists in many parts of Oriental music, its Western form is quite unique. A type of tonality known as *Ansa* in Indian music is fundamentally different, in terms of its meaning and function, and is limited to melodic music (Weber, 1958, p. 34). Arabs, with the *Oud*, have rational and irrational intervals in their tonal system (Weber, 1958, p. 43). However, this tonal system has not developed into a polyphonic type of music.

The development of polyphonic music is what allowed a rationalist combination of many individual elements. Even though polyphonic music has its roots in the Orient, only in the West did it follow a specific developmental progression based on contrapuntalist and diatonic innovations. The process of rationalism plays an evident role in bringing polyphony to the forefront in the West, and, conversely, polyphony is at the forefront in the rationalization of musical development. In this regard, Weber gives special importance to church music and its choirs in the development of polyphonic music. "As shown by the name *organizare* for the creation of many-voiced settings, the organ (and perhaps also the organistrum) played an important role in the rationalization of polyvocality" (Weber, 1958, p. 114). Weber repeatedly expresses that the organ, which has instrumental components that organize playing together, holds a special place in the development of polyphony.

Weber thinks that one of the most important factors allowing the unprecedented development of Western music is the advancements in musical notation. The development of musical notation is not only important in terms of keeping a record of the pieces and allowing them to be played again, but also in terms of the development of polyphonic music. In this regard, musical notation stands parallel to the advancement of Western music towards polyphonicism. With the acceptance of polyvocal music in monastery choirs in the ninth century, the need for a more developed musical notation system to replace *neumes* became more apparent (Weber, 1958, p. 114).[15] *Neumes* represented the recording of the hand movements (chieronomy), showing the rises and falls in a melody while conducting orchestras. The first step in its replacement, according to Weber, was the transposition of *neumes* onto straight lines, making it easier to read while performing music. The transformation of *neumes* into points, squares and long rectangles during the process represents an important phase. In the process following this, the musical notation that is based on symbols developed and made the practice of polyvocal music easier. Notation in modern music is as important as the role of orthography in the shaping of literary arts (Weber, 1958, pp. 83–84). A musical notation based on measures allowed the composition of polyvocal art and supported the development of polyphonal creations. This is because rationalist notation provides strong support of the harmonic rationalization of the tonal system of polyphony (Weber, 1958, pp. 88–89). In addition to these benefits, the use of notes in place of letters when writing music (solmization) and as a tonal alphabet characterized by the relative placement of half-tone steps always played an important role in

---

15   A neume is the basic element of musical notation based on inflective marks that indicated the general shape prior to the invention of modern five-line staff notation (Weber, 1958, pp. 37, 86).

teaching measures in the West. This was particularly the case within the weaving of the tones in a row, or more specifically half-tone steps (Weber, 1958, p. 59).

Even though symbols of notes of some kind can be found elsewhere, there is no correlation with rationalized melodicism. This means that a rational standard musical production was never generated (Weber, 1958, p. 84). For instance, because Arabic music has gradually lost its old notational system consequent to the Mongolian attacks, they were completely dispossessed of the means to the rationalist development of music.

Weber (1958, p. 94) also thinks that musical instruments hold an important place in the rationalization of the musical system (Weber, 1958, p. 62). Here, keyboard instruments and string instruments hold a special place in the West. For instance, the organ and piano allowed independent instrumental music and the division of the octave into 12 equal parts. On the other hand, the organ also played an important part in the development of polyphonic music, while wind instruments functioned in the role of providing harmonic support to the melody (Weber, 1958, p. 114). In this regard, the production technique of musical instruments also directly affects musical rationalism. While the production methods of musical instruments in the past did not encourage harmonic music, modern instruments were designed later as a vehicle of melodic effect (Weber, 1958, pp. 100–111). Conversely, ancient Arabic musical instruments derived from old bagpipes impeded development, and hindered the theoretical development that emerged with the adoption of Hellenic musical theory (Weber, 1958, p. 25).

Weber states that the production of musical instruments was affected by the development of craftsmanship as well as by geographical conditions. When compared to people in the Orient, Nordic inlay work and carpentry were more adept at transforming trees into flat pieces, and this resulted in the development of musical instruments (Weber 1958:105). Weber also states that the industrial production of certain musical instruments played an important role in the rationalization and mass use of music. With the organ, and later on, the piano, becoming available for individual use in various segments of society, the production of musical instruments turned into an industry, resulting in even more advancements. As a result, the piano became an inseparable part of the nineteenth-century bourgeois household, and the performance of music became commonplace.

Finally, Weber believes that the development of musical instruments and the notation system encouraged individual performance and competitive compositions. In this regard, in relation to his own theory of charisma, Weber states that the basis of musical production is for the composer to create rationalist music. In particular, the virtuoso composer represents a heroic individual. Weber imbues the composer with something similar to the leadership role of prophets. In this regard, the composer ensures the development of music as if he were a disciplined devotee (Kemple, 2009, pp. 189–193). Weber poses mystical music as a means to escape this world against this Western type, repeating the Orient–Occident dilemma that pervades his sociology.

Weber offers a similar analysis for other arts, demonstrating that he thinks his statements on music are also valid in all artistic fields. In this regard, for instance, even though cornered arches exist as a method of decoration outside the Western world, placing them side by side or across from each other to form a row of arches is not known. Likewise, the use of the Gothic arch as a vehicle to support surfaces shaped in certain ways, or its use as a tool to diffuse weight took place first and only in the West. The same is said about its development as a solution to problems inherent in the dome, as well as the use of various arts combined with statues and paintings as the foundation of a particular architectural style. "Every type of "classical" rationalization of the entire art world—as occurred in painting through the rational use of both linear and spatial perspective—was also lacking outside the West, where it began with the Renaissance" (Weber, 2009, p. 207).

Weber's work on art, especially on music, is important in demonstrating how he attempted to establish the West's unique nature in all aspects of social life. In this regard, his sociology on music is constructed to supplement this basic goal. According to him, even though individual pieces that demonstrate the unique nature of Western music might exist in other systems, and even though these pieces might sometimes reach more rational and advanced points, in the end they do not totally reach the rationalist level of Western music.[16] Weber analyzes the spirit that uniquely brings these pieces together and as a result distinguishes the West. This spirit is the reflection of rationalism into music. There are both contextual as well as methodical similarities between Weber's analysis of music and the development of other modern institutions. For him, each individual field mutually interacts with and affects other fields within life's general orientation and changes in thought. Frequently referring to comparisons with Oriental societies in this regard, Weber adamantly maintains that the general style of life in the Orient hinders rationalism in the Western sense.

In conclusion, as it is discussed above, Weber tries to complete his all-encompassing comparison by examining all areas of life from religious thought to economic activity, from city to law, from political systems to architecture, and from bureaucracy to music. With this examination he wants to create a total differentiation between Orient and Occident. Focusing on differences in each field, he seeks to create a basis for proving the uniqueness of Western civilization. As it will be discussed in the next chapter, this is the spirit of Weber's sociology.

---

16   For an assessment of how to understand the cases of rational development Weber uses in his analyses and how these can also be understood as a non-rationalizations, see Segady, 1993.

Chapter 12
Weber's Occidental Geist: Defining the West by Using the Orient

In his *Protestant Ethic*, Weber states that even though Benjamin Franklin was not a practicing Protestant, his actions can be analyzed from a Protestant perspective since he has a certain "frame of mind" (Weber, 2009a, p. 74). He stresses that the actor is predetermined and acts according to certain mental patterns. In this regard, he has a acquires a certain frame of mind by placing himself as a member of Western civilization. Weber's perspective toward Oriental societies can be understood from here, as he liked to think that only Western civilization has "a historical line of development with universal significance and empirical validity" (Weber, 2009b, p. 205). He reveals this basic analytical orientation, and continues his work to find an answer to the crisis the West was experiencing both with itself and the rest of the world.[1]

The central theme of Weber's sociology is to clarify the historical place of modern Western society and to show its unique nature. This central theme is closely related to the era Weber lived in. From the end of the nineteenth century on, the belief in modernity began to come under criticism. From the beginning of the twentieth century onwards, a prevalent pessimism emerged with the belief that the utopian expectations imposed on modernity would not be achievable. Even though Weber sometimes harbored a Nietzschean pessimism,[2] he still made it his mission to combat the loss of belief in modernity, which was particularly prevalent among the youth.[3]

---

1   "The peak of Weber's intellectual maturity coincides with the emergence of the greatest crisis of this century in the Western world, both socially and politically, and within itself and the rest of the world—the First World War" (Parsons, 1971, p. 28).

2   An extensive evaluation and comparison of the position of Nietzsche and Weber in relation to modernity may be found in David Owen (1994).

3   Marianne Weber tells the story of Weber's duel with Spengler who was the popular representative of this thought. "At that time there was a discussion in Weber's seminar of Oswald Spengler's work *Der Untergang des Abendlandes* [The Decline of the West], which was attracting universal attention. Weber saw in it a conception of the philosophy of history by a very clever and scholarly "dilettante" who has squeezed the results of historical research into his speculative constructions. Some members of seminar who knew the author personally desired a debate between him, Weber and a few other thinkers. The men were prepared to cross swords. On a cold, clear winter day they met at the city hall. The young people, sitting in several rows, clustered about the small group of scholars; they consisted predominantly of *Freideutsche Jugend*, but young Communists and sectarians of all kinds

Weber's sociological analyses offered a new perspective to assertions on the unique nature and hegemony of the West, which was a product of nineteenth century positivism and evolutionary perspectives. But its validity quickly came under scrutiny and questioning, and Weber took on massive projects with the goal of fulfilling the mission he thought was his responsibility, that is, to put forth the historical meaning of Western civilization.[4] As a result, the worn out empirical and theoretical basis of old explanations had to be renewed and the historical significance of modernity was to be emphasized.[5]

In this regard, Weber thinks that "[a]ny heir of modern European culture will, unavoidably and justifiably, address universal historical themes with a particular question in mind: What combination of circumstances led in the West, and only in the West, to the appearance of a variety of cultural phenomena that stand—at least, we like to imagine—in a historical sine of development with *universal* significance and empirical validity?" (Weber, 2009b, p. 205) In light of this question, he took on the analysis of non-Western civilizations in a multi-dimensional way, defining the "particular character of the West's social order" (Weber, 2009b, p. 214). Along these lines, he attempted to put forth, once again, the unique nature of the West and to rejuvenate the loss of hope in modernity.[6]

---

were also present. The intellectual tournament lasted for a day and a half and was extremely exiting (Marianne Weber, 2008, p. 674).

4 Weber ends his *Science as a Vocation* speech by answering Goethe's question: "But what is your duty?" He answers, "We must set to work and meet the "demands of the day" humanly and vocationally." (Weber, 2008, p. 53 note 237 by editor)

5 In reality, it is this choice which secures Weber's place in the following generation and makes him one of the founders of twentieth century social theory. Instead of being an expert exploring the depths of his own field, Weber chose to be a general theoretician delivering explanations for the most basic problems in his own period, civilization and society.

6 Within the context above, we can say that 1909 was a year which served as a turning point for Weber. After getting over his psychological illness, which began in 1897, he started to work in 1903 with the intention of empirically explaining development of Western society. At the same time, in order to produce these works, he was occupied with clarifying his own methodology. But as explained above, the transformation of the doubts in modernity which led to it being questioned and discredited, starting from Germany and moving throughout European cultural circles, caused Weber to transform his work into comparative studies in civilization. Even though he explains that the reason he decided not to pursue the work he had previously planned to undertake as a continuation of Protestant Ethic because his close friend, Troeltsch, had completed a better analysis than he could ever make, he does not explain why he set out to analyze world religions after this remittal. It is important that the first product of this period is The Agrarian Sociology of Ancient Civilizations, a work which developed out of the massive expansion of a short text he had previously written in 1896 and 1897. Weber starts his analysis of world religions in this text, and takes on the foundations for dividing the field of these two civilizations through an expansive Oriental–Occidental comparison.

In order to tackle this duty, created by the conditions he found himself in, Weber used Oriental societies as an object of comparison. Because, for exploring the *causal* relationships in the other societies "to the extent necessary for the discovery points of *comparison* with the West's development"[7] (Weber, 2009b, p. 217). In this context, by utilizing the comparative analyses on the framework of socio-historical models, which he constructed based on concept of type, Weber attempted to reach a universal explanation of Western civilization. He did this through works spread over a wide spectrum of subjects, from religious thought to the city, bureaucracy to monastery systems, law to technological developments and music to architecture.

When making such comparisons between civilizations, Weber benefited from the institutionalized research of Orientalist studies. Even though he was not an expert in any of the fields of Orientalism or classical studies, he made use of the resources they provided, using and interpreting the available data and offering analyses of the structure of Oriental societies. Weber never felt the need to question the empirical or theoretical validity of this literature. He repeated many of the preconceived judgments they contained, and placed a passive and stagnant Orient against an active and dynamic West. Thus, he exemplifies the maxim that he uses "an ingenious error is more fruitful for science than stupid accuracy" (Weber, 2003, p. 30).

To make a comparison over such a lengthy period and wide geographic area possible, Weber determined the basic characteristics which needed to be used. In this regard, he uses rationalism as what determines and separates the West, and patrimonialism as the factor that determines and separates the Orient. Accordingly, Western societies have a rationalism which does not exist in other societies. As a result of various factors and expanding into every field, this rationalism is the source of the progressivism of Western societies. Weber discovers the foundation of this rationalism in the four pillars of the West, the Greek, Roman, Jewish and Christian past. According to him, it is the result of an *elective affinity* of conditions. Even if advanced rationalism took place in different fields outside of the West, these developments were either blocked by other factors or they were unable to form an affinity as they did in the West. In contrast to this, the central political apparatus that formed as a result of the need to carry out agriculture based on irrigation,

---

7   In the previously mentioned letter, Weber tells the historian Georg von Below that Economy and Society will deal with "the topic comparatively and in a normative fashion." In this letter, Weber demonstrates the place of the comparison in his work and says, "The special characteristics of a thing, for instance of a middle-age city, can be defined by determining which of these characteristics other cities (classical China and Islamic) do not have. This is the historian's task, as we have already agreed. This is a general rule. The next task of the historian is to offer casual explanations to these special characteristics." According to this, analyses of non-Western societies should be made to make the characteristics of Western societies more evident (Von Below, 1925, p. xxiv; see also Marianne Weber, 2008, p. 200, 226 fn. 36).

which was also related to the geographic conditions of Oriental societies, gave birth to patrimonialism. These factors caused Oriental societies to have a stagnant, as opposed to progressive, social structure. By thus analyzing the situation, Weber formulated two ideal types—Orient and Occident—that opposed one another, and based the uniqueness of Western societies upon the comparison of the two.[8]

According to Weber, the West is unique because it gave birth to capitalism. The economic backwardness of Oriental societies results in their historical lack of a social or political basis from which to produce capitalism. Consequently, according to Weber, the Orient does not have a valid science, a systematic theology, and, moreover, its astronomy lacks mathematical foundations. Chinese history cannot be on par with the history of the Greek historian Thucydides. Oriental art lacks perspective, while Oriental music lacks harmony, sonatas, and polyphony. To summarize, the Orient does not possess the rationalism which makes the West successful. Acting from this viewpoint, Weber developed these statements while violating a series of methodological principles, including those he had defined himself. Many samples of eclecticism, anachronism and the juxtaposition of unrelated evidences to one another are all flaws present in Weber's work, casting a shadow on his claims of objectivity.[9]

Objectivity is very important for Weber when defining his own methodology. He states that a series of subjectivities in cultural sciences, starting from the choice of topic, is an inseparable part of the task. His theory is that objectivity should not be a result of a value judgment on the topic, but that rather it should appear as a result of an objective analysis of the data. Weber is extremely meticulous about using sources and providing evidence in regards to objectivity. His most significant work, in which we see this, is *Protestant Ethic*. Here he attempts to prove his statements by providing a wide range of evidence. Yet it cannot be said that Weber continues with the same approach in his analysis of Oriental societies. He often bases his central argument on a single source and defends himself by saying that he is not an expert in the field, and therefore, his contributions should be considered to be sociological observations. However, it is surprising that such wide and ambitious analyses are based on one dimensional research. For instance, Weber bases his analyses on Islamic cities on one single source, a work of the Hurgronje. On the other hand, he sees no problem in carrying over the latter's coarse and hostile claims about Prophet Muhammad (and in particular, claims about Prophet Muhammad's family life and sexuality). On this topic, he neither

---

8   The disassociation of the Orient and the West was so extreme in Weber's work that it also led him to separate Oriental Christianity from Western Christianity, Oriental Judaism from Western Judaism, and the state of Hellenism in the Orient from that in the West (Weber, 1967b, p. 362).

9   Those who think that Weber created multiple and multi-faceted analyses independently from values are reading only from his writings on methodology. A comparative analysis of this methodology with works on Oriental societies demonstrates that Weber did not adhere to his own methodology.

finds it necessary to adhere to the principle of his own interpretive sociology, which offers a method of contextual analyses and a viewpoint of the meaning the actors attach to themselves, nor does he find it necessary to corroborate the topic from other sources. As the claims in question support his own thesis, he takes them as is.

Another of the most frequent methodological problems in Weber's works is eclecticism. He selects the premises according to the model he wants to form, particularly when forming ideal types related to Oriental societies. As a result, it is questionable whether these ideal types represent the social fact he is actually analyzing or not. Eclecticism, in this regard, results from the nature of Weber's research, as explained above. Because the basic goal is to formulate an Orient whose character opposes that of the West, Weber does not observe, in any way, the context of the data he selects. For instance, when discussing the unique nature of the West, he places an example from Buddhism as the opposite of a feature of the West, yet using examples from Islam, Babylon and China for others; in the end he uses data all together and establishes an Orient–Occident clash. In his analysis, he totally disregards the differences these societies have with one another, and feels free to pick and choose, and include qualities from each society when they support his own theories.

Another problem which parallels Weber's eclecticism, and consequently appears as a methodological problem, is chronological discrepancy and anachronism. Such criticisms have always been made against Weber. For instance, huge gaps in time exist when presenting proof and this is the most criticized part of *Protestant Ethic*. However, such problems are an almost natural part of his analyses on Oriental societies. Weber disregards the gap in time, which amounts to almost thousands of years, between the data he uses. He presents examples from antiquity and modern times side by side when providing evidence for a fact. It can be assumed that the reason behind Weber not paying attention in this regard to the examples he uses with Oriental societies is related to his theses that Oriental societies do not change internally and that they are stagnant. In reality, even though Weber does not state this openly, a stagnant, unchanging Orient is what appears in the picture he paints. That key examples are selected from various timeframes and presented in a manner in which they support one another, as was the case with his Orientalist predecessors, should not be disregarded.[10]

For instance, when tackling the topic of patrimonialism in Islam, Weber uses a combination of evidence from Prophet Muhammad in the seventh century, the feudalization of land tenure from the twelfth century and Ottoman *waqfs* from the sixteenth century, creating the impression that patrimonialism is a repeating fact. According to this, Islamic societies are patrimonial societies and always re-patrimonialize. Likewise, in his analysis and assessment of Indian villages, Weber does not state a time and lists characteristics which can be seen at different time

---

10   In reality, a similar picture can be painted for the West with a similar disregard for chronological consistency and a similar eclecticism.

periods and different locations. It thus seems as if he is mentioning a fact that remains the same throughout time, with continuous examples (Weber, 1967a, pp. 78–79).

The problem of chronology, of course, brings with it the problem of anachronism. Weber criticized the anachronism and declared it to be a "modernizing perspective" (Weber, 1988, p. 45). According to him, such an approach is misleading and reduces the value of the event being analyzed. However, his analyses of Oriental societies are anachronistic. This problem arises at the root, when assigning the purpose of his work. The question, "Why did the advancements of the West not appear in the Orient?" naturally pushes Weber towards anachronistic assessments. He takes on all issues of the Orient from a retrospective point of view, and questions why the Western developmental chain could not arise in these societies. Weber at least wants to see the series of changes necessary to take these societies to modernity.

Around the framework of these methodological problems, Weber tries to find empirical evidence for his idea of Europe's supremacy. Due to this, because he is aware that the Orient was actually more advanced during many of the periods he is dealing with, Weber creates various arguments to make this discrepancy ambiguous. For instance, in many places in his works, he mentions the Orient's more rational and advanced practices, but he immediately states afterwards that these advancements did not successfully continue, or that their effects were unexpectedly negative or that they were restrained by other factors. By doing so, he states that the result of any such developments did not spark developments in the social system and that therefore total social backwardness continued. He creates an image of himself as being fair and objective by mentioning the successes of the Orient and its contributions to the West, but immediately afterwards he offers strong evidence for his general thesis, reporting that these successes did not have the same result as in the West and were not sustained. A chain of development as a result of various supporting factors appears only in the West, which the rest of the world's civilizations can be sure that they will lack. This deprivation causes a long list of insufficiencies to appear in places where the Orient is in question. As a result, to establish the unique nature of the West, he analyzes the Orient from a Western perspective. In this analysis there is no room for the advancement of the Orient.[11]

In these comparisons, Weber takes the West and the Orient as a single phenomenon. Even though he compares Oriental societies with one another and mentions many differences, in the end, he designates similarities that reconcile these differences in the Orient, presenting it as the West's negative other. The main goal of Weber's analysis of Oriental societies is not to explain or understand Oriental societies, but to prove his analyses on Western societies. In this context, to demonstrate the uniqueness of the West, Weber designs a counter-Oriental model.

---

11   Weber talks about so many deficiencies in so many fields that listing them is a task of its own. But his incorporation of the facts in the most general eclectic way with the form in which they exist in the West is the most important reason for these deficiencies.

PART III
Converging Poles of Sociology

Chapter 13
A Comparison of Marx and Weber's Analyses of Oriental Societies

Weber's Relationship with Marx

As stated in the introduction to this study, in modern sociological literature Marx and Weber have been placed in opposing positions. This reading, which developed within American sociology, has not only spread throughout the world, but has become a sociological theory in its own right. According to this perception, all of Weber's theories were formed in confrontation with the specter of Marx.

At the time of Weber's youth, the works of Marx were widely read and analyzed in the German intellectual community, and at the same time, Marxism had also started to develop.[1] Within this background, particularly following the rapid development of the German Social Democratic Party after 1880, Marxist explanations of a number of matters began to be presented in party circles. What is more, due to the discussions around the birth of capitalism and the roots of modern society, Marx's theories on modernity began to receive attention in wide academic circles. During this period, historical materialism became popular amongst the German intelligentsia. This situation, in turn, triggered a response to Marx and Marxism in the bourgeoisie environment.

Within this context, Weber's relationship with Marx developed in two opposing ways. The first was negative due to Weber's class consciousness as a member of the German bourgeoisie. In this, he approached the matter partially from the contemporary position of Marxism, and based his attitude on the future prospects of the German government. This opposition, which appeared in particular in political analyses and methodological approaches, is more associated with the determination of national politics. Weber's second point of contact is his relationship with Marx as a scholar. Weber was aware of the scope of the context Marx had developed, and his importance in Western society gave him a position Weber recognized. This was because Weber, like Marx, examined modern society from a comparison with Oriental societies.

In this sense, the first item which needs to be examined regarding Marx and Weber is the ways in which they analyzed Oriental societies. For both of them, the reasoning behind the analysis of the Oriental world is the same, that is, they formed

---

1 After 1880 in Germany, *Manifesto of the Communist Party, A Contribution to the Critique of Political Economy, Capital* (3 vols), *Anti-Dühring, Poverty of Philosophy and The Origin of the Family, Private Property and the State* were accessible.

their arguments around the question about why modern society had only developed in the West. While Marx explained this phenomenon with reference to capital accumulation, Weber refers to transformations in the Western *weltanschauung* and the development of a kind of rationalism that covered all spheres of social life. When Oriental societies are examined, the question arises as to why the same form that is found in modern societies is not found within them. Marx did not ask this question as directly or repeatedly as Weber did. However, he did establish his own model in the context of this question, with implicit references.

Marx's dialectic method has an important role in establishing this hypothesis. In his method, which was formed along Hegelian lines, it is only possible to define something according to its opposite. Consequently, Marx used Oriental societies as a mirror to define Occidental societies, and in the most fundamental way, an "ideal type," that is, the AMP, was formed to show what the West was not. The same can be said for Weber. In order to demonstrate the unique nature of the modern West, Weber resorted to Oriental societies and attempted to demonstrate how the developmental elements did not occur in the same way in the Orient as they did in the Occident.

Comparing Orient with Modernity: Bases of Western Exceptionalism

It is only possible to present the respective differences to their approaches to the Orient by examining the various situations in which both thinkers found themselves. While Marx writes at a time when the form of modern society had not yet completely been formed, Weber produces work at a more settled and developed period. The same can be said for the Western dominance over the world that determined the approach towards Oriental societies. During Marx's life, the West was politically superior, however Weber wrote at a time when this had reached its peak, and it is reflected in statements the latter makes about the Orient. Even though for Marx the Orient was taken as a whole, this integrity was only used as a vehicle for othering. For Weber, on the other hand, the Orient was transformed into a model that was opposed to the West in every way. This was because in the period in which Marx lived, the form of modern society was still debatable. During the era in which Weber lived, this debate had ended and the form of modern society had taken on a settled order in the West. For this reason, Weber was able to take this structure and create a more detailed othering. In essence, it seems that as the world domination of the West increased, the differences in tone between the Occident and the Orient became more pronounced.

Within this context, as an important methodical mean, comparison plays a vital role for both thinkers. Weber clearly states that it is necessary to compare the two forms of society using a general and systematic method, while Marx places comparison in a central position in his argument due to the dialectic method mentioned above. For these reasons, in regards to the analyses carried out on modern society, the examination of Oriental societies becomes unavoidable. In this context, the Oriental societies were dealt with and approached as a combined single structure, ignoring different historical and social conditions, religious and political situations, in sum, the thousands of years that formed the civilizations of the entire Orient. With the limits of time and place in the generalizations broadened, the empirical side of the comparisons decreased as the role of discourse increased. Although Weber is in comparison to Marx, more aware of the differences in Oriental societies, he still confuses these differences and does not refrain from creating an Orient that is formed of a society opposed to the West as a whole in order to establish a base for his analysis.

The overlapping approach to Oriental societies affects the main conceptualizations. Even if different terminology is used, one of the most important similarities is that they labeled the modern society that appeared in Western Europe as the most developed form in history, while Oriental society was seen as the least developed. Within the context of this perspective, while Marx has a progressive taxonomy of social types, Weber's model is developmental. Marx states that the stages of social forms followed one another in the bases of different modes of production. According to this, while modern society, which is based on CMP, represents the most advanced form, Oriental societies, represented by AMP, are place in a primitive position. Similarly to the analyses given above, Marx argues that Oriental societies have a stagnant and introverted social structure. According to him they are unaware of historical developments.

There is no such idea of linear progression in Weber. In fact, Weber's methodological approach was shaped in opposition to progressive and evolutionary historical theories in the nineteenth century. In this context, Weber believes that societies have a developmental history, and, according to him, the modern social formation that accompanies the development of rationality represents the most developed form. Even if Oriental societies are rational in certain areas, they have lagged behind due to the fact that rational structures have not developed in an integrated manner. As can be seen, Marx and Weber's different viewpoints and concepts arrive at the same conclusion: the modern social form is the most advanced form of society.

In relation to this, they held an idea that while the Occident is dynamic, the Orient is stagnant. For Marx, history is the history of humanity's struggle against nature. This makes it possible for humanity to create more advanced social structures. The class struggle is the engine of historical development, and in the West, a class society and dynamic social form appeared as a result of the birth of private property, while in the Orient, as there was no private property, no class struggle occurred. In explaining the birth of capitalism, Marx determines his perspective of a dynamic Western history with its own unique progress by placing a stagnant Orient in an opposing pole. This active–passive dialectic, which Marx developed around his progressive materialist philosophy of history, is recreated by Weber around the rationalization of religion and formation of different political systems. Weber proposes that Western rationalism controlled nature and dominated it, but that no such thing occurred in the Orient. While Western religion is characterized as controlling the world and aesthetically orientated, pursing mastery of the world, the religious world of the Orient is characterized as being in accord with the order of the world and traditions, and identified with mysticism, which strives to escape from everything worldly. Similarly, the explanation of a patrimonial system erects various obstacles that lead to the formation of a stagnant society. While Marx and Weber's explanations have different forms, they are in agreement in representing the Occident as having an active social form, and the Orient being an opposingly passive society.

This passive–active dialect used by Marx and Weber in their definition of the West and the Orient is reflected even in the conceptualizations they used. They generally define the Orient in terms of place, while the West is generally defined via time. Thus, the grounds for ideas regarding changes in the West and the continued stagnation in the Orient are prepared, as the fluctuation and passage of time sits in contrast to the fixity of location. There is nowhere else in Marx where the effect of the physical environment is emphasized to the extent that it is in the Oriental societies. He explains the static state and lack of development in the Orient with geographical factors. In this context, he names the means of productions that belong to the West with the concepts concerned with time (antique, modern, etc.) and concepts concerned with location (Asiatic and Oriental) with the Orient. Thus, the Western pre-capitalist modes of productions are the first link in the dynamic process that leads to capitalism, and the Asiatic form, which is seen to be atypical and abnormal, is the dead-end of history. While referring to the Orient in many places, Weber gives country names, but when referring to the West he uses terms such as the Middle Ages or Antiquity. Thus, with the idea that was widely accepted in modern Europe and which was expressed by Hegel for Africa, that is, that the Orient did not belong to time but to space, both thinkers attribute a temporal dynamism to Europe and a locational stagnation to the Orient.

Developing Orientalism: Overlapping Sources and Common Fallacies

It can be stated that these perspectives were the result of the widespread ideas in Western thought of the nineteenth century. In this context, it should be stated that Marx and Weber are consistent in their popular Orientalist sources. They recreated a sociological interpretation from the perspective of these sources, and it can be said that both used the Orientalist perspective in a non-critical way. However, the development and situation of Orientalist research affected the way the two thinkers dealt with the issues in question. In regard to the development of Orientalist studies, in particular German Orientalism, Weber had an advantage in the matter of sources.

By Weber's time, Orientalism had developed into subcategories and had specialized into regions. The division of labor among countries in the West had a role to play in this. The development of comparative linguistic and religious studies in German Orientalism created a base for Weber's work as he carved out a respectable niche for himself in the public eye and the universities, while working from an individual curiosity. As the function and working of Orientalism became clear and Orientalist turned into an expert who worked in an institutional framework with state funds and support. This helped to resolve, to a large extent, its methodological problems. Newly developing sciences, like ethnology and archaeology, concretized the division of labor in Orientalist researches and cooperation in the field, and thus the accumulation of knowledge on the Orient became detailed. It was now possible to analyze the Orient more thoroughly and extensively.

Within this framework, Marx generally bases his more logical and discursive explanations of the Orient on the Enlightenment and the period immediately after. The confusing heritage of the British political economists, political philosophers of the French Enlightenment and the German philosophers helped to shape his ideas regarding the Orient. In order to detail his analyses, Marx used historical, economic, social and political data from travelogues and colonial officials. At the same time, this information, which had been attained purely from observations and shaped by the observer's perspective (sometimes fantasy), was generally unreliable. Due to Marx's personal (refugee status) and financial situation, he was unable to easily obtain a variety of sources. For this reason, Marx's lack of a detailed analysis can be understood. However, he chose to make these problematic sources even more problematic. Even though he was aware that they were limited and biased, he did not hold back from making bold and sweeping generalizations, even ones that go beyond his own sources and attains a result that strains his source contents.

Weber, as stated above, had access to a wide range of alternative sources based on expert research. In particular, he made a detailed discussion using an accumulation of information formed in the area of the comparative history of religion that was part of the German Orientalist tradition. Not only did the specialized journals, publishers and courses make following the information produced easier, Weber's financial and academic opportunities also played an important role. He could reach extensive sources, from England, France, the United States, and the Netherlands to Russia, Sweden and many other places in the West. In addition to these, by this time Weber was able to use translations of Oriental classics in a number of Western languages. Through the use all of these materials, he was able to carry out sociological analyses upon those aspects of Orientalism that had been previously neglected.

Thus, Weber developed analyses based on concrete data in keeping with Marx's general templates. While Marx makes more general and abstract comments regarding the subjects at hand, Weber takes advantage of more detailed empirical research and is able to carry out more penetrating factual analyses. Yet, despite the great variety in the source materials, the continuity of the Orientalist discourse and perspectives establish a connection between Marx and Weber. An Orientalist spirit that is far from an accurate understanding of the Orient permeates both the work of Marx and Weber. The Orientalist perspective, which adopts a superior, judgmental and stereotypical attitude, can easily be observed in both authors. Both view the Orient not as its own actor, but rather approach it asking why it was left behind during Western advance and development.

When comparing the sources, it is clear that Weber, who works with broad and comprehensive materials, is in a much better position than Marx as far as both resources and opportunities are concerned. This can easily be seen when the volume and depth of their studies are examined together. In contrast to Marx's limited analysis of the Orient, Weber produced detailed and comprehensive work.

In fact, their shared sources and perspectives lead to similar analyses of the Orient. There is to be found an Orient–Occident distinction in the bases of Marx and Weber's studies. This distinction starts from the antique period, establishing two opposite poles in the history of humanity. In this way, the Orient and Occident developed in different directions and were eternally separated from one another. Thus, the Orient formed in an opposing form to the West.

Unending Despotism: Geographical and Climatic Bases of Old Same Distinctions

The most important of distinctions established around the base of social life consists of geographical effects. From the time of the Enlightenment, European thought approached the Orient from the view of climatic and geographical factors. Accordingly, the differentiation between Oriental and Western societies was based upon the differing geographical and climatic conditions. In the beginning, these not only shaped the agricultural mode, but also the mode of ownership, state organization and, later, the religion and mentality.

Adopting these categorical differentiations, Marx and Weber started by accepting that the type of soil and the climatic conditions in the Orient created a need for irrigation in agriculture, which created a centralized political system. According to them, due to these conditions despotism emerged. In contrast, the Western climate and geography removed the need for irrigation, and thus the need for a bureaucratic centralized state did not emerge. As a result, a more democratic political system came into being. While Marx labeled *Oriental despotism* as AMP, Weber refers to it as *patrimonialism*. This difference, reflected in the different names the two thinkers gave to the same phenomenon, is actually the result of Weber's attempt to establish his own conceptual system.

By placing despotism at the center of his analyses, Marx committed himself to an economic reading in which no private property or classes appeared in the Orient. Weber analyzed the political system with the same conditions, but based around the formation of a centralized bureaucracy. In the place of Marx's economic determinism, Weber forms a determinism based upon politics and *weltanschauung*. While Marx speaks of the formation of two completely different worlds in the framework of economic conditions, Weber claims that the same thing was the result of a difference in political formations.

According to Marx, due to the geographic conditions in Oriental societies, a person was not able to solve the problem of irrigation individually. The construction and management of dams and canals was more than the individual could achieve, and, as a result, a powerful authority foreign to society was necessary whereby the development of despotism was assured. As the highest authority of the state, the despot owned all lands and only in return for taxes-in-kind and corvée did an individual have a right to use it. As the individual did not own any land, no class system was generated and equality continued. Thus, the relationship between the individual and society differed from that in Western societies, which was based on private property. The *autonomous individual,* to whom Marx gives great importance, does not appear in the Orient. In a certain way, the individual is dependent on society and this dependence creates stagnation. When Marx speaks of a generalized slavery in Oriental societies, he is speaking of this dependence of the individual on society.

Weber believes that the problem of irrigation, determined by the geographic conditions, formed a centralized bureaucratic political system. According to him, the elementary types of agriculture and settlement in the Orient were realized within great civilizations that were established along fertile valley bases. The need for irrigation and defense generated a society that was organized by a centralized bureaucracy managed by a despotic ruler.

The basic element of this system, which Weber characterizes as patrimonialism, is control of the country via the ruler's officials. Weber never stated that there was no private property in the Orient. However he asserts the opinion that the primary form of land property was public ownership. Through this public ownership, or *timar* system, the basis for the state's bureaucracy, military and administrative (and even legal) branches was established. The ruler would allocate a property to the officials and thus, a problem-free administration could be ensured. In contrast, as there was no need for extensive irrigation in the West, an independent military and political power formed instead of a centralized bureaucracy. Thus, a more dynamic social system could arise.

Does irrigation in the Orient really hold such a fundamental position? Marx, working from sources that are both limited and unreliable, places irrigation at the center of social formation, although it is mentioned in his sources for only a limited region of the Orient. On the other hand, Weber understands that irrigation systems were peculiar only to certain areas. For example, while mentioning that there is an agricultural and political system based on irrigation in Ceylon, he does not speak of any such thing for southern India. However, Weber still generalizes that the political formation (patrimonialism) and social structure were based on irrigation. He is aware that on a factual level, differentiation and diversity in the Orient do not allow for generalizations. Nevertheless, in the end he makes one in his discourse, claiming that all the differences in the Orient led to the same result.

Equally, it may be asked whether there was ever any need in the West for an irrigation system. Marx and Weber, even if only occasionally, mention the need for irrigation, and that this was answered by a collective structure. However, both thinkers place different factors into the mix and try to gloss over why such activity in the West did not produce the same results as it did in the Orient. Here, Marx states that in Europe (particularly in Italy and Flanders), as the irrigation systems were carried out on a voluntary social organization basis, the same factors that existed in the Orient did not emerge. Correspondingly, Weber produces the same argument for the Ancient Greek irrigation systems. Thus, when the Orient is being discussed, the irrigation that leads to AMP or patrimonialism, and which are attributed solely to geographical factors, is dealt differently from when it is tackled in the West, that is, other social factors are included in the analysis.

For both Marx and Weber, the political system in the Orient, which they qualify as being detached from the people, is a source of legitimacy and thus they both make similar explanations as to the question of its continuance. Both thinkers believe that the persistence of the Oriental political structures are not only being independent from society but also foreign to it, was connected to the successful implementation of public works. According to both Marx and Weber, as long as what the system needed was produced, it would pose no problems if the Orient was administered by foreign imperial conquerors. This political system according to Marx was more absolute; for Weber it had a need of greater legitimacy. Marx held that the Oriental government was a superior authority akin to a plunderer. However, Weber suggested that the dynamics of the system can be further analyzed and associated with welfare and order. According to Marx, while the Oriental political system is a frozen one, for Weber it is not frozen, but rather stagnant.

Within this context, the basic characteristic that determines the relations between the state and the people is the absence of private property, while the other is the corvée employed in carrying out large public works. As a result, both thinkers reiterate the view that was generally accepted in Europe: everyone in the Orient is a slave of the ruler. According to Marx, production relations in AMP are social not economic. In return for the use of the despot's land, there is compulsory service in which the people carry out major public works to ensure a regular supply of water. With time the corvée went beyond irrigation, being expanded to include the construction of roads, castles, palaces, temples and fulfilling military service. Thus, according to Marx, while the individual in the West does not have individual freedom and thus has slavery imposed on them, in the Orient labor, as a whole, is not free, and there is a "general slavery." According to Weber, the use of slaves in production in Oriental societies did not develop in a way comparable to Western ones. Rather, a public service and corvée system developed to undertake public works under the gaze of the ruler's bureaucrats. The Great Wall of China, the Pyramids and the Tower of Babel were all results of such a system. Cities were also formed in the same way on the orders of the ruler. All the political and production systems were shaped via the individual's dependence on the patrimonial administration. Thus, corvée was located at the base of the continuation of societies.

According to Marx and Weber, the fact that labor was organized in this way is the reason why independent craftsmen did not appear. Marx states that in the Orient the craftsmen that did exist produced not for the market, but for the palace and its environs. He writes that it was for this reason that there was no specialization which would lead to the emergence of a separate craft sector. For this reason the necessary infrastructure for the development of capitalism did not form. Similarly, Weber states that in the Orient there was no independent craftsmanship, that the craftsmen were dependent on the ruler and his officials for both raw materials and market procurement, and that with corvée all artisans became officers of the court. Likewise, the trade guilds in the Orient were not organized like those in the West, but rather were formed for purposes of control. The reason why craftsmanship did not develop, according to Marx, was that the economic system was not productive or efficient in and of itself. Rather, labor in the Orient did not include the elements needed for social change. Weber insists that the absence of an independent craftsmanship meant that a bourgeoisie class did not appear. Thus, Oriental societies were deprived of the rationalization that the bourgeoisie brought. Weber, like Marx, also believed that capitalistic organizations did not develop for the same reason.

Another argument in Marx carried out in parallel to these was that the stagnation of village communities constituted the basis of Oriental despotism. According to Marx, there are economically enclosed and self-sufficient village communities in the Orient, which allowed the integration of agriculture and craftsmanship. In every village community, in addition to weaving, spinning and agriculture that every family carried out to meet their own needs, there were crafts divided into 12 professions. According to Marx, the existence of the introverted village communities is dependent on the monopoly of the state over the water and land. These village communities have a constant need for a central administration to carry out public works and due to their natural isolation, they are not interested in political affairs such as whether the monarch is living or dead or whether they have changed. Every village is trapped within its own borders, and Marx, influenced by the Utilitarian thought of the era, evaluated the elimination of village communities as the sign of progress of the civilization.

Although he did not enter the discussion of village communities to the same extent, Weber also believed that the villages were a vital component of the Orient. Due to the oppressive system of the patrimonial structure, villages were located at the center of society. According to Weber, as there were no independent craftsmen, the tribal ties did not disappear, and due to state policies, the village had more autonomy than the city. Each village had its own administrative system. Because this autonomy did not overstep its own boundaries or conflict with the general political structure, it was easier to impose them the responsibilities such as corvée, taxes and mandatory military service. In this sense, within Weber's corpus the only direct positive reference to Marx is that of the Indian village, where the position of the craftsmen in the village demonstrates this socio-political agreement (Weber, 1967a, p. 111).

According to Marx and Weber, as the village is the base of the Orient, there is no city. Rather the city, which has the conditions for the development of capitalism, only exists in the West. Due to the position of the craftsmen and the despotic character of the political structure in the village communities that Marx speaks of, cities only appeared temporarily as the ruler's headquarters or around the palace. For Marx, the nature of the division of labor in the village did not open the way to specialization because there was no market that had the conditions necessary for it. The necessary surplus production that was needed for change to occur was not created or was only created in response to instant and temporal demands within the village. The fact that there was no change or specialization constitutes Marx's reason for why no cities appeared in Oriental societies. Without the appearance of a market, the craftsmen remained tied to the land, and without the appearance of independent craftsmen, cities in the Orient would only appear in places that were suitable for foreign trade or where the head of state or the *satrap* exchanged their income (surplus products) for labor and where what was given for the labor was spent.

Weber gives the city a vital position in the appearance of modern society and thinks that cities like those in the West did not develop in the Orient. According to him, the necessary conditions for the appearance of a city did not exist in the Orient. There was no independent craftsmen class since craftsmen only produced for the palace and the court, that is, those who could consume their products. Nor was there an autonomous bourgeoisie class or military strata, both of which had led to the growth of the city in the West. Oriental patrimonialism completely obliterated the political horizon. In the Orient, cities could only appear when established by the ruler to increase their income, and the prosperity of the village was restricted by the future of this political structure. Thus, the ruler may change the location of the city and its name. As cities were not autonomous, there was no bourgeoisie, and no grounds for the development of capitalism. Weber and Marx's observations concerning the role of the city in historical development and the fact that there were no cities in the Orient agree to a surprising extent.

In connection to the factors mentioned above, both were of the opinion that there were the necessary grounds for the formation of capitalism in the West and that in the Orient there were grounds that prevented the same. In this sense, Marx and Weber, to a large extent, are in agreement. According to them, one of the important conditions for capitalism was free labor. With the collapse of feudalism, which partially restricted free labor in the West, complete freedom appeared. But the system in the Orient continued without changing and the traditional ties such as the patrimonial system and general slavery remained, and this prevented free labor. As expressed above, the two authors have similar views on the matter of the role of the city. In the same way, they agree on the place and importance of the organization of capital. Weber ratifies the idea of rationalism and the rational organization of labor; Marx also looks from the same perspective, allocating capitalism as the highest point of rationalism. They are in agreement that this type of rationalization in the organization of labor did not occur in the Orient. Even though he states that there was partial rationalization in the Orient, Weber rejects the presence of a total rationalization.

Marx and Weber are both of the opinion that modern conditions were the result of specific mediaeval social formations. The basic perspective concerning the preparation of internal dynamics and development was established around the Middle Ages, which was a preparatory period for the world to come. While Marx locates feudalism at the base of capitalism, in keeping to his main thesis that one mode of production is born from the internal conflicts of the previous one, Weber emphasizes the importance of the social and ideological conditions formed by feudalism previous to the development of capitalism. While Marx emphasizes the social dynamism that was the result of conflict among social classes and the role of capital accumulation, Weber, in a similar way, states that the division of power formed by feudalism prevented a centralized state and bureaucracy from appearing. Again, this separation of powers formed competition, creating a rationalization and dynamism in social life. Both thinkers state that this type of feudalism does not belong to the Orient, and thus are united in holding the position that there is no chance of a capitalist development there. Of course, while Marx emphasizes the accumulation of capital for the development of capitalism, Weber emphasizes the rationalization process and the appearance of the capitalist spirit as a result of all these processes. Indeed, it is at this point that the two diverge. Nevertheless, both share views about the conditions for the development of capitalism and that these conditions will not appear in the Orient.

Within this context, like Marx, Weber distinguishes modern capital from primitive accumulation. The basis of this separation reflects Marx's view that *capitalist* accumulation is the result of *exchange*. According to Weber, primitive accumulation is attained through violence, while capital is formed around *profit* by the opportunities of exchange (Weber, 2009b, pp. 208–209).[2] As for Marx, he separates mediaeval merchant wealth and capital, and like Weber, presents modern capital as a dynamic structure that is organized in a rational way and overcomes a number of obstacles that appear before it. At the base of this separation lies the desire to demonstrate that the primitive accumulation which appears in Oriental societies is not transformative or dynamic like modern accumulation. In this sense, while using clearer and more succinct phrases in making the comparison, Weber also tries to present the rational structure of modern capitalism in a more transparent way and tries to demonstrate that the existence of the other types of capitalism which appear in the Orient are not associated with the rational political system. Marx defends that capital and capitalism are unique to the West and that nothing similar appears anywhere else in history. Thus, Marx underlines that a capitalism which carries the society to an advanced stage of history is peculiar to the West.

As a progressive thinker, Marx believes that the conditions in the Orient can be changed. This belief led him to highly controversial views on colonialism. As a humanist, Marx believes that Oriental societies can be brought to civilization

---

2   In the footnote in which Weber (2009b, p. 209 fn. 9) adds this sentence the difference in perspective between him and Lujo Brenteno, whom he criticizes, is put forward.

even if by force. However, having analyzed the social structures that appeared from these values, Weber claims that in societies where there are values opposed to those of Western civilization, Western modernity would be impossible. Even though he has a similar outlook to Marx in regards to forcibly opening of the Orient, he is of the opinion that in the end the way to realize modernization has been blocked. Thus, in contrast to Marx, Weber speaks of two poles that are more divided and impossible to bring together.

Neglected Methodologies: Self-Revealed Mistakes

Weber himself clearly states that where he most differs from Marx is methodology. This is the main point on which the famous story of Marx–Weber opposition has been produced. However when dealing with Oriental societies they converge by not obeying their own methodology. While Marx examines the successive modes of productions and related social forms that follow each other in a materialist dialectical framework, Weber's analytical sociology examines different societies in the framework of ideal types and *verstehende*. Weber's criticism of Marxism as a single-sided analysis of society is based on this framework. The fact that Marx is progressive causes him to establish a hierarchical relationship between the historical stages. Different social forms are shaped in stages that follow one upon another. But while the different social stages are presented in the West in a dynamic way, in the Orient the existence of the same single social form is maintained throughout history. Marx finds a need for a basic methodology when dealing with this unchanging social form. Because of this, he uses a fictional Orient to answer the need to define the form of Western society in compliance with the dialectic method. This is done by ascribing the opposite characteristics that were hypothesized for the West to the Orient.

While Weber methodologically rejects determinist approaches which form chains of cause and effect, he makes analyses that are multi-factorial and therefore multi-dimensional. In contrast to Marx's logical and philosophical inferences, he performs analyses that are based on empirical details. Weber's analysis is therefore able to examine the different dimensions of an event to a greater degree. However, the problem here lies in the fact that he ignores some basic fundamentals in his own methodology. Weber's interpretive sociology defends the necessity of studying the conditions that appear as part of a problem, but this was not implemented much when the subject in question was Oriental societies. He makes analyses with a selective approach to his own model, collecting and confirming anachronistic examples without taking into account the context, time or social environment. In this context, no matter how much his examination is based on facts, due to the methodical inconsistencies, they present a fictional model.

When it comes to Oriental societies, there is similarity between Marx and Weber in that both thinkers neglect their own methodologies. In fact, both Marx and Weber turn upside down the formats of their analyses and methods. For example, in Marx's substructure–superstructure model, economic factors are the primary bases of all things in a social structure. But when examining Oriental societies, he carries out analyses concerning how the economy in AMP is determined by the political structure. As it has been seen, for Marx, the effect of the political formation on the economic structure that surrounds Oriental despotism forms the basic shape of Oriental societies. In a similar way, when Oriental societies are in question, Weber's analyses are based on the religious mentality of political life as he deals with the connections between religion and economy. According to him, the patrimonial political form affects all social life, starting with the type of belief in God. Thus, when Oriental societies are examined, both Marx and Weber abandon their own methods and become united in the idea that the determining factor is the political structure.

As a result, when dealing with Oriental societies both Marx and Weber set off with similar goals and carry out their studies with similar attitudes. They diverge on the character of capitalism due to their political views, but unite from a Western standpoint and come to the same line when analyzing the Orient. The agreement in their sources, the general trends in the nineteenth-century European thought and a similarity in the position that they give to Oriental society in their sociology define their line. Acting from the same discourse, they reiterate the same view of passive and stagnant Orient of the nineteenth-century Orientalists. This closeness in their discourse and analyses has an important place that nullifies the significance of the comparison that divides sociological theory into two opposing poles represented by these key figures.

Chapter 14
Epilogue

As the new social forms became crystallized at the beginning of the nineteenth century, defining the form of modern society and explaining the position of the Western civilization in the inter-civilizational relationships became important topics in the intellectual circles of Europe. In this context, particularly in the *fin de siècle*, it can be observed that an important development took place in the philosophy of history. Intense efforts were made in the philosophy of history to explain the success of the West historically. It divided the world history into several stages from a progressive perspective, and within this series modernity was placed last, representing the pinnacle of that history. Parallel to this staging, classification of societies also took place. This classification served to discover the laws of historical progress and thus to position modernity in inter-societal relationships. For this, they turned to comparison with other forms of societies as seen in the Orient.

In this philosophical atmosphere, the nineteenth-century sociology appeared as a science whose main function was to explain modern society that had appeared as a result of philosophical, political, economic and social transformations. There were two basic dimensions of this function. There was a need to create solutions for the wide-ranging social problems. This was the main reason for the formation of a distinction between the traditional and the modern, which determined almost all of classical sociological thought. Another aspect of sociology is, again, related to this distinction. This was the positioning of modern social forms by comparing them to others of their kind that had been seen throughout human history. Here, the philosophy of history and Orientalism provided the philosophical grounds for sociology on the matter of Oriental societies. In this context, the Orient was placed at the beginning and the Occident at the end in the thought of sociology during this founding period. Generally, the Orient was described as being stagnant in contrast to the progress of Western societies, and this ensured the unique nature of modern social forms by ousting the Orient from historical progress. Thus, the analyses made about Oriental societies were ultimately not to explain the Orient, but to transform it into an opposite model contrasting with the Occident.

In the era in which sociological thought was formed, the nature of these widespread classifications to a large extent determined its character. Marx and Weber acted from the base that had been formed by this classification of societies in their fundamental analyses. In the context of identifying modern society, they, like those before, turned to the Orient as a component of comparison, an opposing model, the "other." Marx and Weber, benefitting from Orientalist research, can be seen to have carried out their classifications in the context of questions concerned with development and the future of modern society. The basic aim in these classifications was to demonstrate modern society as developed, progressive and unique. The reason for this was that even though Marx and Weber offered different explanations concerning the development and future of modern society, the historical role they attributed to it was similar. Thus, in contrast to their traditional sociological opposition to one another, they are in complete agreement in their analyses of Oriental societies.

There are two basic aims in Marx's examination of Oriental societies. The first of these deals with the probable effects of developments on a European revolution. In this context, Marx is interested in India, China, Russia and the Ottomans in the context of their possible effect on European balance. This is because, according to him, developments that have essential importance for the future of humanity take place in modern society. The others are worth attention and examination to the proportion that they affect modern society. Beyond this political plane, Marx's analyses of Oriental societies are carried out for a second fundamental aim, that is as a model that he needs as a contrast in his explanations of modern society. Thus, in parallel with the thought of the era, Marx uses the Orient as an instrumental device to define the Occident.

On the other hand, as another classic and founding name of sociology, Weber analyzed Oriental societies in the context of the economic ethics of world religions in order to complete the explanations about the birth of modern society around Protestantism. His individual studies of Chinese, Indian and Ancient Mesopotamian societies are complemented by his evaluations of Islamic societies found in different studies. Weber directed these wide-ranging comparative studies towards the struggle against the loss of belief in modernity, which was occurring in the cultural world of the era. This is because after the first 10 years of the twentieth century, pessimism pervaded intellectual environments. Weber, in order to refresh the belief in modernity and to demonstrate that modern society was unique, was able to carry out a comprehensive study of Oriental societies using well-established Orientalist sources.

In this context, the basic question in the sociology of Marx and Weber concerns explaining modern Western society. In the framework of this common aim, they tried to develop a comparative explanation with the Oriental societies, as it was in the early sociological theory. Here they take their place in the tradition of Western thought that defines the Occident by means of othering the Orient.

As Marx and Weber relied on Orientalist sources and explanations, they developed similar analyses of Oriental societies via similar conceptual frames. Their analyses were explanations of the theses of Oriental despotism which were based on geographic and climatic explanations, and which were the most fundamental patterns of the Orientalist thought. According to these explanations, the Orient had a despotic political structure because the transition to settled life resulted from the need for irrigation being at the center of life. However, while Marx does not turn the despotism theses into a comprehensive theoretical explanation, Weber develops a model based around patrimonialism, which would be closely followed after his time. This difference between their explanations is closely related to the development of their sources, since Orientalism, which was still in its developmental stage when Marx lived, underwent a profound transformation and was institutionalized after the 1870s, thus widening and deepening. It can be seen very clearly when a comparison of Weber and Marx's sources is made. While Marx had a limited number of works, Weber used different sources that contained expert and detailed information. This meant that in subjects that Marx was only able to mention, Weber was able to carry out comprehensive empirical analyses and, working with theoretic models, delve deeper into them.

In addition to this change in the sources, the evolution that occurred in modern social form itself affected their approaches. As Oriental societies were being evaluated according to the modern society, the changes that were experienced in Europe shaped the way that Oriental societies were approached. Marx wrote his works in an era when the form of modern society had been determined but not ensured. In contrast, Weber wrote when the modern social form had reached irrevocability and was stable in the West. As a result, his studies display a comprehensive and systematic explanation of Oriental societies. However, in order to demonstrate the unique nature of modern society Marx applies to Oriental societies merely as a comparative object, unlike Weber who totally otherizes them. The latter fills in the empirical gaps in Marx's theory, which result from an indecisive attitude due to his critical approach to modern society. In this light, Weber is grounded more on the concrete and factual, while Marx presents a more abstract and philosophical approach.

Fundamentally, the comparison that lies at the base of both thinkers' works is the idea that the Occident is progressive while the Orient is stagnant. Based on the Oriental hydraulic despotism thesis, both Marx and Weber claim that stagnation reigns in the Orient because of the position of private property and political structure. Marx renders historical progress peculiar to the Occident with reference to class struggle, while Weber does this with rationalization. As Marx places the West in the last stage of a progressive historical concept, Weber accomplishes this with a developmental perspective. Both interpret history by looking backwards, and interpret the history of modern society, starting from Ancient Greece onwards, as one that is special, distinct and unique in its progress. According to them, due to the special conditions the West developed around, the rest of the world was trapped in endless stagnancy.

When the subject was Oriental societies, the two pioneers of sociological methodology did not feel compelled to adhere to their own methods. This is incredibly astonishing for anyone who is aware of how sensitive they were in the matter of method when it comes to their theoretical studies. Marx gives up historical materialism based on determining economic factors and emphasized the determinative political factors in Oriental societies. According to him, economic conditions in the Orient were determined by despotic political inclinations. As for Weber, a neglect of some basic rules of his interpretive sociology is evident. Rather than analyzing Oriental societies according to their own conditions and meanings, he examines them from a Western perspective. He achieves this frequently by using selective sources in an anachronistic way. In sum, when Oriental society was being examined, both authors abandoned their methodological consistency in their analyses in order to realize their aims.

Finally, the basic nature of the sociological theories of Marx and Weber was to interpret modernity. With this basic aim, the approach they had towards Oriental societies was determined by the needs and inclinations of society, civilization and the intellectual world. Both Marx and Weber tried to analyze modern society by comparing it to Oriental societies. Thus, Oriental societies were a part and supplementary factor of their analyses of modern society.

In the light of these evaluations, the position of Marx and Weber in the history of sociology should be re-examined. Their juxtaposition as theoretical opponents, which still continues to dominate sociological literature, should be questioned in the context of the basic aims they shared in sociology. Political divergence about the roots and future of modern society gave way to a convergence of ideas gleaned from the world-historical meaning of modernity. In the end, Marx and Weber not only overlap to a large extent in their similar explanations and concepts on Oriental societies, they even complete one another.

Bibliography

Abdel-Malek, A. (1963). Orientalism in Crisis. *Diogenes*, (44) 104–112.

Allen, K. (2004). *Max Weber: A Critical Introduction*. London: Pluto Press.

Althusser, L. (1969). *For Marx*. Harmondsworth: Penguin Books.

Anderson, P. (1979). *Lineages of the Absolutist State*. London: Verso.

Antoni, C. (1962). *From History to Sociology: The Transition in German Historical Thinking*. London: Merlin.

Antonio, R. J. (1985). Introduction. In R.J. Antonio and R.M. Glassman (eds), *A Weber-Marx Dialogue* (pp. 20–43). Lawrence: University Press of Kansas.

Antonio, R. J., and Glassman, R.M. (1985). Introduction. In R.J. Antonio and R.M. Glassman (eds), *A Weber-Marx Dialogue* (pp. xi–xxi). Lawrence: University Press of Kansas.

Aristotle. (1996). *The Politics and the Constitution of Athens*. Cambridge, UK: Cambridge University Press.

Aron, R. (1965). *Main Currents in Sociological Thought: Montesquieu, Comte, Marx, Tocqueville, and The sociologists and the Revolution of 1848*. New Brunswick, New Jersey: Transaction Publishers.

Avineri, S. (ed.). (1968a). *Karl Marx on Colonialism and Modernization; His Despatches and Other Writings on China, India, Mexico, the Middle East and North Africa*. Garden City: Doubleday.

Avineri, S. (1968b). Introduction. In S. Avinery (ed.), *Karl Marx on Colonialism and Modernization; His Despatches and Other Writings on China, India, Mexico, the Middle East and North Africa* (pp. 1–31). Garden City: Doubleday.

Avineri, S. (1969). Marx and Modernization. *The Review of Politics*, 31(2), 172–188.

Avineri, S. (1971). *Social and Political Thought of Karl Marx*. Cambridge: Cambridge University Press.

Avineri, S. (1990). The Hegelian Origins of Marx's Political Thought. In B. Jessop and C. Malcolm-Brown (eds), *Karl Marx Social and Economic Thought, Critical Assesments Vol. 1* (pp. 154–168). London: Routledge.

Bacon, F. (1632). *Essays or counsels civil and moral*. London.

Bailey, A.M., and Llobera, J.R. (1974). The Asiatic Mode of Production: An Annotated Bibliography. *Critique of Anthropology*, 1(2), 95–107.

Bailey, A.M., and Llobera, J.R. (1979). Karl A. Wittfogel and The Asiatic Mode of Production: A Reappraisal. *Sociological Review*, 27(3), 541–559.

Bailey, A.M., and Llobera, J.R. (1981). *The Asiatic Mode of Production: Science and Politics*. London, Boston: Routledge & Kegan Paul.

Baron, S.H. (1975). Marx's Grundrisse and the Asiatic Mode of Production. *Survey*, (21), 128–147.

Bendix, R. (1945). Bureaucracy and the Problem of Power. *Public Administration Review*, 5(1), 194–209.

Bendix, R. (1947). Bureaucracy: The Problem and Its Setting. *American Sociological Review*, 12(5), 493–507.

Bendix, R. (1960). *Max Weber: An Intellectual Portrait*. Garden City: Doubleday.

Bernal, M. (1987). *Black Athena: The Afroasiatic Roots of Classical Civilization. Vol. 1: The Fabrication of Ancient Greece, 1785–1985*. London: Free Association Books.

Bernier, F. (1914). *Travels in the Mogul Empire, A.D. 1656–1668*. (A. Constable, trans.). London & New York: H. Milford & Oxford University Press.

Bimber, B. (1990). Karl Marx and the Three Faces of Technological Determinism. *Social Studies of Science*, 20(2), 333–351.

Birnbaum, N. (1953). Conflicting Interpretations of the Rise of Capitalism: Marx and Weber. *British Journal of Sociology*, 4(2), 125–141.

Blaut, J.M. (1993). *The Colonizer's Model of the World: Geographical Diffusionism and Eurocentric History*. New York: Guilford Press.

Blaut, J.M. (2000). *Eight Eurocentric Historians*. New York: Guilford Press.

Bodin, J. (1967). *Six Books of the Commonwealth*. Oxford: B. Blackwell.

Bottomore, T. (1975). *Marxist Sociology*. London: The Macmillan Press Ltd.

Bottomore, T. (1978). Marxism and Sociology. In T. Bottomore and R. Nisbet (eds), *A History of Sociological Analysis* (pp. 118–130). New York: Basic Books.

Bottomore, T. (1984). *Sociology and Socialism*. Brighton: Wheatsheaf Books.

Bottomore, T., and Outwaite, W. (1993). Introduction to Translation. In T. Bottomore and W. Outwaite (eds), *Max Weber and Karl Marx*. London: Routledge.

Boucock, C. (2000). *In the Grip of Freedom: Law and Modernity in Max Weber*. Toronto: University of Toronto Press.

Brubaker, R. (1984). *The Limits of Rationality: An Essay on the Social and Moral Thought of Max Weber*. London: Allen & Unwin.

Camic, C., Gorski, P.S., and Trubek, D.M. (2005). Introduction. In C. Camic, P.S. Gorski, and D.M. Trubek (eds), *Max Weber's Economy and Society: A Critical Companion* (pp. 1–30). Stanford: Stanford University Press.

Campbell, G. (1852). *Modern India: A Sketch of the System of Civil Government*. London: J. Murray.

Carver, T. (1990). Marx and Hegel's Logic. In B. Jessop and C. Malcolm-Brown (eds), *Karl Marx Social and Economic Thought, Critical Assesments* (Vol. 1, pp. 188–203). London: Routledge.

Chakrabarty, D. (1996). Marxist Perception of Indian History. *Economic and Political Weekly*, (13), 1838–1840.

Chesneaux, J. (1964). Le mode de production asiatique: quelques perspectives de recherche. *La Pensee*, 114 (Jan–Feb).

Cohen, J., Hazelrigg, L.E., and Pope, W. (1975). De-Parsonizing Weber: A Critique of Parsons' Interpretation of Weber's Sociology. *American Sociological Review*, 40(2), 229–241.

Collins, R. (1981). *Sociology Since Midcentury: Essay in Theory Cumulation.* New York: Academic Press.

Collins, R. (1986). *Max Weber: A Skeleton Key.* Beverly Hills: Sage Publications.

Connell, R.W. (1997). Why is Classical Theory Classical? *American Journal of Sociology*, 102(6), 1511–1557.

Cooper, R. (1925). The Logical influence of Hegel on Marx. *University of Washington Publications in Social Sciences*, 2(2), 79–182.

Coşkun, İ. (1989). Modernleşme Kuramı Üzerine. *Sosyoloji Dergisi, 3. Dizi*(1), 289–304.

Coşkun, İ. (1991). Niyazi Berkes Üzerine. *Sosyoloji Dergisi, 3. Dizi*(2), 49–86.

Coşkun, İ. (2000). Modernliğin Kaynakları: Rönesans Üzerine Bir Değerlendirme. *Sosyoloji Dergisi, 3. Dizi*(6), 45–70.

Coşkun, İ. (2008). Sosyoloji, Antropoloji, Şarkiyatçılık ve Öteki. *Sosyoloji Dergisi, 3. Dizi* (16), 11–26.

Cox, O.C. (1950). Max Weber on Social Stratification: A Critique. *American Sociological Review*, XV(2), 223–227.

Crone, P. (1999). Weber, Islamic Law, and the Rise of Capitalism. In T.E. Huff and W. Schluchter (eds), *Max Weber and Islam* (pp. 247–272). New Brunswick: Transaction.

Çizakça, M. (1996). *A Comparative Evolution of Business Partnerships: Islamic World and the West, with Specific Reference to the Ottoman Archives.* Leiden: E.J. Brill.

Dewey, C. (1972). Images of the Village Community: A Study in Anglo-Indian Ideology. *Modern Asian Studies*, 6(3), 291–328.

Dibble, V.K. (1968). Social Science and Political Commitments in the Young Max Weber. *European Journal of Sociology*, 9(1), 92–110.

Dirlik, A. (1982). Chinese historians and the Marxist concept of capitalism: A critical examination. *Modern China*, 8(1), 105–132.

Divitçioğlu, S. (1966). *ATÜT ve Az Gelişmiş Ülkeler.* İstanbul: Elif Yayınları.

Divitçioğlu, S. (1967). *Asya Üretim Tarzı ve Osmanlı Toplumu.* İstanbul: İstanbul Üniversitesi İktisat Fakültesi Yayınları.

Djait, H. (1985). *Europe and Islam.* Berkeley: University of California Press.

Draper, H. (1985). *The Marx-Engels Chronicle: A Day-By-Day Chronology of Marx And Engels' Life And Activity.* New York: Schocken Books.

Dumont, L. (1966). The "Village Community" from Munro to Maine. *Contributions to Indian Sociology*, 9, 67–89.

Dunn, S. (1982). *The Fall and Rise of the Asiatic Mode of Production.* London: Routledge & Kegan & Paul.

Eisen, A. (1978). The Meanings and Confusions of Weberian 'Rationality'. *British Journal of Sociology*, 29(1), 57–70.

Eisenstadt, S.N. (1999). Weber's Analysis of Islam and the Specific Pattern of Islamic Civilization. In T.E. Huff and W. Schluchter (eds), *Max Weber and Islam* (pp. 247–272). New Brunswick: Transaction.

Ellul, J. (1964). *The Technological Society.* (J. Wilkinson, trans.). New York: Vintage.

Elphinstone, M. (1889). *The History of India: The Hindú and Mahometan Periods.* London: J. Murray.

Engels, F. (1976a). The Discovery of America (Minutes of Engels's Lecture to the London German Workers' Educational Society on November 30, 1847). *MECW* (Vol. 6, pp. 627–629). New York: International Publishers.

Engels, F. (1976b). Abd-El-Kader. *MECW* (Vol. 6, pp. 469–472). New York: International Publishers.

Engels, F. (1977). Democratic Pan-Slavism. *MECW* (Vol. 8, pp. 363–371). New York: International Publishers.

Engels, F. (1980). Karl Marx, A Contribution to the Critique of Political Economy. *MECW* (Vol. 16, pp. 465–477). New York: International Publishers.

Engels, F. (1982). Engels to Marx in Manchester, 23 May 1851. *MECW* (Vol. 38, pp. 361–364). New York: International Publishers.

Engels, F. (1983). Engels to Marx in London, June 6, 1853. *MECW* (Vol. 39, pp. 335–342). New York: International Publishers.

Engels, F. (1986). Persia – China. *MECW* (Vol. 15, pp. 278–283). New York: International Publishers.

Engels, F. (1989). Preface to the First German Edition of Socialism: Utopian and Scientific. *MECW* (Vol. 24, pp. 457–459). New York: International Publishers.

Engels, F. (1990a). The Origin of the Family, Private Property and the State. *MECW* (Vol. 26, pp. 129–276). New York: International Publishers.

Engels, F. (1990b). Ludwig Feuerbach and the End of Classical German Philosophy. *MECW* (Vol. 26, pp. 353–398). New York: International Publishers.

Engels, F. (1998a). Preface [Capital Vol. 3]. *MECW* (Vol. 37, pp. 5–26). New York: International Publishers.

Engels, F. (1998b). Supplement to Capital, Volume Three. *MECW* (Vol. 37, pp. 873–900). New York: International Publishers.

Engels, F. (2004). Engels to W. Sombart in Berlin, March 11, 1895. *MECW* (Vol. 50, pp. 460–461). New York: International Publishers.

Ertürk, R. (1997). *Türk Sosyolojisinde ve Cumhuriyet Döneminde Köy Tartışmaları.* İstanbul: İstanbul Üniversitesi Edebiyat Fakültesi Yayınları.

Feher, F. (1987). Weber and the Rationalization of Music. *The International Journal of Politics, Culture and Society*, 1(2), 147–162.

Ferrarotti, F. (1982). *Max Weber and the Destiny of Reason.* Armonk: M.E. Sharpe.

Ferrarotti, F. (1987). *Max Weber and the Crisis of Western Civilization.* Port Washington: Associated Faculty Press.

Fischoff, E. (1944). The Protestant Ethic and the Spirit of Capitalism–The History of a Controversy. *Social Research*, 11(1), 53–77.

Freund, J. (1968). *The Sociology of Max Weber.* New York: Pantheon Books.

Freund, J. (1978). German Sociology in the Time of Max Weber. In T. Bottomore and R. Nisbet (eds), *A History of Sociological Analysis* (pp. 149–186). New York: Basic Books.

Gane, N. (2002). *Max Weber and Postmodern Theory: Rationalization Versus Re-Enchantment*. Houndmills: Palgrave.

Garaudy, R. (1967). *Karl Marx: The Evolution of His Thought*. New York: International Publishers.

Gellner, E. (1985). Soviets Against Wittfogel; or, the Anthropological Preconditions of Mature Marxism. *Theory and Society*, 14(3), 341–370.

Gerth, H.H. (1968). Prefatory Note. In H.H. Gerth (ed.), *The Religion of China: Confucianism and Taoism* (pp. ix–xiii). New York: Free Press.

Gerth, H.H. (ed.) (1958). *The First International: Minutes of the Hague Congress of 1872 with Related Documents*. (H.H. Gerth, trans.). Madison: University of Wisconsin Press.

Gerth, H.H., and Martindale, D. (1952). Preface. In H.H. Gerth and D. Martindale (eds), *Ancient Judaism* (pp. ix–xxvii). New York: Free Press.

Gerth, H.H., and Mills, C.W. (1946). Introduction: The Man and His Work. In H.H. Gerth and C.W. Mills (eds), *From Max Weber: Essays in Sociology* (pp. 3–74). New York: Oxford University Press.

Giddens, A. (1970). Marx, Weber, and the Development of Capitalism. *Sociology*, 4(3), 289–310.

Giddens, A. (1971). *Capitalism and Modern Social Theory: An Analysis of the Writings of Marx, Durkheim and Max Weber*. Cambridge: Cambridge University Press.

Giddens, A. (1972). *Politics and Sociology in the Thought of Max Weber*. London: Macmillan.

Giddens, A. (1984). *The Constitution of Society: Outline of the Theory of Structuration*. Berkeley and Los Angeles: University of California Press.

Giddens, A. (1995). *Politics, Sociology and Social Theory: Encounters with Classical and Contemporary Social Thought*. Stanford, California: Stanford University Press.

Godelier, M. (1964). *La Notion du mode de production asiatique et les schémas marxistes d'évolution des sociétés*. Paris: Centre d'études et de recherches marxistes (CERM).

Goldhammer, H., and Shils, E. (1939). Types of Power and Status. *The American Journal of Sociology*, 45(2), 171–182.

Goody, J. (1996). *The East in the West*. New York: Cambridge University Press.

Görgün, T. (1996). Ignaz Goldziher. *DİA İslam Ansiklopedisi*. İstanbul.

Habib, I. (1985). Classifying Pre-Colonial India. *Journal of Peasant Studies*, 12(2), 44–53.

Habib, I. (1999). *The Agrarian System of Mughal India (1526–1707)*. New Delhi and New York: Oxford University Press.

Hambly, G.R.G. (1982). Towns and Cities: Mughal India. In T. Raychaudhuri and I. Habib (eds), *Cambridge Economic History of India*, Vol. 1 (pp. 434–52). Cambridge: Cambridge University Press.

Harstick, H.-P., Sperl, R., and Strauß, H. (1999). Die Bibliotheken von Karl Marx und Friedrich Engels: Annotiertes Verzeichnis Des Ermittelten Bestandes. *MEGA Band 32*. Berlin: Akademie Verlag.

Hegel, G. W. F. (1988). *Introduction to The Philosophy of History: With Selections from The Philosophy of Right*. (L. Rauch, trans.). Indianapolis: Hackett Publishing.

Hennis, W. (1983). Max Weber's "Central Question". (K. Tribe, trans.) *Economy and Society*, 12(2), 135–180.

Hilav, S. (1970). Asya–Tipi Üretim Tarzı ve Türkiye Sosyalist Hareketi. In İ. Keskinoğlu (trans.), *Asya Tipi Üretim Tarzı* (pp. 9–22). İstanbul: Ant Yay.

Hindess, B. (1987). Rationality and Characterization of Modern Society. In S. Whimster and S. Lash (eds), *Max Weber, Rationality and Modernity* (pp. 137–153). London: Allen & Unwin.

Hindess, B., and Hirst, P.Q. (1975). *Pre-capitalist Modes of Production*. London: Routledge & Kegan Paul.

Hobsbawm, E.J. (1965). Introduction. *Pre-Capitalist Economic Formations* (pp. 9–66). New York: International Publishers.

Hobson, J.M. (2004). *The Eastern Origins of Western Civilisation*. Cambridge, New York: Cambridge University Press.

Honigsheim, P. (1946). Max Weber as Rural Sociologist. *Rural Sociology*, 11(3), 208–218.

Honigsheim, P. (2000). *The Unknown Max Weber*. (A. Sica, ed.). New Brunswick: Transaction Publishers.

Hook, S. (1950). *From Hegel to Marx; Studies in the Intellectual Development of Karl Marx*. New York: Humanities Press.

Huff, T.E., and Schluchter, W. (eds) (1999). *Max Weber and Islam*. New Brunswick, New Jersey: Transaction Publishers.

Hughes, H.S. (2002). *Consciousness and Society*. New Brunswick, New Jersey: Transaction Publishers.

Inalcik, H. (1992). Comments on "Sultanism": Max Weber's Typification of Ottoman Polity. *Princeton Papers in Near Eastern Studies*, (1), 49–73.

Institute of Marxism-Leninism. (1934). *Karl Marx: Chronik Seines Lebens*. Moscow: Marx-Engels-Verlag.

International Institute of Social History. (2008). Karl Marx / Friedrich Engels Papers. Amsterdam: International Institute of Social History. Retrieved August 13, 2008, from http://www.iisg.nl/archives/pdf/10760604.pdf

Isin, E.F. (2003). Historical Sociology of the City. In G. Delanty and E. F. Isin (eds), *Handbook of Historical Sociology* (pp. 312–325). London: SAGE Publications.

Isin, E.F. (2006). Theorizing the European City. In G. Delanty (ed.), *Handbook of Contemporary European Social Theory*. London and New York: Routledge.

Jones, D.M. (2001). *The Image of China in Western Social and Political Thought*. New York: Palgrave.

Kaesler, D. (2004). From Academic Outsider to Sociological Mastermind: The Fashioning of the Sociological "Classic" Max Weber. *Bangladesh e-Journal of Sociology*, 1(1) Special Issue: Patrimonialism, Culture and Religion: A Reexamination of Max Weber), 4–16.

Kaiser, B., and Werchan, I. (1967). *Ex libris Karl Marx und Friedrich Engels: Schicksal und Verzeichnis einer Bibliothek*. (B. Kaiser, ed.). Berlin: Dietz.

Kalberg, S. (1994). *Max Weber's Comparative-Historical Sociology*. Chicago: University of Chicago Press.

Kalberg, S. (ed.). (2005). *Max Weber: Readings and Commentary on Modernity*. Malden: Blackwell Pub.

Kaviraj, S. (1983). On the Status of Marx's Writings on India. *Social Scientist*, 11(9 (Karl Marx)), 26–46.

Kayalı, K. (2008). Sol'da Kemal Tahir Tartışmaları. In M. Gültekingil (ed.), *Modern Türkiye'de Siyasi Düşünceler* (Vol. 8 (Sol), pp. 1089–1095). İstanbul: İletişim Yayınevi.

Kemple, T. M. (2009). Weber/Simmel/Du Bois: Musical Thirds of Classical Sociology. *Journal of Classical Sociology*, 9(2), 187–207.

King, R. (1999). *Orientalism and Religion: Postcolonial Theory, India and the Mystic East*. London and New York: Routledge.

Kippenberg, H.G. (2005). Religious Communities and the Path to Disenchantment: The Origins, Sources, and Theoretical Core of the Religion Section. In C. Camic, P.S. Gorski, and D.M. Trubek (eds), *Max Weber's Economy and Society: A Critical Companion* (pp. 164–182). Stanford: Stanford University Press.

Koebner, R. (1951). Despot and Despotism: Vicissitudes of a Political Term. *Journal of the Warburg and Courtauld Institutes*, *14*(3/4), 275.

Korsch, K. (1938). *Karl Marx*. New York: John Wiley & Sons.

Koselleck, R. (2007). *İlerleme*. (M. Özdemir, trans.). Ankara: Dost Yay.

Kozyr-Kowalski, S. (1968). Weber and Marx. *Polish Sociological Bulletin*, (1), 5–17.

Krader, L. (1974). *The Ethnological Notebooks of Karl Marx (Studies of Morgan, Phear, Maine, Lubbock)*. (L. Krader, trans.). Appen: Van Gorcum.

Krader, L. (1975). *The Asiatic Mode of Production: Sources, Development and Critique in the Writings of Karl Marx*. Appen: Van Gorcum.

Krader, L. (1982). Theory of Evolution, Revolution and the State: The Critical Relation of Marx to His Contemporaries Darwin, Carlyle, Morgan, Maine and Kovalevsky. In E.J. Hobsbawm (ed.), *The History of Marxism* (pp. 192–226). Bloomington: Indiana University Press.

Lekas, P. (1988). *Marx on Classical Antiquity: Problems of Historical Methodology*. New York: St. Martin's Press.

Lenin, V.I. (1972). Materialism and Empirio-Criticism. *Lenin Collected Works* (Vol. 14, pp. 17–362). Moscow: Progress Publishers.

Lichtheim, G. (1961). *Marxism: An Historical and Critical Study*. London: Routledge & Kegan Paul.

Lichtheim, G. (1969). *The origins of socialism*. New York: Praeger.

Llobera, J. R. (1979). Techno-Economic Determinism and the Work of Marx on Pre-Capitalist Societies. *Man, New Series*, 14(2), 249–270.

Love, J. (2000). Max Weber's Orient. In S.P. Turner (ed.), *The Cambridge Companion to Weber* (pp. 172–199). Cambridge: Cambridge University Press.

Lowe, D.M. (1966). *The Function of "China" in Marx, Lenin, and Mao*. Berkeley: University of California Press.

Löwith, K. (1993). *Max Weber and Karl Marx*. (H. Fantel, trans.). London: Routledge.

Lukacs, G. (1972). Max Weber and German Sociology. *Economy and Society*, 4(1), 386–398.

Lukács, G. (1981). *The Destruction of Reason*. Atlantic Highlands, N.J.: Humanities Press.

Machiavelli, N. (2005). *The Prince*. (P. E. Bondanella, trans.). Oxford; New York: Oxford University Press.

MacIntyre, A. (1968). *Marxism and Christianity*. New York: Schocken Book.

Madan, G. R. (1979). *Western Sociologists on Indian Society: Marx, Spencer, Weber, Durkheim, Pareto*. London and Boston: Routledge & Kegan Paul.

McCarney, J. (2000). Hegel's Legacy. In T. Burns and I. Fraser (eds), *The Hegel-Marx Connection* (pp. 56–78). Basingstoke: Macmillan Press.

McCarthy, G.E. (1988). *Marx' Critique of Science and Positivism: The Methodological Foundations of Political Economy*. Boston: Kluwer Academic.

McNaron, D.L. (1999). Social Sciences and Verstehen Thesis. In T. M. Powers and P. Kamolnick (eds), *From Kant to Weber: Freedom and Culture in Classical German Social Theory* (pp. 101–124). Malabar: Krieger Publishing Company.

Manasse, E.M. (1947). Max Weber on Race. *Social Research*, 14, 191–221.

Mandel, E. (1971). *The Formation of Economic Thought of Karl Marx: 1843 to Capital*. (B. Pearce, trans.). London: Monthly Review Press.

Marshall, G. (1982). *In Search of the Spirit of Capitalism: An Essay on Max Weber's Protestant Ethic Thesis*. London: Hutchinson.

Marx, K. (1970). *Notes on Indian History (1664–1855)*. Moscow: Foreign Languages Publishing House.

Marx, K. (1975a). Letter from Karl to his Father in Trier, 10 November 1837. *MECW* (Vol. 1, pp. 10–21). New York: International Publishers.

Marx, K. (1975b). Debates on Freedom of Press. *MECW* (Vol. 1, pp. 132–181). New York: International Publishers.

Marx, K. (1976a). Contribution to the Critique of Hegel's Philosophy of Right [Introduction]. *MECW* (Vol. 3, pp. 175–187). New York: International Publishers.

Marx, K. (1976b). On Jewish Question. *MECW* (Vol. 3, pp. 146–174). New York: International Publishers.

Marx, K. (1976c). The Poverty of Philosophy. *MECW* (Vol. 6, pp. 105–206). New York: International Publishers.

Marx, K. (1976d). Contribution to the Critique of Hegel's Philosophy of Right. *MECW* (Vol. 3, pp. 3–130.). New York: International Publishers.

Marx, K. (1976e). Wage Labour and Capital. *MECW* (Vol. 9, pp. 197–229). New York: International Publishers.

Marx, K. (1978a). The Eighteenth Brumaire of Louis Bonaparte. *MECW* (Vol. 11, pp. 99–197). New York: International Publishers.

Marx, K. (1978b). The Class Struggles in France, 1848 to 1850. *MECW* (Vol. 10, pp. 45–146). New York: International Publishers.

Marx, K. (1979a). The British Rule in India. *MECW* (Vol. 12, pp. 125–133). New York: International Publishers.

Marx, K. (1979b). The Future Results of British Rule in India. *MECW* (Vol. 12, pp. 217–222). New York: International Publishers.

Marx, K. (1979c). Declaration of War. – On the History of the Eastern Question. *MECW* (Vol. 13, pp. 100–108). New York: International Publishers.

Marx, K. (1980). Trade With China. *MECW* (Vol. 16, pp. 536–539). New York: International Publishers.

Marx, K. (1982). The Revolt in the Indian Army. *MECW* (Vol. 38, pp. 297–300). New York: International Publishers.

Marx, K. (1983a). Marx to Ferdinand Lasalle in Düsseldorf, 21 December 1857. *MECW* (Vol. 40, pp. 225–227). New York: International Publishers.

Marx, K. (1983b). Marx to Engels in Manchester, 16 January 1858. *MECW* (Vol. 40, pp. 248–251). New York: International Publishers.

Marx, K. (1983c). Marx to Engels in Manchester, 2 June 1853. *MECW* (Vol. 39, pp. 330–335). New York: International Publishers.

Marx, K. (1983d). Marx to Engels in Manchester, 14 June 1853 . *MECW* (Vol. MECW, pp. 344–348.). New York: International Publishers.

Marx, K. (1984). The North American Civil War. *MECW* (Vol. 19, pp. 32–42). New York: International Publishers.

Marx, K. (1986). Economic Manuscripts of 1857-58 (Grundrisse). *MECW* (Vol. 28). New York: International Publishers.

Marx, K. (1987a). Marx to Engels in Manchester, 25 March 1868. *MECW* (Vol. 42, pp. 547–549). New York: International Publishers.

Marx, K. (1987b). A Contribution to the Critique of Political Economy. *MECW* (Vol. 29, pp. 257–420.). New York: International Publishers.

Marx, K. (1987c). From The Prepatory Meterials [Original Text of Critique of Political Economy, 1858]. *MECW* (Vol. 29, pp. 430–507). New York: International Publishers.

Marx, K. (1987d). Preface (A Contribution to the Critique of Political Economy) . *MECW* (Vol. 261–265, pp. 261–265). New York: International Publishers.

Marx, K. (1987e). Economic Manuscripts of 1857-58 (Grundrisse). *MECW* (Vol. 29). New York: International Publishers.

Marx, K. (1989a). Economic Manuscript of 1861-63: A Contribution to the Critique of Political Economy (Theories of Surplus Value),. *MECW* (Vol. 31). New York: International Publishers.

Marx, K. (1989b). Drafts of the Letter to Vera Zasulich, in November 1881 . *MECW* (Vol. 24, pp. pp.346–369.). New York: International Publishers.

Marx, K. (1991). Economic Manuscript of 1861-63: A Contribution to the Critique of Political Economy (Theories of Surplus Value). *MECW* (Vol. 33). New York: International Publishers.

Marx, K. (1996a). Aferword to the Second German Edition . *MECW* (Vol. 35, pp. 12–20). New York : International Publishers.

Marx, K. (1996b). Capital (Vol.1). *MECW* (Vol. 35). New York: International Publishers.

Marx, K. (1998). Capital (Vol. 3). *MECW* (Vol. 37). New York: International Publishers.

Marx, K., and Engels, F. (1897), ed. E. Marx-Aveling and E. Aveling. *The Eastern Question..* London: Swan Sonnenschein.

Marx, K., and Engels, F. (1962). *On Britain, Moscow.* Foreign: Language Publishing House.

Marx, K., and Engels, F. (1969). *On Colonialism.* Moscow: Foreign Language Publishing House.

Marx, K., and Engels, F. (1976a). German Ideology. *MECW* (Vol. 5, pp. 19–584). New York: International Publishers.

Marx, K., and Engels, F. (1976b). Manifesto of the Communist Party. *MECW* (Vol. 6, pp. 477–520). New York: International Publishers.

Marx, K., and Engels, F. (1977). *Kapitalizm Öncesi Ekonomi Biçimleri.* (M. Belli, trans.) (Genişletil.). Ankara: Sol Yayınları.

Mayer, C. (1975). Max Weber's Interpretation of Karl Marx. *Social Research*, 42(4), 701–719.

Mayer, J.P. (1944). *Max Weber and German Politics, a Study in Political Sociology.* London: Faber and Faber.

Melotti, U. (1977). *Marx and the Third World.* Atlantic Highlands: Humanities Press.

Merton, R.K. (1949). *Social Theory and Social Structure: Toward the Codification of Theory and Research.* Glencoe: Free Press.

Mitzman, A. (1985). *The Iron Cage: An Historical Interpretation of Max Weber.* New Brunswick: Transaction Books.

Mommsen, W.J. (1977a). Max Weber as a Critic of Marxism. *Canadian Journal of Sociology*, 2(4), 373–398.

Mommsen, W.J. (1977b). *The Age of Bureaucracy: Perspectives on the Political Sociology of Max Weber.* New York: Harper & Row.

Mommsen, W.J. (1984). *Max Weber and German Politics, 1890–1920.* Chicago: University of Chicago Press.

Mommsen, W.J. (1989). *The Political and Social Theory of Max Weber: Collected Essays.* Chicago: University of Chicago Press.

Montesquieu, C. B. D. (2008). *Persian Letters.* (M. Mauldon, trans.). Oxford, New York: Oxford University Press.

Montesquieu, C. B. D. (2011). *The Spirit of Laws.* New York: Cosimo Publications.

Mukhia, H. (1985). Marx on Pre-Colonial India: An Evaluation. *Marxian Theory and the Third World* (pp. 173–184). New Delhi: Sage Publications.

Munch, P. (1993). The Thesis Before Weber: An Archaelogy. In G. Roth and H. Lehmann (eds), *Weber's Protestant Ethic: Origins, Evidence, Contexts* (pp. 51–72). Washington, DC: German Historical Institute.

Musto, M. (2008). *Karl Marx's Grundrisse: Foundations of the critique of political economy 150 years later*. (M. Musto, ed.) (With a spe.). London and New York: Routledge.

Nafissi, M.R. (1998). Reframing Orientalism: Weber and Islam. *Economy and Society*, *27*(1), 98–118.

Nafissi, M.R. (2000). On the Foundations of Athenian Democracy: Marx's Paradox and Weber's Solution. *Max Weber Studies*, *1*(1), 56–83.

Nafissi, M.R. (2005). *Ancient Athens and Modern Ideology: Value, Theory and Evidence in Historical Sciences: Max Weber, Karl Polanyi and Moses Finley*. London: Institute of Classical Studies.

Naqvi, S. (1973). Marx on Pre-British Indian Economy and Society. *Socialist Digest*, (7), 36–70.

Needham, J. (1959). Review of K.A. Witttogel's Oriental Despotism. *Science and Society*, *23*(1), 58–65.

Nelson, B. (1965). Dialogs Across the Centuries: Weber, Marx, Hegel, Luther. In John Weiss (ed.), *The Origins of Modern Consciousness; Essays* (pp. 149–165). Detroit: Wayne State University Press.

Nelson, B. (1974). Max Weber's "Author's Introduction" (1920): A Master Clue to his Main Aims. *Sociological Inquiry*, *44*(4), 269–277.

O'Leary, B. (1989). *Asiatic Mode of Production: Oriental Despotism, Historical Materialism, and Indian History*. Massachusetts: Basil Blackwell.

Oakes, G. (1977). Introductory Essay. In G. Oakes (trans.), *Critique of Stammler* (pp. 1–58). New York: Free Press.

Oakley, A. (1983). *The Making of Marx's Critical Theory: A Bibliographical Analysis*. London and Boston: Routledge & Kegan Paul.

Parkin, F. (1982). *Max Weber*. Chichester: E. Horwood.

Parsons, T. (1928). "Capitalism" in Recent German Literature: Sombart and Weber. *The Journal of Political Economy*, *36*(6), 641–661.

Parsons, T. (1929). "Capitalism" in Recent German Literature: Sombart and Weber-Concluded. *The Journal of Political*, *37*(1), 31–51.

Parsons, T. (1963). Introduction. In E. Fischoff (trans.), *The Sociology of Religion* (pp. xix–lxviii). Boston: Beacon Press.

Parsons, T. (1967). Introduction to Max Weber's the Sociology of Religion. *Sociological Theory and Modern Society* (pp. 35–78). New York: Free Press.

Parsons, T. (1968). *The Structure of Social Action: A Study in Social Theory With Special Reference to a Group of Recent European Writers (2 vols.)*. New York: Free Press.

Parsons, T. (1971). Value-freedom and Objectivity. In O. Stammer (ed.), *Max Weber and Sociology Today* (pp. 27–50). New York: Harper & Row.

Parsons, T. (1975). On "De-Parsonizing Weber". *American Sociological Review*, *40*(5), 666–670.

Plamenatz, J. (1992). *Man and Society: Political and Social Theories from Machiavelli to Marx (Vol 3, Hegel, Marx and the Idea of Progress).* (M.E. Plamenatz and R. Wokler, eds) (A new edn). New York: Longman.

Poggi, G. (2006). *Weber: A Short Introduction.* Cambridge: Polity.

Ragin, C., and Chirot, D. (1995). The World System of Immanuel Wallerstein: Sociology and Politcs as History. In T. Skocpol (ed.), *Vision and Method in Historical Sociology* (pp. 276–312). New York: Cambridge University Press.

Riazanov, D. (1990). *K. Marx/ F. Engels: Hayat ve Eserlerine Giriş.* (R. Zarakolu, trans). İstanbul: Belge Yay.

Ringer, F.K. (2004). *Max Weber: An Intellectual Biography.* Chicago: University of Chicago Press.

Robertson, H.M. (1933). *Aspects of the Rise of Economic Individualism: A Criticism of Maw Weber and His School.* Cambridge: Cambridge University Press.

Rodinson, M. (2007). *Islam and Capitalism.* London: Saqi Books.

Rosenberg, N. (1999). Marx as a Student of Technology. In B. Jessop and R. Wheatley (eds), *Karl Marx Social and Economic Thought, Critical Assesments* (Vol. 5, pp. 396–412). London: Routledge.

Roth, G. (1971a). The Historical Relationship to Marxism. In R. Bendix and G. Roth (eds), *Scholarship and Partisanship; Essays on Max Weber* (pp. 227–252). Berkeley: University of California Press.

Roth, G. (1971b). Weber's Generational Rebellion and Maturation. In R. Bendix and G. Roth (eds), *Scholarship and Partisanship; Essays on Max Weber* (pp. 6–33). Berkeley: University of California Press.

Roth, G. (1979). Weber's Vision of History. In G. Roth and W. Schluchter (eds), *Max Weber's Vision of History: Ethics and Methods* (pp. 195–206). Berkeley: University of California Press.

Roth, G. (1987). Rationalization in Max Weber's Developmental History. In S. Whimster and S. Lash (eds), *Max Weber, Rationality and Modernity* (pp. 75–91). London: Allen & Unwin.

Rubel, M., and Manale, M. (1975). *Marx Without Myth: A Chronological Study of His Life and Work.* New York: Harper & Row.

Rubiés, J.-P. (2005). Oriental Despotism and European Orientalism: Boteroto Montesquieu. *Journal of Early Modern History,* 9 (1–2), 109–180.

Said, E.W. (1977). *Orientalism.* London: Penguin.

Salomon, A. (1935a). Max Weber's Methodology. *Social Research, 1*(2), 147–168.

Salomon, A. (1935b). Max Weber's Sociology. *Social Research, 2*(1), 60–73.

Salomon, A. (1935c). Max Weber's Political Ideas. *Social Research, 2*(3), 368–384.

Salomon, A. (1945). German Sociology. In G. Gurvitch and W.E. Moore (eds), *TwentiethCenturySociology*(pp.586–614).NewYork:ThePhilosophicalLibrary.

Sawer, M. (1977). *Marxism and the Question of the Asiatic Mode of Production.* The Hague: Nijhoff.

Sayar, A.G. (1998). *Bir İktisatçının Entellektüel Portresi Sabri F. Ülgener.* İstanbul: Eren Yay.

Sayar, A.G. (2006). Sabri Ülgener'in Bir Türk Weberi Olarak Portresi. *Ülgener Yazıları* (pp. 37–43). İstanbul: Derin Yayınları.

Scaff, L.A. (1981). Max Weber and Robert Michels. *The American Journal of Sociology*, *86*(6), 1269–1286.

Schluchter, W. (1979). The Paradox of Rationalization: On the Relation of Ethics and World. In G. Roth and W. Schluchter (eds), *Max Weber's Vision of History: Ethics and Methods* (pp. 11–64). Berkeley: University of California Press.

Schluchter, W. (1981). *The Rise of Western Rationalism: Max Weber's Developmental History*. (G. Roth, trans.). Berkeley: University of California Press.

Schluchter, W. (1987). Weber's Sociology of Rationalism and Typology of Religious Rejections of the World. In S. Whimster and S. Lash (eds), *Max Weber, Rationality and Modernity* (pp. 92–115). London: Allen & Unwin.

Schluchter, W. (1999). Hindrances to Modernity: Max Weber on Islam. In T.E. Huff and W. Schluchter (eds), *Max Weber and Islam* (pp. 53–138). New Brunswick: Transaction Books.

Schroeter, G. (1985). Dialogue, Debate, or Dissent? The Difficulties of Assessing Max Weber's Relation to Marx. In R.J. Antonio and R.M. Glassman (eds), *A Weber-Marx Dialogue* (pp. 2–19). Lawrence: University Press of Kansas.

Segady, T.W. (1993). Consequences of the Increasing Rationality of Music: A Reassessment of Weberian Rationalization. *Sociological Spectrum*, *13*(4), 451–463.

Sezer, B. (1979). *Asya Tarihinde Su Boyu Ovaları ve Bozkır Uygarlıkları*. İstanbul: Edebiyat Fakültesi Basımevi.

Sezer, B. (2003). Kemal Tahir Üzerine – İki Televizyon Konuşması. In E. Eğribel and U. Özcan (eds), *Sosyoloji Yıllığı 10. Kitap: Kemal Tahir'in 30. Yıldönümü Anısına* (pp. 27–30). İstanbul: Kızılelma Yay.

Shaw, W.H. (1979). "The Handmill Gives You the Feudal Lord": Marx's Technological Determinism,. *History and Theory*, *18*(2), 155–176.Springborg, P. (1992). *Western Republicanism and the Oriental Prince*. Cambridge: Polity Press.

Stalin, J. (1940). *Dialectical and Historical Materialism*. Moscow: International Publishers.

Stalin, J. (1947). *Problems of Leninism*. Moscow: Foreign Languages Publishing House.

Sumiya, K. (2001). Max Weber and Critical Succession of German Historical School. In Y. Shionoya (ed.), *The German Historical School* (pp. 120–138). London and New York: Routledge.

Sunar, L. (2012). *Türkiye'de İş Ortaklıkları*. İstanbul: İTO Yay.

Tavernier, J.-B. (2012). *Travels in India (2 Vols.)*. (V. Ball, trans.). Cambridge, New York: Cambridge University Press.

Tenbruck, F.H. (1980). The Problem of Thematic Unity in the Works of Max Weber. (S. Whimster, trans.)*The British Journal of Sociology*, *31*(3), 316–351.

Thorner, D. (1980). Marx on India and the Asiatic Mode of Production. *The Shaping of Modern India* (pp. 349–383). New Delhi: Allied Publishers.

Toynbee, A. (1958). Wittfogel's "Oriental Despotism". *American Political Science Review*, *52*(1), 195–198.

Turner, B.S. (1974a). *Weber and Islam: A Critical Study*. London: Routledge & Kegan Paul.

Turner, B.S. (1974b). Islam, Capitalism and the Weber Theses. *The British Journal of Sociology*, *25*(2), 230–243.

Turner, B.S. (1978). *Marx and the End of Orientalism*. London: Allen & Unwin.

Turner, B.S. (1981). *For Weber: Essays on the Sociology of Fate*. Boston: Routledge & Kegan Paul.

Turner, B.S. (1992). *Max Weber: From History to Modernity*. London: Routledge.

Turner, B.S., and Holton, R.J. (1989). *Max Weber on Economy and Society*. London: Routledge.

Turner, S.P., and Factor, R.A. (1983). *Max Weber and the Dispute Over Reason and Value: A Study in Philosophy, Ethics, and Politics*. London: Routledge & Kegan Paul.

Türkdoğan, O. (1985). *Max Weber: Günümüzde ve Türkiye'de Weberci Görüşler*. İstanbul: Türk Dünyası Araştırmaları Vakfı.

Ülgener, S.F. (2006a). *Tarihte Darlık Buhranları ve İktisadi Muvazenesizlik Meselesi*. İstanbul: Derin Yayınları.

Ülgener, S.F. (2006b). *İktisadi Çözümlemenin Ahlak ve Zihniyet Dünyası*. İstanbul: Derin Yayınları.

Ülgener, S.F. (2006c). *Zihniyet ve Din: İslam, Tasavvuf ve Çözülme Devri İktisat Ahlakı*. İstanbul: Derin Yayınları.

Valensi, L. (1993). The Birth of the Despot: Venice and the Sublime Porte. (A. Denner, trans.). Ithaca, NY: Cornell University Press.

Varga, E. (1928). Les problemes fondamentaux de la revolution chinoise. *La correspondence internationale*, (561).

Varga, E. (1970). Asya Tipi Üretim Tarzı. In Jean Chesneaux vd. (ed.), *Asya Tipi Üretim Tarzı* (pp. 69–92). İstanbul: Ant Yay.

Venturi, F. (1963). Oriental Despotism. *Journal of the History of Ideas*, *24*(1), 133–142.

Von Below, G. (1925). *Der Deutsche Staat des Mittelalters: Eine grundlegung der deuschen Verfassunfgsgeschichte, Vol. 1, 2*. Leipzig: Verlag von Quelle and Meyer.

Von Savigny, F.K. (2003). *Von Savigny's Treatise on Possession; Or The, Jus Possessionis of the Civil Law*. (S.P. Erskine, trans.) (6th edn). Clark, N.J.: Lawbook Exchange Ltd.

Weber, Marianne. (2008). *Max Weber: A Biography*. New Brunswick: Transaction Books.

Weber, M. (1946a). Religious Rejections of the World and Their Directions. In C.W. Mills and H.H. Gerth (eds), *From Max Weber: Essays in Sociology* (pp. 323–363). New York: Oxford University Press.

Weber, M. (1946b). The Social Psychology of the World Religions. In C.W. Mills and H.H. Gerth (eds), *From Max Weber: Essays in Sociology* (pp. 267–301). New York: Oxford University Press.

Weber, M. (1949a). Objectivity in Social Sciences and Social Policy. In E. Shills and H. Finch (eds), *The Methodology of Social Sciences* (pp. 49–112). New York: Free Press.

Weber, M. (1949b). Critical Studies in the Logic of the Cultural Sciences. In E.A. Shils and H. A. Finch (eds), *The Methodology of Social Sciences* (pp. 113–188). New York: Free Press.

Weber, M. (1958). *The Rational and Social Foundations of Music*. (G. Neuwirth, trans.). Carbondale: Southern Illinois University Press.

Weber, M. (1967a). *The Religion of India: The Sociology of Hinduism and Budism*. (H.H. Gerth and D. Martindale, trans.). New York: Free Press.

Weber, M. (1967b). *Ancient Judaism*. (Hans H. Gerth, trans.). New York: Free Press.

Weber, M. (1968). *The Religion of China: Confucianism and Taoism*. (Hans H. Gerth, trans.). New York: Free Press.

Weber, M. (1975). *Roscher and Knies: The Logical Problems of Historical Economics*. (G. Oakes, trans.). New York: Free Press.

Weber, M. (1978). *Economy and Society: An Outline of Interpretive Sociology*, ed. G. Roth and C. Wittich.. Berkeley and Los Angeles: University of California Press.

Weber, M. (1979). Developmental tendencies in the situation of East Elbian rural labourers. (K. Tribe, trans.) *Economy and Society*, *8*(2), 172–205.

Weber, M. (1988). *The Agrarian Sociology of Ancient Civilizations*. (R.I. Frank, trans.). London: Verso Books.

Weber, M. (1994). The National State and Economic Policy. In P. Lassman and R. Speirs (eds), *Weber: Political Writings* (pp. 1–28). London: Cambridge University Press.

Weber, M. (1995). *The Russian Revolutions*. (P. Baehr, trans.). Ithaca: Cornell University Press.

Weber, M. (2001). *The Protestant Ethic Debate: Max Weber's Replies to His Critics, 1907–1910*. Liverpool: Liverpool University Press.

Weber, M. (2003a). *General Economic History*. (F.H. Knight, trans.). Mineola: Dover Publication.

Weber, M. (2003b). *The History of Commercial Partnerships in the Middle Ages*. (L. Kaelber, trans.). Lanham: Rowman & Littlefield Publishers.

Weber, M. (2008a). Science as a Vocation. In J. Dreijmanis (ed.), *Max Weber's Complete Writings on Academic and Political Vocations*. New York: Algora Publishing.

Weber, M. (2008b). *Roman Agrarian History: In Its Relation to Roman Public and Civil Law*. (R.I. Frank, trans.). Claremont: Regina Books.

Weber, M. (2009a). *The Protestant Ethic and the Spirit of Capitalism with Other Writings on the Rise of the West*. (S. Kalberg, trans.) (4th edn). New York: Oxford University Press.

Weber, M. (2009b). Prefatory Remarks to Collected Essays in the Sociology of Religion [Vorbemerkung]. In S. Kalberg (ed.), *The Protestant Ethic and the Spirit of Capitalism with Other Writings on the Rise of the West* (4th edn, pp. 205–220). New York: Oxford University Press.

Weiss, J. (1986). *Max Weber and the Marxist World*. (E. King-Utz and M.J. King, trans.). London: Routledge & Kegan Paul.

Whimster, S. (2005). Max Weber. In G. Ritzer (ed.), *Encyclopedia of Social Theory* (Vol. 2, pp. 877–883). Thousand Oaks: Sage Publications.

Wilks, M. (1869). *Historical Sketches of the South of India: In an attempt to Trace the History of Mysoor; From the Origin of the Hindoo Government of That State, to the Extinction of the Mohammedan Dynasty in 1799* (Vol. 1). Madras: Higginbotham.

Wittfogel, K.A. (1958). Reply to Arnold Toynbee. *American Political Science Review*, *52*(2), 502–506.

Wittfogel, K.A. (1981). *Oriental Despotism: A Coparative Study of Total Power*. New York: Vintage Books.

Wittfogel, K.A. (1990). The Ruling Bureaucracy of Oriental Despotism: A Phenomenon that Paralyzed Marx. In B. Jeppop and C. Malcolm-Brown (eds), *Karl Marx Social and Economic Thought, Critical Assesments* (Vol. 6, pp. 428–435). London: Routledge.

Wrong, D. (1970). Introduction: Max Weber. In D. Wrong (ed.), *Max Weber* (pp. 1–76.). Englewood Cliffs: Prentice-Hall.

Wrong, D. (1984). Marx, Weber, and Contemporary Sociology. In R.M. Glassman and V. Murvar (eds), *Weber's Political Sociology: A Pessimistic Vision of a Rationalized World* (pp. 69–81). London: Greenwood Press.

Yang, C.K. (1968). Introduction. In Hans H. Gerth (ed.), *Religion of China: Confucianism and Taoism* (pp. xiii–xliii). New York: Free Press.

Zeitlin, I.M. (1968). *Ideology and the Development of Sociological Theory*. New Jersey: Prentice-Hall.

Zijderveld, A.C. (2005). Neo-Kantianism. In G. Ritzer (ed.), *Encyclopedia of Social Theory* (2 vols) (pp. 529–530). Thousand Oaks: Sage Publications.

Zimmerman, A. (2006). Decolonizing Weber. *Postcolonial Studies: Culture, Politics, Economy*, *9*(1), 53–79.

Index

For Product Safety Concerns and Information please contact our
EU representative GPSR@taylorandfrancis.com Taylor & Francis
Verlag GmbH, Kaufingerstraße 24, 80331 München, Germany